Kindred Hands

Kindred Hands

Letters on Writing by British and
American Women Authors, 1865 – 1935

Edited by Jennifer Cognard-Black
and Elizabeth MacLeod Walls

UNIVERSITY OF IOWA PRESS | IOWA CITY

University of Iowa Press, Iowa City 52242

http://www.uiowa.edu/uiowapress

Copyright © 2006 by the University of Iowa Press

Printed in the United States of America

Design by April Leidig-Higgins

The University of Iowa Press is a member of Green
Press Initiative and is committed to preserving
natural resources.

Printed on acid-free paper

Library of Congress Cataloging-in-Publication Data
Kindred hands: letters on writing by British and
American women authors, 1865 – 1935 / edited by
Jennifer Cognard-Black and Elizabeth MacLeod
Walls.
   p.   cm.
Includes bibliographical references and index.
ISBN 0-87745-964-9 (cloth)
1. Women authors, English — Correspondence.
2. Women authors, American — Correspondence.
3. English prose literature — 19th century. 4. English
prose literature — 20th century. 5. American prose
literature — 19th century. 6. American prose literature
— 20th century. 7. English letters. 8. American
letters. 9. Authorship. I. Cognard-Black, Jennifer,
1969 –. II. Walls, Elizabeth MacLeod, 1974 –.
PR111.K56 2006   2005048144
823'.8080357 — dc22

06 07 08 09 10 C 5 4 3 2 1

CONTENTS

Kindred Hands

Letters are, by definition, common artifacts. Their contents capture the transitory, finite experience of the everyday—the private expression and connection that, historically, has delimited both British and American women's lives. The letters contained in this collection exemplify a world dependent upon epistolary communication. However, while these letters are in some ways prototypic examples of the daily correspondence endemic to nineteenth- and early twentieth-century society, they are also, and quite uncommonly, rhetorical artifacts depicting women's entrée into the world of professional writing. The letters presented in this collection were written by published authors, all of whom used informal and formal correspondence to negotiate their roles within the literary arena. Thus these letters by women authors are also about writing—the vagaries of creating, publishing, reading, and selling their work. Read together, they provide both a glimpse into women's public and private lives and a map of women's progress through largely masculine territory: the literary marketplace.

Letter writing aided the women featured in this collection as they attempted to articulate and identify their authorial selves, create camaraderie with other authors, and negotiate the literary world. For example, in an unpublished letter to George Eliot, Harriet Beecher Stowe writes about the experience of reading Eliot's fiction, thereby defining the purpose and power of writing. "A book is *a hand* stretched forth in the dark passage of life to see if there is another hand to meet it," Stowe believes. "Now in your works if you could read my marked edition of them you would see how often the hand has met the kindred hand. Reviews and book notices are commonly so dreary—so *un*sympathetic."[1] Thus, Stowe constructs herself as an intimate, appreciative reader distinct from the popular social mind and that scourge of sympathy, the book reviewer. Stowe receives Eliot's work via the metaphor of the hand, transforming the cerebral experience of "kindred" text to the tactile experience of literal kin, a touch or a clasp, thus making art palpable and comforting. In turn, the receiving hand scripts

Stowe's understanding of Eliot into another version of materiality. The hand of sympathy becomes the instrument of true interpretation, creating a continuous embrace, one hand meeting another across the "dark passage of life." To Stowe, fine literature and, by association, fine authors speak soul-to-soul, author-to-reader, in a manner defying the mere economics of book distribution.

Recovering British and American Women Authors

In one sense, publishing the letters of women writers from the nineteenth and early twentieth centuries contributes to the important recovery efforts that have already transfigured literary and historical scholarship on forgotten artists and their writings. *Kindred Hands* complements the fundamental reclamation work achieved by such collections as Sally Ledger and Roger Luckhurst's *The Fin de Siècle: A Reader in Cultural History c. 1880–1900*, Judy Simons's *Diaries and Journals of Literary Women from Fanny Burney to Virginia Woolf*, Judith Fetterley's *Provisions: A Reader from 19th-Century American Women*, Molly Meijer Werthheimer's edition of *Listening to Their Voices: The Rhetorical Activities of Historical Women*, the Schomburg Library of Nineteenth-Century Black Women Writers Series, edited by Henry Louis Gates Jr., or the Rutgers University Press series of primary work by American women writers, coedited by Joanne Dobson, Judith Fetterley, and Elaine Showalter.

Yet, in another sense, this collection steers existing recovery scholarship along an uncharted path. The letters that appear in this collection share an important commonality: they explore the idea, the act, and the meaning of writing. Writing—entering and surviving in the profession or maintaining career, reputation, and artistic integrity—dominates the casual communications of these figures. Some of the authors are well known, even canonical; others have been forgotten by the very industry that gave them celebrity. Three of these women— Frances E. W. Harper, Palma Pederson, and Jessie Redmon Fauset—personify the outsider in almost every sense, using their letters to reinforce the power of identity alongside the purpose of art. And all of these authors relied upon letters to codify a certain approach toward writing or the marketplace. These letters, then, offer more than historical curiosity: they are manifestoes, autobiographies, philosophies, and commentaries delivered with dignity and restraint to a variety of friends and foes, loved ones and feared ones, family members and utter strangers. For these reasons, the letters signify the power of writing to the nineteenth- and twentieth-century authors who defined women's place in the literary arena of the modern age.

Accessing Unpublished Correspondence by Women Authors

Letters have served both as a perfunctory form of communication and as a treasured mechanism for articulating women's artistry. Given their import and their interiority, the letters in this collection provide a glimpse into the intellectual, political, and social revolutions that transformed women's lives. Culled from their private ruminations, these letters are evidence of women's authorial evolution. In the case of George Eliot and Harriet Beecher Stowe, scholars and teachers usually trace their authorship through their fiction or historical record. We know these writers primarily as two of the most influential women writers of their time; we recognize their work as crucial to the advent of proto-feminist literature. Yet, because Stowe's complete correspondence with Eliot remains unpublished — accessed only through partial and inaccurate nineteenth-century sources and fragments in modern-day biographies — we have not, to date, understood that Stowe and Eliot's ideas about authorship were collaborative, that their aesthetic vision was shared, or that the influences they had on the literary world were linked. Moreover, Stowe's unpublished letters complicate neat scholarly categories that separate sentimental women writers such as Stowe from high-realist authors such as Eliot.

A collection such as this, therefore, unearths concealed connections that shaped not only women's general experiences but also the scope and ethos of nineteenth- and early twentieth-century fiction and poetry. Our title for this collection is taken from Stowe's own metaphor: *Kindred Hands: Letters on Writing by British and American Women Authors, 1865 – 1935*. Drawing upon Stowe's phrase, the collection expands our understanding of British and American women writers living between 1865 and 1935, featuring letters by women that detail the experience of writing within a marketplace often categorized as antagonistic, impersonally professional, and nationalistic. These letters address the pragmatics of writing as well as illuminating such issues as authorship, aesthetics, collaboration, inspiration, and authorial intent.

The collection also represents a range of authors, including transatlantic correspondents, women of color, canonical writers, and regional writers; in other words, these documents provide new sources about women's writing for scholars engaged in reception theory, women's studies, social history, composition theory, modernism, and nineteenth-century studies. This collection also serves as an archive for rediscovered and reclaimed contributions to British and American literary history. Almost all of the letters presented in this collection are previously unpublished and thus made available to scholars here for the first time. For this same reason, the collection is useful to teachers. Through these letters, students will discover different viewpoints on Victorian and modern gender roles, empire, socioeconomic disparity, and the idiosyncrasies of daily life. And because they are letters—handwritten documents created in haste and with little thought to their preservation—these primary documents will introduce students to a detailed and complex world that is so often disguised by the mask of fiction or the impersonal facts of history.

The Epistle-as-Literature, the Epistle-as-History

One could argue that letter writing facilitated the success of female authors throughout the nineteenth and twentieth centuries. Epistles served numerous functions for the writer: professional networking, plot and character development, opportunities for refining and encouraging reader reception, refuting or offering criticism, authorial commiseration, establishing a base of loyal readers, and pre-writing or invention—an epistolary function that still thrives in composition classrooms today. Of course, letter writing is not confined to the previous two centuries; *ars dictaminis*, the art and practice of letter writing, emerged through study of biblical and classical literature. Some of our best-known Enlightenment authors relied on epistles as a crucial, private supplement to their very public, artistic lives. And it is perhaps no coincidence that Samuel Richardson's *Pamela* fused daily correspondence with a stylized narrative that ultimately solidified the place of the novel in the Anglo-American world. This kind of one-sided colloquy between sender (narrator) and receiver (reader) represented what authors knew: a genre they could at once master and manipulate. Thus, epistolary communication became the style on which not only Richardson's *Pamela* relied but also Alexander Pope's poetry, Jonathan Swift's essays, and Hannah Foster's or Jane Austen's novels.

Until very recently, moreover, letters symbolized high cultural status and value: literacy, resources, and authority. Letters were often (though not always) preserved and venerated. They provided a written record of policy, philosophy, or practice, as in Paul's letters to his followers or James Madison's letters to Alexander Hamilton. Epistolary theorists from Alberic, an eleventh-century Italian monk, to Lewis Carroll, a Victorian author and academic, refined *ars dictaminis* to a science and established clear rhetorical rules for their composition. Moreover, numerous studies in the past two decades have shown that the art and craft of the epistle was not reserved for male writers; notable among these is Elizabeth Goldsmith's edited anthology, *Writing the Female Voice: Essays on Epistolary Literature*, and James Daybell's recent collection, *Early Mod-*

ern Women's Letter Writing, 1450–1700. Indeed, letter writing has provided a crucial outlet for female artists and intellectuals otherwise restricted by their domestic responsibilities and various other social strictures. David Barton and Nigel Hall's *Letter Writing as Social Practice,* William Merrill Decker's *Epistolary Practices: Letter Writing in America before Telecommunications,* and Christe Geisler's *Gender-Based Variation in Nineteenth-Century English Letter Writing* have all grounded the female letter-writing experience — and the liberation it so often provided — within a nineteenth-century context. These and other critical analyses of nineteenth-century letter writing as both an expedient communication tool and a testing ground for female artistry confirm that women authors throughout the Victorian and modern periods used letters to help create, enhance, publicize, and defend their writing.

This collection presents letters that achieve each of these ideological ends. In so doing, the collection underscores the centrality of letters in fostering women's creative expression in the nineteenth and twentieth centuries. For example, for Mary Cholmondeley and Rhoda Broughton, letter writing provided an opportunity for authorial connection, a safe space in which the men's clubs at the heart of London's literary marketplace were quietly extended into the drawing rooms, bedrooms, and gardens of women's country homes. For Henrietta Stannard, Mary Corelli, and Annesley Kenealy, letter writing subverted the exclusive meeting room or office space of Fleet Street, offering instead a rhetorical conduit for communicating discreetly — yet intentionally — with male literati. For Palma Pederson or Jessie Redmon Fauset, letter writing provided at once professional connection and personal release, specifically the chance to explore what it meant to be an author, and an Other, in arenas ill-suited to supporting alternative perspectives. This collection, then, exposes a cross section of epistolary history and its connection to British and American literature, demonstrating that letter writing provided authors an essential, fundamental experience — an extension of the self into a personal, yet public, space: a "kindred hand" with which to touch and be touched by another congruent mind.

Transatlanticisms

This collection is deliberately transatlantic. Whereas other primary source anthologies tend to identify as either British or American, the aim of this collection is to mirror the nineteenth- and early twentieth-century marketplace in which our selected authors wrote — and that market was inherently Anglo-American. Indeed, from the early 1860s on, transatlantic thought was a way of life. As Malcolm Bradbury notes, the 1860s marked a new "cosmopolitanism, and the trans-atlantic contacts multiplied, decade by decade" (180). Between 1860 and 1900, over ten million immigrants came to America (Palma Pederson arrived in 1894), and hundreds of thousands of Americans made European tours (Jessie Redmon Fauset spent over a year in Europe, from 1924 to 1925). News, art, politics, commercial ventures, technology, and the family were all bound by transatlantic interests — at least through World War II with the clear establishment of the United States as its own superpower in addition to the advent of second- and third-generation immigrants becoming the bulk of the American population.

As a result, British and American authors saw their audience as twofold, constituted of both American and British readers. The letters reproduced here demonstrate this twofold audience in a number of ways. First and foremost, some of the authors write to acquaintances, friends, and/or fellow authors across the Atlantic: Stowe and Phelps both write to George Eliot; Rosamund Watson writes to Mark Twain biographer Albert Bigelow Paine; and, from Paris, Fauset corresponds with Langston Hughes. In addition, some authors felt it their duty to help encourage their fellow citizens to read more literature from abroad. In one of Phelps's letters to Eliot, she details a series of lectures she gave on Eliot at Boston University, explaining, "I write to tell you how great the interest seems to have been in my *subject*. Hundreds were turned away from the little College Classroom, for whom there was no admittance."[2]

Furthermore, it could be argued that all published narratives produced in America and Britain during this period were transatlantic narratives — and not in the limited sense of travelogues or Jamesian expatriate novels. One cannot appreciate, for instance, the widespread social and political dynamics of *Uncle Tom's Cabin* (1852) unless one reads British responses to the novel, including George Eliot's comments on the establishment of a number of anti-slavery societies in England and Scotland as a direct result of Stowe's two visits across the Atlantic. Reciprocally, in order fully to understand Eliot's influence on American realism, one must read what Stowe and Phelps (as well as James, Howells, and others) have to say about Eliot's fiction. And these are but two examples, for each and every popular narrative, whether by Harper, Malet, Egerton, or Pederson, had a dual life on both sides of the ocean, through critical notices and commentaries as well as in the parlors and back bedrooms of many households.

Thus the British and American publishing markets of the nineteenth century were never limited to an author's home country, and this interconnection became increasingly important with the proliferation of transatlantic travel as well as with the communications and mass distribution technologies that gained prominence in the latter half of the century. As such, the selections in this collection mirror these inherent transatlanticisms.

1865 to 1935: The American and British Milieu

Although this collection begins with letters dating from the early 1860s, the culture of authorship in Britain and America during the first half of the nineteenth century directly affected how women writers thought of their work in the literary marketplace after 1860. As Nina Baym, Barbara Christian, Judith Fetterley, Jane Tompkins, Jean Fagan Yellin, and others have argued about American women writers, between the turn of the century and the end of the Civil War, such authors demonstrated both determination and a sense of purpose in the act of picking up the pen.[3] Generally speaking, writers such as Catharine Sedgwick, Fanny Fern, Harriet Jacobs, Susan Warner, Harriet Beecher Stowe, Gail Hamilton, and Elizabeth Stuart Phelps claimed neither ignorance nor innocence about writing for a reading public; rather, they maintained a keen awareness, an earnest engagement with what it meant to be an "author." And this self-possession is all the more striking given that their subject matter was not romance, a New World wilderness, or the narrative of a hero in search of intellectual autonomy; they were not writing the stuff of James Fenimore Cooper, Nathaniel Hawthorne, or Ralph Waldo Emerson. Rather, their subject matter was women and their everyday lives, the private sphere. And antebellum women writers invariably wrote what they knew: the domestic and its concern with morals, manners, and social limits. This focus proved both popular and lucrative. The sales and distribution patterns of a work such as Stowe's *Uncle Tom's Cabin* invented the very category of the "bestseller" and led to Nathaniel Hawthorne's oft-quoted sneer against the "d——d mob of scribbling women" with which he had to compete.

In turn, British women writers from the early 1800s to the 1860s, among them Mary Shelley, Mary Prince, Margaret Oliphant, the Brontës, Mary Elizabeth Braddon, and Elizabeth Barrett Browning, showed greater unease with the role of the writer, perhaps due to a millennia-long tradition of masculine authorship, or perhaps to a stronger national emphasis on authors as self-conscious artists, set apart from society and meant to critique it from a position of superiority. Sandra Gilbert and Susan Gubar have argued that British women writing in the first half of the nineteenth century worked under an anxiety of authorship, a fundamental separation from the word "author," which connotes "a father, a master or ruler, and an owner" (7).[4] To "kill" the passive, inconstant, and objectified female archetypes that abound in British literature — and thereby "free" themselves to write — Gilbert and Gubar as well as Mary Poovey and Elaine Showalter have claimed that early and mid-Victorian writers chose to publish under male pseudonyms and/or populate their works with dead mothers, Angels of the House, and characters such as governesses and nurses who could conceivably walk class, race, and gender boundaries. Prior to the 1860s, British women writers shared the marketplace with highly successful male contemporaries — Lord Byron; Charles Dickens; Alfred, Lord Tennyson — and found that both the precepts of traditional femininity as well as the literary power of the domestic sphere were appropriated by such writers, often to great monetary gain.

Yet the ensuing seventy years represented here are arguably the most transformative for women authors in the transatlantic world. For British women in particular, the years 1865 to 1935 represent a corridor in history that transfigured the lives of all people, but especially women's. By 1865, Britain had long since undergone an industrial upheaval that had precipitated working-class movements, Reform laws, and a monumental economic and political foray into overseas empire. The publication of John Stuart Mill's *The Subjection of Women* (1869) coincided with the second Reform Bill, which for all intents and purposes inaugurated the Victorian women's suffrage movement. Women writers, including not only Austen and the Brontë sisters but also Barrett Browning and Christina Rossetti, had penetrated the consciousness of the British reading public — and by 1872, with the publication of *Middlemarch*, George Eliot solidified her reputation as one of England's preeminent novelists. Perhaps most significant for the context of this collection, however, is the profound revolution in women's political and personal rights that occurred between 1870 and the conclusion of World War I.

Between 1870 and 1901, the year of Victoria's death, Parliament passed numerous Education Acts granting women participation on educational boards and committees; Married Women's Property Acts establishing a woman's right to keep her possessions after marriage; a spate of suffrage bills; and the 1884 Reform Bill granting universal manhood suffrage. Throughout the 1880s and 90s, reform-minded legislators concentrated their efforts on class and gender inequity in British society. Workers went on strike; women agitated in greater numbers for rights both within marriage and in the civic arena. Spurred by the politics of the moment, a new generation of women novelists emerged in the 1890s. Their "New Woman" novels reflected the experiences of young married women living at the cusp of a new century. Such didactic and otherwise shocking narratives complemented the new tone of frankness. Decadence coupled with disquiet over the controversial 1899 Boer War dulled the jingoism for which the Victorians were especially known.

Victoria's death in 1901 severed most remaining ties to nineteenth-century propriety and sociopolitical repression. In 1903, militant suffrage ignited and was fueled by working- and middle-class unrest as well as by a severe governmental backlash. During this period, literature by and about women reflected the new concern over women's place in this changing British society—from the "modern girl" novels of E. M. Forster and H. G. Wells to the experimental fiction developed by Dorothy Richardson and Virginia Woolf. Following World War I, married women and women over thirty finally were granted the vote; ten years later, all women in Britain achieved this fundamental right. Literature experienced a corresponding shift in tone, approach, and theme, from the publication of the nihilistic *Wasteland* in 1922 to the transformative *To the Lighthouse* in 1928. By the 1930s, then, women writers had earned elevated status and many of the same legal rights as their male counterparts, though at the onset of World War II, unfettered access to the most influential publishers in Britain was still out of reach for most of them.

In turn, the period between 1865 and 1935 in America is marked by an ethos of expansion: imperialism, an effort to expand human rights and reform human inequities, a concomitant expansion of indignities against ethnic and racial minorities, and the widespread growth of mass culture. On the one hand, the reformist impulse throughout this period meant that certain marginalized groups increased their civil and social rights. In 1865, the Civil War ended, and the Thirteenth Amendment to the Constitution abolished slavery. Three years later, Elizabeth Cady Stanton founded the National Woman Suffrage Association, an organization that worked to secure white female suffrage as well as more extensive property rights, birth control, and equal access to education and employment. And by the 1890s, African-American women gained national prominence with the establishment of the National Association of Colored Women. By 1905, Eugene V. Debs created the Industrial Workers of the World; by 1909, Ida B. Wells and W. E. B. DuBois founded the National Association for the Advancement of Colored People; by 1920, with the passage of the Nineteenth Amendment, white women secured the vote; and in 1925, Alain Locke published *The New Negro*, an anthology that galvanized the Harlem Renaissance, bringing African-American artistic endeavors into the national spotlight. On the other hand, with the end of legal slavery came Reconstruction and then the Jim Crow era in which segregation was legalized and lynchings were commonplace. Though the first transcontinental railroad was a symbol of national progress, those who drove home the last spike in 1869 were Chinese laborers—unable to speak English, underpaid, overworked, and subject to accidents that cost them limbs as well as lives. In 1886 the Statue of Liberty was completed, yet only one year later, the Dawes Act seized tribal lands and distributed them to whites, an act that led to the 1890 massacre of the Lakota at Wounded Knee. At the turn of the century, the Spanish-American War was fought in the Pacific and the Caribbean; in 1914, America entered World War I; in 1929, the New York stock market crashed and Hoovervilles became the habitats for the many millions of unemployed Americans; and come 1936, Adolph Hitler initiated his armed occupation of Europe, thereby precipitating American interest in World War II.

Within this climate of expansion, both negative and positive, American women writers were, perhaps, most affected by the growth of "professionalism," an economic and social movement that revolutionized a wide array of institutions, from education to government to religion to most vocations—including authorship. For writers such as Harriet Beecher Stowe, Frances E. W. Harper, Gail Hamilton, and Elizabeth Stuart Phelps, this advent of professionalism meant a radical shift in literary taste from a feminized, *laisser-faire* aesthetic to a masculine, professionalized one—from an amateur and romantic style of authorship to one that was typified by training, realism, and traditional masculinity. As letters in this collection attest, after 1865, American women writers could no longer publish the kinds of emotionally centered literature they had built entire careers on nor take for granted that their "genteel publishers" would treat them equitably. More often than not, such writers fought the mercenary, even clinical feel of the new professional climate in the same moment that they relied on romantic, "feminized" arguments to persuade publishers and others of their right to fair treatment.

In addition to this shift from an amateur publishing market to one typified by professionalism, the new literary marketplace was fueled by mass culture: technologies of popular communication (the steamship, railroad, telegraph, and telephone) that created and maintained the profession of authorship through the buying and selling of words as commodities. For although the American literary climate at the turn of the twentieth century favored realism and objectivity, high-art aesthetics and a reified distance from marketplace pursuits, the profession of authorship became increasingly aligned with commercialism— with the look of inspiration over its substance.

As a result, "lowbrow" wordsmith occupations such as muckraking, technical writing, and political propagandizing embraced the same precepts of professionalism, thus making their labor increasingly more precise, fact-based, and socially aware—more "masculine." Aided by the new technologies of the telephone, papermaking, printing, and photojournalism that lowered production costs and virtually guaranteed the instantaneous transmittal of the word to a mass readership of Britons and Americans, in the first quarter of the twentieth century, modern features of professional discourse were established: literary agents, promotional campaigns for books and periodicals, headlines and by-lines, and a full synergy of visual advertisements (goods) with text (ideas). By the 1920s, then, a new cadre of professional writers came to the fore as popular authors. Like Palma Pederson, writers such as Jack London, Stephen Crane, and Upton Sinclair came out of journalist backgrounds previously held in low esteem. Among these progressives, differences in ethnicity, region, politics, or class mattered less than a common language with which to engage concepts of efficiency, social progress, industrial deregulation, and a democratic, nonpartisan access to ideas. As such, the culture of professionalism radically shifted the popular image of an author from the previous century's woman of letters to a "voice of the people" that continually had to convince the public of the validity of that voice. And this tension is crucial to understanding a central contradiction for both British and American women writers working from 1865 to 1935: the tension between high-art, intellectual work supposedly performed for social good and texts that were marketed for individual or corporate profit through systems of mass media.

Thus, the letters included in this collection mirror, in the most personal and direct fashion, the monumental historical shifts that occurred in Britain and America between 1865 and 1935. Compare, for example, the irreverence of George Egerton or the overt pride of Jessie Redmon Fauset in the 1930s to the prim self-effacement of Gail Hamilton or the careful optimism of Frances E. W. Harper in the 1860s and 70s: these letters expose a range of rhetorical approaches to the literary and social world that correspond to specific historical expectations. Yet all of the letters included here — whether published at the height of Victoria's reign or within the unsettling "Long Weekend" separating World War I and World War II — also betray a common element. Each author uses correspondence to define her multiple — and sometimes contradictory — writing personae; and each uses letters specifically to articulate and justify the inherent value of writing and the artistry of her craft.

Letters about Writing by Women Authors

This collection is as invested in encouraging awareness of women's professional evolution in the modern period as it is in encouraging awareness of writing itself: writing as art, communication, politics, and most importantly, as a declaration of self. Through the interconnections between writing and womanhood imbedded in these letters, the reader of this collection will discover that, often, the two were inextricably part of a single identity. Indeed, during this historical period, women and writing became partnered in the minds of many as a union that was steadily transforming all parts of modern life. The publishing world in the late nineteenth and early twentieth century was at once — and paradoxically — increasingly dominated by men and yet still accepting of certain women writers. Professional writing, like most vocations that required skill and education from its practitioners, was self-selecting; men had the education, leisure, and encouragement to write, while women often possessed neither the formal education nor the freedom necessary to write lasting, meaningful texts. Yet the profession of authorship, while tied to skill and instruction, did not preclude those with talent and a moderate amount of cultural and historical knowledge from entering the marketplace. Moreover, writing was not simply produced within the perfect solitude of a venerated office; rather, the art of writing could also be accomplished within the confined and often chaotic sphere of the home. Creating text is an ongoing practice and quite often a concealed one. In the American context, wherein popular women writers dominated the marketplace at mid-century, publishing women's fiction was commonplace and accepted, although this acceptance waned as realism and aesthetics and, eventually, progressive modernism came into vogue. In Britain, the climate remained largely unwelcoming for women writers; thus it was that, in the nineteenth century, women writers ranging from Jane Austen to George Eliot entered the literary marketplace either disguised via a male pseudonym or marketed quite intentionally as harmless creatures penning works "by a lady," to cite Austen's frequent disclaimer.

Writing, then, emerged as an artistic terrain upon which women could stake an intellectual and professional claim. It is no surprise that their letters chart a parallel path along this new terrain — private ruminations alongside the public journey toward authorship, recognition, and achievement. Letters about writing offer a rare perspective into the dual and often competing existences of women authors. The letters included in this collection underscore their authors' humanness as private citizens generating personal observations for specific readers. Yet the letters also depict these authors as professionals harboring ambition and delivering careful rhetorical arguments regarding their place in the literary landscape. Because the common theme among the letters is writing, one recognizes that all of these letters used this topic to explore professionalism behind a carefully constructed veil of the everyday.

About the Letters and Their Authors

The American writers in this collection span the Romantic Age (when Stowe was nine years old, Washington Irving published his *Sketch Book*) to the Modern

Age (Jessie Redmon Fauset died in 1961, the same year John Glenn first orbited the earth). As a whole, their letters demonstrate an enduring engagement with politics, reform, religion, and other aspects of the public realm; an ambivalent and often agitated relationship to the professionalization of authorship; a careful negotiation of their respective subcultures within the larger setting of a mass national culture; and a desire to speak and speak passionately about why words matter and why getting them into print matters even more. As Jennifer Cognard-Black and George V. Griffith's contributions demonstrate, Harriet Beecher Stowe and Elizabeth Stuart Phelps both felt a strong need to speak about the importance of words in what they saw as a time of moral decline. Their shared desire to foster moral fiction is directed to George Eliot, a writer who epitomized the common human feeling an author should inspire in her readers. The similarities in how Stowe and Phelps address Eliot are striking: they both find in their British peer a "dear friend," a "sister," a fellow "woman," a common "soul," a symbol of true womanhood — what Phelps called the "Apostle of the 'Woman Question.'" They also lament the lack of Christian ideology in her later work, especially *Middlemarch* and *Daniel Deronda*, for they see in Eliot a writer who could, potentially, reform a group Stowe termed the "children of this generation sitting in the marketplace eager only for sensation & with no time to think."[5]

But where Stowe and Phelps claim that words have a kind of spiritual or philosophical importance, Frances Smith Foster and Sharon M. Harris's selections reveal that Frances E. W. Harper and Rebecca Harding Davis are more interested in the politics of words, their power to shape public policy and practice. In a letter from 1860, for example, Harper lauds Charles Sumner's speech on the floor of the U.S. Senate, asserting that Sumner's words are what might be called a kind of speech-act, "melt[ing] every fetter and dissolv[ing] every chain."[6] And Davis, too, sees words as a means for advocacy and agitation: throughout her life, her writing protested oppressions of all kinds, whether directed at women, factory workers, or African Americans. In letters to James T. Fields and F. P. Church, Davis advocates for better treatment of women authors at the hands of her own "genteel publishers," thereby illustrating her own belief in the real-world force of words to change minds.

Mary Abigail Dodge [Gail Hamilton] and Jessie Redmon Fauset also found themselves having to agitate for fair treatment as the genteel publisher of the first half of the nineteenth century gave way to the business-oriented professional publisher. As Susan S. Williams shows, after Hamilton read an article revealing that male authors were paid higher royalties, she actively protested the discriminatory practices of certain publishing houses. She writes to Sophia Hawthorne, Nathaniel's spouse, that their mutual publishers, "are either from dishonesty or mismanagement utterly untrustworthy[.]"[7] In turn, where Hamilton and Hawthorne were mistreated by publishers, Kimberly J. Banks's collection of letters by Fauset reveal an author under the double oppressions of gender and race within the publishing practices of the Harlem Renaissance—practices that valued the masculine over the feminine as well as writing that white liberals approved over writing found to be subversive. To Alain Locke, the editor of *The New Negro* (1925), Fauset articulates her frustration at Locke's masculinist critiques of her novels. "I have always disliked your attitude toward my work," she tells him, "[. . . and it] has always both amused and annoyed me to read your writings."[8]

This negotiation of a double identity within a specific cultural movement is also found in the letters translated and edited by Kristin A. Risley. Risley works with Palma Pederson, a Norwegian immigrant who actively participated in creating the literary heritage of the *Vesterheimen* or "western home"—a term coined by Norwegian Americans to define their ethnic and geographic home in the United States. The ethos of the *Vesterheimen* was overwhelmingly masculine, and, like Davis and Hamilton, Pederson engaged that masculinity with a mixture of both pride and self-doubt—and a good measure of wit.

Taken together, then, the American authors approach the work of writing with humor and seriousness, grace and anger, assertion and anxiety. They are united in the passion that they bring to their work as well as in their staunch belief that what they are doing matters—for themselves, their readers, their gender, their ethnicity, and their nation.

In turn, the letters presented in this collection composed by British women authors convey myriad perspectives and ideals, but they also share one unifying goal: the desire to communicate the value of their art within the larger context of British literary history. Moreover, as symbols of women's place within the literary marketplace, these letters possess a unique value. Spanning the final decades of the nineteenth century through the turbulent first thirty years of the twentieth, they reflect a remarkable moment in the creation and reception of women's art.

Jennifer Phegley's presentation of Mary Elizabeth Braddon's correspondence yields new insight into the import of the so-called sensation novel to nineteenth-century British society; namely, these letters speak to the ability of vociferous "sensation" writers and their "shocking" fictions to alter the scope and quality of publishing for women. Linda Peterson's contribution—the compelling correspondence between novelists Rhoda Broughton and Mary Cholmondeley—signifies a bridge between sensationalism (Broughton) and a didactic New Womanhood (Cholmondeley). Here, Peterson presents letters that speak to Cholmondeley's sense of alienation alongside Broughton's persistent struggle with what is just versus what is possible. Above all, by demonstrating a profound connection between these two writers from different periods in British literary history — what Peterson terms a mother/daughter relationship — these letters underscore the value of women's literary endeavors not simply as a means of securing intellectual fortune but also as a venue for deepening friendship and understanding between two women writers. Patricia Lorimer Lundberg describes Mary St. Leger Harrison [Lucas Malet] as "modernist," "radical," and "bold" — all of which might well be applied as adjectives to describe her letters, which constructed a clear relationship between fiction and women's lived experience in the 1890s. Malet's letters betray rare glimpses of the New Woman as she was: not as a caricature but indeed as a flawed yet also much beloved persona, outspoken and intellectual, who viewed fiction as the natural extension of one's own understanding of the world (and, in particular, the publishing world).

Molly Youngkin's selections — the letters of Henrietta Stannard, Marie Corelli, and Annesley Kenealy — explore the dynamics of authorship and women's efforts to gain entrée into the annals of professionalism and power in the *fin-de-siècle* marketplace. Perhaps more than any other contribution to the collection, Youngkin's cache of letters paints a scene of celebration, longing, expiration — the many and common responses among women writers working to survive in the literary marketplace. In her presentation of the correspondence of Mary Chavelita Dunne Bright [George Egerton], Elizabeth MacLeod Walls draws a connection between Egerton's letter writing and the growing modernist movement to exploit a Victorian aesthetic. Egerton, a forgotten, passé aesthete, uses her correspondence with an upstart young modernist to declare her independence from this self-serving generation of writers and, simultaneously, to redefine who she is and whom she wishes to become at the end of her popularity. Finally, as Linda K. Hughes underscores with her contribution of the letters of *fin-de-siècle* poet and aesthete, Rosamund Marriott Watson [Graham R. Tomson], letters by women authors regarding their writing sometimes generated a unique opportunity to articulate one's artistic achievement outside of the confines of a particular sociohistorical milieu. Tomson's letters, as Hughes explains, reflect the gamut of experience — and fame — encountered by so many women writers of the 1890s. And thus Tomson's correspondence offers an appropriate denouement to the letters by British writers in this collection. Proud yet at times uncertain, accepting though still assured, Tomson's letters encompass the vacillating opportunities, personalities, and strategies employed by British women writers during this seventy-year period.

Editorial Note

As the general editors of this collection, our two chief concerns have been to make the following letters convenient for modern-day scholars, teachers, and students, while intruding as little as possible upon the quirks, abbreviations, and outright mistakes in the original nineteenth- and early twentieth-century correspondence. As such, our selected letters are almost exact transcriptions.

The correspondence adheres to individual author's idiosyncratic spelling habits, abbreviations, distinctive uses of punctuation (or lack thereof), omissions, and inaccuracies. When a writer such as Harper spells the Reverend Francis Grimke's name "Grimkie," we have not corrected it — and the same is true for words such as "coffe," "entended," and "instil." Neologisms, too, have been left intact: "competest," "tragical," "stayless," or "jollitude." And we've preserved nineteenth- and early twentieth-century spellings — "aweful" for "awful" — as well as, of course, British spellings: "favour," "honour," "criticise," etc. We have also retained all abbreviations, from "tho" to "Xmas" to "yr" (for "your") to "shld" to the ubiquitous ampersand (&), and we've left all capitalizations as they are in the original manuscripts.

In terms of punctuation, some authors employ dashes rather than periods to end their sentences, and in all cases, the dash has been left as the syntactic break. To maintain consistency, here and there we have inserted, with brackets, a missing pair of quotation marks or part of a parentheses which was overlooked. In addition, we've chosen not to insert dropped apostrophes — so words such as "dont," "wont," and "Ive" remain as they were originally written — nor to add entire words that authors accidentally omitted (chiefly articles such as "a" or "the" or conjunctions). We have used a period for all personal titles (Dr., Mrs.).

Throughout the selections, we have normalized the dates and salutations at the beginning of each letter as well as the formatting (spacing, placement on the page, etc.) of all signatures and postscripts. Crossed text, added text, and marginalia have been incorporated either into the body of the letters themselves or into endnotes, depending on readability; and all text that was originally deleted by an author appears in endnotes within carets, e.g., ‹whether›. When handwriting has proved illegible, these instances are also expressed in endnote citations with the phrase ‹indecipherable word›, and when one of our contributors has made an educated guess as to what a word might be, we have retained that word in the letter itself, cordoned it with brackets, and added a question mark, e.g., [more?].

In their endnotes, our individual contributors have cited all references to published works, people, places, and events. When such identification has been impossible, they have indicated that the information is not available. In addition, they have attempted to provide the sources of all direct quotations and most literary allusions used by the authors.

Notes

1. Harriet Beecher Stowe to Mary Ann Evans [George Eliot], Hartford, Connecticut, 25 May 1869, Berg Collection of English and American Literature, the New York Public Library, Astor, Lenox and Tilden Foundations, New York; hereafter Berg Collection, NYPL.

2. Elizabeth Stuart Phelps to Mary Ann Evans [George Eliot], 27 July 1875, Beinecke Rare Book and Manuscript Library, Yale University, New Haven; hereafter Beinecke Lib., Yale U.

3. For a group that she designates as "literary domestics," Mary Kelley argues the opposite: that, in fact, women writers were uneasy in their relationship to professional authorship. See Kelley's *Private Woman, Public Stage* (1984).

4. While Gilbert and Gubar focus almost exclusively on English women writers, they also treat Emily Dickinson; see Gilbert and Gubar's *The Madwoman in the Attic* (1979). In turn, Nancy Armstrong takes Gilbert and Gubar to task, arguing that their focus on the psychology of patriarchal authorship ignores history, particularly the rise of the novel as a feminine and domestic culture text. See Armstrong's *Desire and Domestic Fiction* (1987).

5. Harriet Beecher Stowe to Mary Ann Evans [George Eliot], Hartford, Connecticut, 23 September 1872, Berg Collection, NYPL.

6. Frances Ellen Watkins [Harper], 7 July 1860, *National Anti-Slavery Standard*.

7. Mary Abigail Dodge to Sophia Hawthorne, Hamilton, [Massachusetts], 2 September 1868, Berg Collection, NYPL.

8. Jessie Redmon Fauset to Alain Locke, 9 January [1934], Alain Locke Collection, Moorland-Spingarn Research Center, Howard University, Washington, DC; hereafter Moorland-Spingarn Research Center, Howard U.

References

American Women Writers Series. Ed. Joanne Dobson, Judith Fetterley, and Elaine Showalter. 17 vols. New Brunswick: Rutgers U P.

Armstrong, Nancy. *Desire and Domestic Fiction: A Political History of the Novel*. NY: Oxford U P, 1987.

Barton, David, and Nigel Hall. *Letter Writing as Social Practice*. Philadelphia: John Benjamins Publishers, 2000.

Baym, Nina. *Woman's Fiction: A Guide to Novels by and about Women in America, 1820–1870*. Ithaca: Cornell U P, 1978.

Bledstein, Burton J. *The Culture of Professionalism: The Middle Class and the Development of Higher Education in America*. NY: W. W. Norton and Co., 1976.

Blumin, Stuart M. *The Emergence of the Middle Class: Social Experience in the American City, 1760–1900*. Cambridge: Cambridge U P, 1989.

Bradbury, Malcolm. *Dangerous Pilgrimages: Trans-atlantic Mythologies and the Novel.* NY: Viking Penguin, 1996.

Charvat, William. *The Profession of Authorship in America, 1800–1870.* 1968. Ed. Matthew J. Bruccoli. NY: Columbia U P, 1992.

Christian, Barbara. *Black Women Novelists: The Development of a Tradition, 1892–1976.* Westport: Greenwood Press, 1980.

Cohen, Monica. *Professional Domesticity in the Victorian Novel: Women, Work and Home.* Cambridge: Cambridge U P, 1998.

Daybell, James, ed. *Early Modern Women's Letter Writing, 1450–1700.* NY: Palgrave, 2001.

Decker, William Merrill. *Epistolary Practices: Letter Writing in America before Telecommunications.* Chapel Hill: U of North Carolina P, 1998.

Fetterley, Judith, ed. *Provisions: A Reader from 19th-Century American Women.* Bloomington: Indiana U P, 1985.

Geisler, Christe. *Gender-Based Variation in Nineteenth-Century English Letter Writing.* Amsterdam: Rodopi, 2003.

Geison, Gerald L., ed. *Professions and Professional Ideologies in America.* Chapel Hill: U of North Carolina P, 1983.

Gilbert, Sandra M., and Susan Gubar. *The Madwoman in the Attic: The Woman Writer and the Nineteenth-Century Literary Imagination.* New Haven: Yale U P, 1979.

Goldsmith, Elizabeth, ed. *Writing the Female Voice: Essays on Epistolary Literature.* Boston: Northeastern U P, 1989.

Haight, Gordon, ed. *The George Eliot Letters.* 9 vols. New Haven: Yale U P, 1955.

Hall, Nigel. *The Materiality of Letter Writing: A Nineteenth Century Perspective.* Amsterdam: Benjamins, 1999.

Kelley, Mary. *Private Woman, Public Stage: Literary Domesticity in Nineteenth-Century America.* NY: Oxford U P, 1984.

Larson, Magali Sarfatti. *The Rise of Professionalism: A Sociological Analysis.* Berkeley: U of California P, 1977.

Levine, Lawrence W. *Highbrow/Lowbrow: The Emergence of Cultural Hierarchy in America.* Cambridge: Harvard U P, 1988.

Marcus, Sharon. "The Profession of the Author: Abstraction, Advertising and *Jane Eyre*." *PMLA* 110.2 (March 1995): 206–219.

Perkin, Harold. *The Rise of Professional Society.* NY and London: Routledge, 1990.

Phelps [Ward], Elizabeth Stuart. *Chapters from a Life.* Boston and NY: Houghton, Mifflin, and Co., 1897.

Poovey, Mary. *The Proper Lady and the Woman Writer: Ideology as Style in the Works of Mary Wollstonecraft, Mary Shelley, and Jane Austen.* Chicago: U of Chicago P, 1984.

Richards, Thomas. *The Commodity Culture of Victorian England: Advertising and Spectacle, 1851–1914.* Stanford: Stanford U P, 1990.

The Schomburg Library of Nineteenth-Century Black Women Writers Series. Ed. Henry Louis Gates Jr. 40 vols. NY and Oxford: Oxford U P, 1988–2002.

Showalter, Elaine. *A Literature of Their Own: British Women Novelists from Brontë to Lessing.* Princeton: Princeton U P, 1977.

Standage, Tom. *The Victorian Internet: The Remarkable Story of the Telegraph and the Nineteenth Century's On-line Pioneers.* NY: Walker and Co., 1998.

Tompkins, Jane. *Sensational Designs: The Cultural Work of American Fiction, 1790–1860.* NY: Oxford U P, 1985.

Trachtenberg, Alan. *The Incorporation of America: Culture and Society in the Gilded Age.* NY: Hill and Wang, 1982.

Yellin, Jean Fagan, ed. *Incidents in the Life of a Slave Girl: Written by Herself.* By Harriet A. Jacobs. 1861. Cambridge: Harvard U P, 1987.

Zboray, Ronald J. *A Fictive People: Antebellum Economic Development and the American Reading Public.* NY and Oxford: Oxford U P, 1993.

Chapter 1

JENNIFER COGNARD-BLACK

Harriet Beecher Stowe (1811–1896)

That Harriet Beecher Stowe would become, at age forty, the best-known and best-paid author of nineteenth-century America was, in part, the accident of having been born and raised in antebellum New England — a time and a place in which women writers dominated the American literary scene. The seventh child of Roxana Foote Beecher and Lyman Beecher, Stowe was born in Litchfield, Connecticut on June 14, 1811. Roxana was a novel reader, while Lyman practiced evangelical ministry, and this combination came to fruition in the adult Stowe: a natural preacher and a voluminous reader and writer of popular novels. These aspects of Stowe's personality were fostered by her early education and marriage. From 1824 to 1827, Stowe attended Hartford Female Seminary, founded by her sister Catherine. This seminary was unlike any other, operating on a kind of collaborative pedagogy and offering a curriculum commensurate with that taught to boys. Stowe began teaching as soon as she arrived, which enabled her to advocate her liberal Protestantism as well as her love of good books, all to an audience of young girls (future "readers"). In turn, in 1836 after Stowe moved to Cincinnati and married the professor Calvin Ellis Stowe, she gained both the intellectual support of a literary husband and the opportunity, as a woman in charge of her own home, to practice and hone what Stowe's most recent biographer, Joan Hedrick, has termed "parlor literature."

For it is in the parlor that Stowe began her writing career, crafting short stories for a Cincinnati reading club, sending letters to the sick and bereaved, and writing entertaining correspondence for family gatherings — a kind of real-life, epistolary "novel" read out loud. Akin to teaching at the seminary, Stowe's audience was primarily women, and her early writing is indicative of the voice of everyday comfort and virtue that she would later develop in her novels. Throughout the 1830s and 40s, Stowe published a book of local color narratives, *Primary Geography for Children* (1833); stories and essays in the periodicals *Godey's Lady's Book*, the *Western Monthly Magazine,* and the *New-York Evangelist*; and a collection of fifteen of these stories entitled *The Mayflowers* (1843). With these early publications, Stowe gained her first national audience, an audience that sought relief from poverty, industrialization, disease, and high mortality rates — especially among children. This audience looked to the kind of parlor-based morality that Stowe offered: feminine, evangelical, and egalitarian.

This morality became the basis for the narrative voice of *Uncle Tom's Cabin*, which Stowe wrote as a reaction against the 1850 Fugitive Slave Law. Stowe's novel has repeatedly been credited as one of the factors that precipitated the Civil War, and Stowe herself has been called the "voice of the nation" on abolition. *Uncle Tom's Cabin* appeared as weekly serializations in the *National Era* from June 1851 through April 1852, and with it Stowe acquired international fame as well as the full-time vocation of an author[1] — "author," here, meaning a pre-professional practice in the antebellum marketplace.[2] Until the late 1860s, parlor literature was precisely what the nation wished to read. As a result, Stowe's books were both profitable and popular: her account of the stories that inspired her to write on slavery, *The Key to Uncle Tom's Cabin* (1853); her travelogue, *Sunny Memories of Foreign Lands* (1854); her second slavery novel, *Dred* (1856); her local color books, *The Minister's Wooing* (1859), *The Pearl of Orr's Island* (1862), and *Oldtown Folks* (1869); her Italian romance, *Agnes of Sorrento* (1862); and her domestic sketches, *Household Papers and Stories* (1865 – 1867) and *Little Foxes* (1866). In 1853, Stowe had written to an English admirer: "I wrote what I did because as a woman, as a mother I was oppressed & broken-hearted, with the sorrows & injustice I saw, because as a Christian I felt the dishonor to Christianity — because as a lover of my country I trembled at the coming day of wrath."[3] Stowe took for granted that her position of woman, Christian, and citizen provided her with a right to authorship as well as an inherent appeal to her American readers, and these assumptions proved accurate throughout the first three decades of Stowe's career.

In 1869, however, Stowe published an article, "The True Story of Lady Byron's Life,"[4] in which she accused Lord Byron of an incestuous relationship with his half sister Augusta Leigh — an accusation she made to engage the national debate on woman's rights by holding Lady Byron up as a model of wronged womanhood. Immediately, Stowe received widespread censure from both the British and American press that threatened her prior authorial ethos. Put simply, the press held Stowe to standards of what was fast becoming a professional literary marketplace typified by a growing interest in realism over romance, an objective narrative voice, and a masculine audience of academics, editors, and members of men's clubs.[5] As a result, Stowe's uncontested position as the nation's moral voice came to an end.

During this pivotal time, Stowe sent her first letter to George Eliot,[6] five months before the outbreak of the "Byron whirlwind."[7] Perhaps because Stowe was already working on her article, in this first letter, Stowe asserts her belief in the power of artistic femininity to shape national culture. "What strikes me most in your writings is the *morale*," Stowe tells Eliot. "[S]ometimes I read your writings supposing you man but come to the contrary con clusions from internal evidence[.] No my sister, there are things about us that no *man* can know & consequently no man can write — & being a woman your religion must be different from mans[.]"[8] What Stowe seeks in Eliot is a writer after her own heart: a writer whose moral acuity and feminine insight match her own, despite Eliot's choice of a masculine pseudonym.

The key to such sympathy is to receive this fellow writer's spiritual, emotional, and moral teachings through her novels. Time and again, Stowe refers to how supported she feels reading Eliot's work. As part of her initial letter, Stowe lists the novels by Eliot that she has just reread, explaining that "when my soul is walking as it often does alongside of your soul [. . .], it speaks aloud in a sort of soliloquy — This knowledge of a mind purely from its writings when we have never seen the bodily presence is to me the purest expression of what disembodied communion may be[.]"[9] Over the next decade, reading each other's work becomes a conversation that continues beyond the bounds of the letters themselves. In the correspondence that follows this initial letter, Stowe voices her strong reactions against Tom Tulliver in *The Mill on the Floss*, *Middlemarch*'s Edward Casaubon, and *Daniel Deronda*'s Mallinger Grandcourt as well as her equally strong approbation of the heroines from *Middlemarch* and *Daniel Deronda*, Dorothea Brooke and Gwendolen Harleth. She conflates Eliot's real life with her fictional ones, assuming, for instance, that Casaubon is a thinly veiled complaint against Eliot's own "husband," George Henry Lewes,[10] for being a scholar without the discipline to finish his projects. Stowe even goes so far as to tutor Eliot when her aesthetic or religious teachings "stray" — such as when Deronda becomes a Jew instead of a Christian — from engaging an audience Stowe repeatedly designates as the "children sitting in the marketplace"[11] in need of instruction and guidance.

In turn, Eliot's replies to Stowe are just as warm, intimate, and heartfelt. In her response to Stowe's first letter, Eliot writes that "The best joy your words give me is the sense of that sweet, generous feeling in you which dictated them, and I shall always be the richer because you have in this way made me know you better" (Haight V: 29). Akin to Stowe, Eliot privileges the novel as an ideal means of communication, commenting that "Letters are necessarily narrow and fragmentary, and when one writes on wide subjects are liable to create more misunderstanding than illumination" (V: 31). Yet Eliot trusts Stowe's capacity for true interpretation, even of her "narrow" and "fragmentary" letter: "But I have little anxiety of that kind in writing to you, dear friend and fellow-labourer — for you have had longer experience than I as a writer, and fuller experience as a woman, since you have borne children and known the mother's history from the beginning" (V: 31). Here Eliot creates a picture of her correspondent that Stowe herself would have cherished. Eliot connects Stowe's artistic sympathy to the compassion of friendship, calling her both a "dear friend" and a "fellow-labourer." In addition, she locates Stowe's distinctive authorial powers in her knowledge and experience as a woman and as a mother.

The warm camaraderie that permeates Stowe and Eliot's correspondence is perhaps surprising, given that Stowe is now studied and taught as a sentimental or political writer, Eliot as a realistic, erudite one. Their mutual banter about America and its dual promises of "future" and "jollitude," or their confessions about respective ailments and personal losses, or their worries over how their work will be received across the Atlantic, or even their disagreements about the form in which the soul lives after death are windows that reveal both their private relationship as well as how these two icons desired to shape their public in similar ways. In the years in which Stowe went through the greatest literary trial of her authorial life — and the years in which she self-consciously attempted to professionalize her voice into a more impersonal, high-culture, and realistic one with such works as *Lady Byron Vindicated* (1870) or *Woman in Sacred History* (1874) — her letters to Eliot show how dedicated she remained to the pre-professional notion that the novel, not the magazine or newspaper, was the vehicle for bettering hearts and minds; that parlor literature remained the world's best hope for achieving moral uplift; and that the duty of every writer was to speak with the voice of and for the multitude, not the self. In Eliot, Stowe found a kindred voice, one interested in teaching others how to feel right through reading: "[Y]ou are," Stowe insisted to her friend, "as Dorothea said part of the great current for good in our times[.]"[12]

Letter 1. Harriet Beecher Stowe to Mary Ann Evans [George Eliot],
Mandarin, Florida, 15 April[13] 1869[14]

My Dear Friend

A year ago my friend Mrs. Henry Fields[15] called upon me at my daughter's
in Stockbridge,[16] & gave me what was to me most interesting an account of her
visit to you — & ended with what was to me most delightful of all a word of kind
message from you. Forthwith I resolved then and there that I would write to
you immediately and tell you some of the *many* many thoughts *you* have caused
me — But I was at that time heavily taxed writing a story that I am just now with
fear & trembling giving to the English world[17] It is so intensely American that
I fear it may not out of my country be understood, but I cast it like a waif on
the waters Instead of writing to you, at that time I took Silas Marner[18] and re
read carefully pencil in hand & then the Mill on the Floss.[19] Then then Adam
Bede[20] & then Romola[21] — I have *studied* all these *more* than read them — & you
will therefore see why it is that I *must* begin a note to you "My dear friend" — I
have also made careful studies of Scenes from Clerical life[22] — and it is my
opinion that some things in those sketches have never been executed in your
best works — "Janet's Repentance"[23] is a theme that might have been expanded
into a novel of greater length & has in it some of the most effective elements
of the great underlying tragedy of life treated in a most original way. What
strikes me most in your writings is the *morale.* You appear to have a peculiar
insight into the workings of the moral faculties — and the religious development
through all its phases which is very similar to that of Goethe[24] — so complete
is the understanding that you seem to have with each phase that one cannot
divine which of all that you have drawn is the one with which you yourself
most deeply sympathise — but following you through all the lanes & winding
high ways & by ways of religious thought one often asks *where* does this pilgrim
find *home*? — What is the *rest* of this explorer? I see your footsteps sometimes
in places where one is both glad & sorry to see that another has been — glad
because the heart always throbs at sympathetic tokens sorry because; there was
there no water and no rest —

You are by nature so *thoroughly English* — Your mind, has in the most airy
play of its imagination that English definiteness that refuses to exhale in a mist
& turn to a mere cloud — so that I cannot believe that you have come out into
pantheism in the German way[25] — It requires pipes & tobacco & indefinite coffe
to bring that about — besides you are as thoroughly *woman* as you are English.
For sometimes I read your writings supposing you man but come to the con-

trary con clusions from internal evidence No my sister, there are things about us that no *man* can know & consequently no man can write — & being woman your religion must be different from mans — & I often ask myself what is the innermost by which she lives — that that gives her courage to meet life such as a nature like hers must find it to be — to bear what such a nature must bear — & to look forward to death with joy? —

I do not ask you to tell me but when my soul is walking as it often does alongside of your soul up & down paths of thought and suggestion, it speaks aloud in a sort of soliloquy — This knowledge of a mind purely from its writings when we have never seen the bodily presence is to me the purest expression of what disembodied communion may be.

I know your husband[26] only thro the life of Goethe which my husband[27] finds interesting as he is a perfect monomaniac on that subject. He has I believe collected every possible edition of the Faust and is at present busy in most profound studies on the second part which he designs to embody in an article on the Theology of Goethe — I hope he may do it but he is one forever mining delving studying & slow to work out what he gets into the uses of popular language[28] I understand Mr. Lewes has published a philosophy that is to solve & settle all things[29] May he do it! — When they are all right let me know — and I want everything made clear as a looking glass but I dont want to go through the process of doing it —

My husband has just returned from a summer spent in Spain & we have been reading your[30] poem[31] — What a host of capabilities for romance in that old Spain — what intertwisting of possibilities in the three religions all picturesque and then the mystery of the gypsy race But I like prose — English prose better than poetry — I wish you had written it as a romance. Our language is a hard one for poetry — You write exquisite poetry in your prose — some parts of Adam Bede to wit & you are unfettered by metre —

Did you ever think of the rhythmical power of prose how every writer when they get warm fall into a certain swing & rhythm peculiar to themselves the words all having their place and sentences their cadences But in blank verse proper or any form of metrical rhyme the flow of the idea has to be turned backward to suit the fetters — You are a poet — but I dont like *English* poetry so well as English prose — I wish Mrs. Browning had written more prose[32] —

Shall you ever come to America — If so come & see us? — please do —

When my next book comes out I shall ask the publishers to send you an Early Copy — & if my good husband *does* get his article on the Theology of Goethe done he will make an offering of it to you

I do wish you would come to America We should give you a hearty welcome & there are things here worth seeing —

I am just now with my son[33] in Florida where we are planting an orange grove and starting a settlement — We live in an orange grove & are planting many more — It is a lovely country — My northern home however is my permanent address —

Box 1217 Hartford Conn
I am with true regard & affection
Ever Yours
HB Stowe

Letter 2. Harriet Beecher Stowe to Mary Ann Evans [George Eliot], Hartford, Connecticut, 23 September 1872 [34]

My Darling Friend

For once, I am going to write a letter for no other reason but *just because I feel like it* I have just had a letter from my Rabbi[35] & he has just had he says such a lovely letter from you as quite sets him up into the seventh heaven[36] —

Then again dear, I have been following you brokenly and by snatches thro "Middlemarch" for I have been travelling all summer & could only see the paper that had it in, at intervals.[37] Just the other day I came across a saying of Dorothea to young Ladislaw or whatever his name is to the effect that whatever is honestly & purely attempted for good becomes part of the great force that is moving for good thro the universe[38] — Well — I thought — good — I will cut out that sentence as one article of my creed — I have not the paper by me now & cannot reproduce it.

My darling I confess to being very much amused & sympathetic with Dorothea's trials with a literary husband.[39] Of course I see that he was a stick & all that but the wifely feeling of Dorothea is exactly what you & I and all of us who make real marriages marry with & then these husbands! — Now, dont show this to Mr. Lewes but I know by my own experience with my Rabbi that you learned how to write some of those things by *experience*. Dont these men go on forever getting ready to begin — absorbing learning like sponges — planning sublime literary enterprises which never have a *now* to them? — Years ago my husband made all the researches for writing a life of Martin Luther[40] He imported tons of books — he read he lectured he fired me into a flame of eagerness he prepared & prepared & prepared but his ideal grew & he *never* came to the time of completion — & now alas — never will. Still he goes on reading studying investigating subject after subject apparently for no object but to entertain me & when I try to make him write the books he ought to he is *never* ready — & I believe I sometimes make myself a sort of trouble some outside conscience to him by trying to push him up to do what he has been so long getting ready to do — So you see I sympathise with poor Dorothea but then her husband is too much of a stick! — How could she marry him! — Yet I understand too that girls often make a false marriage & plight their faith to an unreal shadow who they suppose inhabits a certain body — I am intensely curious to know what is to become of her.

You write too well my darling — altogether too well to be pitched into Harpers Weekly[41] along with Edmond Yates[42] & Mifs Braddon[43] & the sensation mongers of the day — Your story is for the thoughtful — for the artist for the few — when it is all out I shall try and interpret it to the many. Generally you live & speak in a surge of thought above the average of society. Dickens was intelligible — I saw a beautiful & very true article by Mr. Lewes about him lately[44] —

Your forte is the morale — & you are as Dorothea said part of the great current for good in our times I would have hope of a young girl or young man that I could get to read Romola but I cannot often do it I did see its effect once on a young officer who having traveled in Florence could understand the scenery so he was powerfully affected shaken with the terrible moral of Tito[45] — The same idea runs in Adam Bede the 'facilis descensus &c'[46] — it is terrible! —

But what shall we say of the children of this generation sitting in the marketplace eager only for sensation & with no time to think?[47] — What shall people so solemnly impressed with real living as you do with them? —

As to the spirits — I only wanted to show you & Mr. Lewes that there is an immense field of *facts* there, unexplored unclassified — undeveloped & to me it is intensely a practical question.[48] For in a certain way I am a pastor & confessor of hundreds who know me only thro the spirit[49] — & the sorrows of life lie open to me — Even this summer I have been the confidant of many who have had the central nerve of life cut in the tearing from them a friend without whom life seems not worth having — Then they ask me the question — Is there a way of communication Would you seek relief this way? —

Now if I had not patiently & sympathetically explored if I had scornfully denounced or declared all such things imposture I should have no power. But now I say as I lately said to a heartbroken mother who asked me Are there such facts — I answer Yes — there are — I have seen I have examined patiently I have listened & no spiritualist could tell more extraordinary facts than have passed under my own observation — Trust me then, when I tell you that this field is a dangerous one for you with your weakened nerves & suffering heart to explore.[50] It is a *real* force but an *unknown* — *unregulated* one, & one which in the present state of knowledge would be unsafe for you to trust yourself to —

There is where I differ from Mr. Owen[51] But much must be pardoned to a man whose only hope of immortality & consolation in the future have come thro this channel Owen is a charming man & for a while pursued the inquiry in a truly philosophic manner & spirit. But he is a Scotchman & of course has an itching after theology & cannot resist the temptation to make up one —

There we part — I say the facts are facts — so far as I can see they are honestly investigated & presented but these are not yet enough to build any system on & to form any religious conclusions from them would be dangerous. To resort to it as consolation for mourners is dangerous — There my friend & I differ — Yet you too be charmed with Owen did you know him —

I wonder what will be the fate of our poor Undine Katy Fox[52] — poor child what a life hers has been Let us believe in an infinite Love & Pity that cares for all & will bring the blind by a way they know not.

Good bye my darling —
Ever your true love
HB Stowe

I send this to you thro Lowe & co because being away from my papers I have not your address

Letter 3. Harriet Beecher Stowe to Mary Ann Evans [George Eliot], Boston, Massachusetts, 26 September 1872[53]

My Dear Friend.

I think when you see my name again so soon you will think it rains, hails, & snows notes from this quarter.

Just now however I am in this lovely little nest in Boston where dear Mrs. Field like a dove sits "brooding on the charmed wave"[54] & we are both, so much wishing we had you here with us — & she has not received any answer from you as yet in reply to the invitation you spoke of in your last letter to me. It seems as if you must have written & the letter somehow gone astray, because I know of course, you would write

Yesterday we were both out of our senses with mingled pity & indignation at that dreadful stick of a Casaubon — & think of poor Dorothea dashing like a warm sunny wave against so cold & repulsive a rock

He is a little too dreadful for any thing — there does not seem to be a drop of warm blood in him — & so as it is his misfortune & not his fault to be a cold blooded, one must not get angry with him It is the scene in the garden after the interview with the Doctor that rests on our mind at this present.[55] There was such a man as he over in Boston high in literary circles but I fancy *his* wife wasn't like Dorothea & a vastly proper time they had of it treating each other with mutual reverence like two Chinese Mandarins[56]

My love: what I miss in this story is just what we would have if you would come to our tumble down, jolly, improper, but joyous country — namely "jollitude"[57] — (You write & live on so high a plane — it is all self abnegation — we want to get you over here, & into this house[58] where with closed doors we sometimes make the rafters ring with fun — & say any thing & every thing no matter what & wont be any properer than we's a mind to be[)] — I am wishing every day you could see *our America* — travel as I have been doing from one bright thriving pretty flowery town after another & see so much wealth, ease progress, culture & all sorts of nice things

This dove cote where I now am is the sweetest little nest — fronting on a city street with back windows opening on a sea view — with still quiet rooms filled with books pictures & all sorts of things such as you & Mr. Lewes would enjoy Dont be afraid of the ocean now Ive crossed it six times & assure you it is an over rated item Froude is coming here[59] — why not you? — Besides we have the fountain of Eternal Youth here[60] — that is in Florida where I live & if you should come you would both of you take a new lease on life & what glorious poems and philosophies & what not we should have My Rabbi writes in the seventh heaven on account of your note to him[61] — to think of his setting off on his own account when I was away! —

Come now, since your answer to dear Mrs. Fields[62] is yet to come let it be a glad yes & we will clasp you to our heart of hearts —

Your ever loving
HBS

Letter 4. Harriet Beecher Stowe to Mary Ann Evans [George Eliot], Hartford, Connecticut, 25 September 1876[63]

My dear Friend.

Well — Daniel Deronda is at last achieved! — We, my husband & I, have strictly confined ourselves to the *serial* form, taking it in our monthly installments & meditating there on[64] — as if it were a passage of scripture. Great talks have we had together as it proceeded, great searchings of heart as to what was to be done with the various characters.

The story divides itself as a parson might say, into two heads—English life & Jewish life. Here let me give you a little anecdote in point A lady met at one of our fashionable watering places, a Jewish lady of the name of Cohen—She said to her that she was lost in admiration of George Elliot in *daring* to make her hero and heroine Jewish!—I think myself, that tho Scott, Mi*f*s Edgeworth & Disraeli have all done the same, it was somewhat *venturesome*.[65]

Of course the "children sitting in the market place," find the rhapsodies of Mordecai, tomes—& one lively friend of mine describes that part of her reading as "wading through a Jewish morass." to reach the firm land of English character & life—In return, my husband a most enthusiastic old Rabbi who boasts the possession of both the Babylonian & Jerusalem Talmud in his library—who rejoices in the only copies in America of Schudt Mer[c]kwürdigkeiten des Juden & Eisenmenger's Entdecktes Judenthum.[66]—he is most specially devoted to the "Jewish Morass" & therein meditates day & night He has for many years cultivated a personal intimacy with the leading Rabbi, & is a frequent attendant at the synagogue—I, myself share this interest, from some of his spare learning having rubbed off onto me, by mere accident of contact, so that I was prepared to understand & care for that part.

But after all I confess that my hearts blood vibrates more toward Gwendolin than Mirah & that I feel a more *living* interest in her feelings, struggles & sorrows than those of Mirah—the two characters of Gwendolin & Grandcourt are I think the artistic genius. Grandcourt as[67] doing the work of the villain in the play without any of the burnt cork of a stage villain—I cant imagine any character more utterly worthless & disagreeable, yet invested throughout with such an air of worldly respectability and *probability*. There is great reticence in his wickedness. Not a monster by any means. Making suitable & even generous provision for the woman he is tired of—. & treating the woman he marries with every external form of consideration & only occasionally swearing at her in the strictest privacy. The point in the courtship where he ejaculates "damn her!" under his breath is a comment on such marriages worth pages of disquisition[68] & the beauty of it is—that you have no moral reflection The grim distinctness with which you set forth "marriage a la mode" with the rector[69] pointing out to the young girl the duty of securing a brilliant match & comforting himself with the reflection that she cannot know any thing about previous irregularities[70]—is a stroke of satire on English good society which I suppose they hardly appreciate—but I do—

Your clergymen of the English church for the most part give me a cold chill, those in your books. When I think that no man enters that church without solemnly declaring that he is inwardly moved by the Holy Ghost & called according to the will of Christ to take that office — & then see that gentlemenly men take it avowedly for no other purpose than as a genteel livelihood for men of good family[71] — I lose all faith in the power of vows to bind — or threats to terrify — & I cease to wonder at scepticism where the church is so represented. The baptismal service, the ordination vows — marriage vows & burial service of that church are aweful enough to make an angel tremble but seem to be taken lightly enough by good English society

So that if your young Jew Daniel Deronda is educated a member in good standing of the English church I can easily perceive that there is no barrier which should prevent his going back to his people except the barrier of good society. The Jews are 'mauvais ton'[72] — that is all.[73] Christ is nothing to the average young Briton — & it does not appear that any feelings about *Him* stand in Derondas way when Mordicai asks him if he accepts the religion of his people[74] — Christ is not[75] much more to Mr. Gasgoine than to Mordicai — in fact, if unselfishness, & self surrender & sacrifice for a noble cause are Christ like Mordicai has the more Christ like spirit of the two. If Deronda had been *a christian*, after the manner of Paul or John — that scene would have been widely different — Although England wants in *such* christians as that, & we should not hear so much about modern scepticism.

But infinitely the most interesting character to me is Gwendolin — Of the artistic *vitality* of the character I need no other proof than that I have been called at various tea tables to defend her[76] as earnestly as if she had been an actual neighbor giving parties round the corner To my mind, so far from being an exceptionally selfish or worldly woman — she stands in the midst of a heartlessly selfish & utterly worldly state of society a creature of higher impulses sensitive to the very first suggestion of moral right

She is like a young eagle who has been brought up among barn yard chickens with clipped wings — full of uneasy instructs that point to soaring among the clouds of heaven. A frivolous or hard, or worldly selfish woman would have worn the diamonds with a self satisfied grin & taken the good the Gods provided without too many reflections on how or at[77] whose expense she came by them.[78] Now is there any thing in the world to me more painfully pathetic, than the blind struggles of such a soul for its native air — its ideal completeness — and it is mournful to see how utterly Godless are all who undertake to guide her Had Deronda been educated a Jew he might have told her out of his old testament scripture that there was a teacher & Guide who dwells in the soul of those who aspire after good — that the High & Lofty One who inhabiteth the eternity dwells in the stricken spirit of the humble "to revive the heart of the contrite one["][79] — he might have told her of One who "to those of no might increaseth strength"[80] — of One who says "I will bring the blind by a way that they knew not, & I will make darkness light before them & crooked things strait — these things will I do to them *& not forsake them*!["][81] And it appears that the well educated serious minded young English gentleman of our time knows neither the God of the old testament nor the Jesus of the new — the Jesus who came to save his people from their sins — & has nothing to give to this imploring anguish & vague aspiration of a soul longing for purity — literally nothing

If this is the last result of modern culture — if it is only to tutor helpless humanity — do your best & dont hope for comfort or help then what a mockery is our existence! But I *know* in whom I believe — & you when you wrote Dinahs prayer with poor Hetty — & Mr. Fryans[82] counsels to Janet — knew full well what a power there is in the living[83] Christ to say to the impotent "Rise up & walk."[84] It is not instruction *about* goodness people need — They need an almighty inseperable Friend of their souls ever present, pure yet sympathetic wise yet strong — to protect them from themselves & bear them above themselves — & alas — if I am to read your picture of English life as you see it there is no such Friend there. For me, it is now fifty years since that Friend became a living presence to me & ever since He has been the Inspirer — consoler & strength of my life, — & to read of those who struggle for goodness without knowing *him* is painful to me as to read of those who die of hunger when there is bread enough & to spare. Christ is my Life — all I ever have been able to do or suffer — all my hope for the poor & oppressed has been my feeling sense of his living presence & that He is ruling all things —

He shall not *fail* nor be discouraged till he have set judgment in the Earth. —

Your book dear friend is a splendid success artistically — & I am happy to learn, financially. Even genius must have the pounds & shillings & I know what they are worth & I hope you have what will purchase you a season of leisure & rest.

As to the criticisms of our American papers — or any free comments on your personality which may have found their way into them — I can only speak for the *great* ones — the large dailys of N York & Boston are all warm in admiration — & incapable I am quite sure of printing any thing about you or your affairs which might be painful.[85] I am so interested in all that concerns you that if any such thing had appeared in well known papers I should have heard of it. I send you to day the notice of the Christian Union. The religious papers are generally I think approbative — or admiring

My only living son is now at Bonn university — a theological student.[86] He is to be a minister. Perhaps he may see you sometime in your continental wan-

derings or in London — he will visit England next summer — Since *he* is there
the Rabbi & I often look longingly at Germany & discuss the question whether
we could not go over & stay with him awhile. If Mr. Stowe were only ten years
younger how he would enjoy it. — It is not quite improbable & in that case we
should see you. I hope you will have a nice easy time now helping your husband
with his work thro the press[87] — Charley (my son) reads his works — I have not
(head enough left) — I believe he (your husband) knows how fortunate above
mortals he is to have *you* — Well dear sister friend — may the All Loving bless
you — & may he *rest* you as only He can. I know all about the head aches &
weariness of over driven nerves — but there is a rest in God that heals all — Your
own true friend[,]

HBS

    I have tried in vain to get the Rabbi to say *to* you some of the handsome things
he is all the while saying of you — but alas — he is lazy — & the labor of form-
ing those arabic quail tracks in which he expresses himself is too great for him.
He loses himself in a perfect swamp of reading — & he *would* write isnt he too
bad?

    I send you my little, *only* grandson the cherub grown to six years — Your
description of the little Deronda reminded me of Him

Notes

    1. In the first week of its release, the novel sold 10,000 copies, and in the first year, that
number climbed to 300,000. *Uncle Tom's Cabin* sold even more copies abroad than in
America; by the end of 1852, legitimate and pirated editions made for one-and-a-half
million sales in England, and the book was translated into more than forty languages
(Mott 118).

    2. For more on what Ann Douglas has termed the "feminization" of American lit-
erature in the early and mid-nineteenth century as well as the relationship of women
writers to the emerging culture of professional authorship both during and after the
Civil War, see Susan Coultrap-McQuin's *Doing Literary Business* (1990); Ann Douglas's
The Feminization of American Culture (1977); and Jane Tompkins's *Sensational Designs*
(1985).

    3. Harriet Beecher Stowe, letter to Lord Denman, 20 January 1853 (HM 24162), Hun-
tington Library, San Marino.

    4. This article was published simultaneously in the September 1869 issues of the *At-
lantic Monthly* in America and *MacMillan's* in England.

    5. See chapter three of Cognard-Black's *Narrative in the Professional Age* (2004).

    6. Thirteen of Stowe's letters to Eliot survive, archived in the Berg Collection, NYPL.

Partial and often inaccurate transcriptions are published in Charles Stowe's (1889) and Annie Fields's (1898) respective biographies; Marlene Springer's "Stowe and Eliot: An Epistolary Friendship" (1986) ; and Margaret Wolfit's "The Toast to the Immortal Memory" (1989).

7. Oliver Wendell Holmes in a letter to John Lothrop Motley (Morse II: 183).

8. Harriet Beecher Stowe, letter to Mary Ann Evans [George Eliot], 15 April 1869, Berg Collection, NYPL.

9. Harriet Beecher Stowe, letter to Mary Ann Evans [George Eliot], 15 April 1869, Berg Collection, NYPL.

10. Lewes (1817 – 1878), a novelist, playwright, and literary scholar who was never legally Eliot's husband but, rather, her live-in companion, collaborator, editor, and manager. Lewes published his best-known work, *Life of Goethe*, in 1855.

11. A reference to the book of Luke which Stowe uses in her letter to Eliot dated 23 September 1872.

12. Harriet Beecher Stowe, letter to Mary Ann Evans [George Eliot], 23 September 1872, Berg Collection, NYPL.

13. ‹March›

14. Berg Collection, NYPL.

15. Annie Adams Fields (1834 – 1915) was a good friend of the Stowe family, an author in her own right and the wife of James T. Fields, Stowe's Boston publisher.

16. Stockbridge, Massachusetts, where Stowe's daughter, Georgiana, lived with her husband, Henry Allen.

17. Here Stowe means her novel *Oldtown Folks* (1869) — a fictional rendition of stories told by her husband Calvin about his hometown of Natick, Massachusetts.

18. *Silas Marner: The Weaver of Raveloe* (1861) was one of Eliot's most-read novels, especially as public schools in America adopted it as part of their standard curriculum.

19. *The Mill on the Floss* (1860) was Eliot's third novel. In a subsequent letter to Eliot, Stowe comments on what she deems as the patriarchal relationship between the novel's heroine, Maggie Tulliver, and her brother, Tom. "Tom Tulliver has been heretofore the characteristic Englishman," claims Stowe. "Tom has made the laws for women & judged women by them but the day is coming when *Maggie* is to judge Tom & show him that there is a higher style of living than ever *he* dreamed of — Maggie whose weakness was stronger than Tom's strength but who didn't know & does not *yet* know how much more than he, she is — " Harriet Beecher Stowe, letter to Mary Ann Evans [George Eliot], 25 May 1869, Berg Collection, NYPL.

20. According to Frank Mott, upon its publication in 1859, Eliot's second novel, *Adam Bede*, was quickly a best-seller in the United States.

21. *Romola* (1863) was Eliot's "Italian novel," set in fifteenth-century Florence and detailing the story of a scholar's daughter, Romola, who comes to despise her corrupt husband, Tito.

22. Published anonymously, *Scenes of Clerical Life* (1857) was Eliot's first "novel" — a collation of three previously published stories about the lives of clergymen.

23. "Janet's Repentance" (1857) was first published as a stand-alone piece in *Blackwood's Magazine* before it was incorporated as one of the three novellas included in *Scenes of Clerical Life*. The novel traces Janet's addiction to alcohol and her recovery via the assistance of an evangelical minister, Mr. Tyran. It is possible that this particular story moved Stowe more than others given that her own son, Fred, was an alcoholic.

24. Johann Wolfgang von Goethe (1749–1832) was a German poet, dramatist, novelist, and philosopher, known primarily for his dramatic poem, *Faust* (1808).

25. Pantheism, part of the nineteenth-century idealist movement in German philosophy, is the theory that God and the universe are one and the same, suggesting that God does not have a distinct personality or intimate relationship with humans.

26. George Henry Lewes, Eliot's companion.

27. Calvin Ellis Stowe (1802–1886), Stowe's husband and a professor of religious philosophy.

28. Calvin Stowe never completed such an article.

29. Originally published in 1845–1846, Stowe probably means Lewes's 1868 American edition of *The Biographical History of Philosophy: from its origins in Greece down to the present day*.

30. ‹the›

31. *The Spanish Gypsy; a Poem* (1868) was George Eliot's last attempt at a book-length poem.

32. Elizabeth Barrett Browning (1806–1861), a British poet and scholar so successful that, when William Wordsworth died, she was considered for the position of poet laureate.

33. In 1867, Stowe purchased a house and orange grove in Mandarin, Florida, thus joining many New Englanders who had taken to wintering "down South." Stowe's son, Fred, occasionally helped her and Calvin at the Florida plantation.

34. Berg Collection, NYPL.

35. Perhaps because nineteenth-century Americans believed Jews were God's "chosen people," Protestant ministers sometimes wore yarmulkes and were called Rabbi. Calvin Stowe was known, colloquially, as "Old Rab."

36. This letter does not appear in Gordon Haight's *The George Eliot Letters*.

37. From 1871 to 1872, *Middlemarch* was published in eight bimonthly parts in *Blackwood's Magazine*. In turn, from 1871 to 1873, *Middlemarch* appeared in weekly installments in *Harper's Weekly* in America. Stowe read the *Harper's Weekly* edition.

38. See the conversation between Dorothea Casaubon and Will Ladislaw in chapter 39 of *Middlemarch*.

39. In her biography, Joan Hedrick writes, "Calvin Stowe *was* like Casaubon in his vast learning and the difficulty that he had, after marriage, in harvesting the fruits of his laborious scholarship. But his lusty enjoyment of physical pleasures set him apart from the bloodless Casaubon" (101).

40. Another unfinished scholarly project on the part of Calvin Stowe.

41. While Stowe refers here to the kind of popular access to high culture that American periodicals such as *Harper's* espoused throughout the antebellum period, by the

time *Harper's* serialized *Middlemarch*, its editors were actively working to make distinctions between the mass of American readers and a select audience of the highest cultivation that *Harper's* hoped to attract. Eliot's serialized novels played a crucial role throughout the 1870s in shifting the magazine's audience, especially as realism became codified as a high-art approach to literature.

42. Edmund Hodgson Yates (1831–1894), an English journalist and popular novelist whom Charles Dickens appointed as the dramatic critic for the *Daily News*.

43. Mary Elizabeth Braddon (1835–1915), actress, author, and journalist.

44. Stowe probably refers here to Lewes's 1872 article, "Dickens in Relation to Criticism." See Alice Kaminsky's *George Henry Lewes as Literary Critic*.

45. In Eliot's novel, Tito Melema is Romola's husband, a man whose seemingly innocuous interest in comfort, wealth, and politics becomes, ultimately, the basis for his loss of humanity.

46. Latin for "easy fall." Stowe refers to the plight of Eliot's character, Hetty Sorrel, a vain and immature girl who rejects the trustworthy, working-class Adam Bede for a false lord and becomes pregnant. Hetty's child dies from neglect, and she is imprisoned for its murder.

47. "They are like unto children sitting in the marketplace, and calling one to another, and saying, We have piped unto you, and ye have not danced; we have mourned to you, and ye have not wept" (*King James Bible*, Luke 7:32).

48. Beginning with a letter from February 1872, Stowe shares with Eliot both her and her family's keen interest in spiritualism, including practices of mesmerism, automatic writing, and other such "phenomina" (Stowe's term). Here, Stowe specifically refers to a lengthy letter in which she'd recounted various séances, including one in which Stowe supposedly had a two-hour conversation with the spirit of Charlotte Brontë. "The conversation was upon that state where she was sojourning—its laws—modes of being, employments—the replies were all characteristic. It was Charlotte careful, keen, witty, wise, pensive, with a profound sense of a past life of suffering & a most affecting & solemn sense of *eternal peace*." In reply, Eliot said, "*Your* experience with the *planchette* is amazing; but that the words which you found it to have written were dictated by the spirit of Charlotte Brontë is to me (whether rightly or not) so enormously improbable, that I could only accept it if every condition were laid bare, and every other explanation demonstrated to be impossible" (Haight V: 280). Harriet Beecher Stowe, letter to Mary Ann Evans [George Eliot], 11 May 1872, Berg Collection, NYPL.

49. Stowe means through reading *Uncle Tom's Cabin*; she's being modest with the number.

50. In Eliot's letter to Stowe from March 1872, she explains, "Last year we spent our summer months in Surrey [. . .]. Unhappily the country was not so favourable to my bodily health as to my spiritual, and on our return to town I had an illness which was the climax of the summer's malaise. That illness robbed me of two months, and I have never quite recovered a condition in which the strict duties of the day are not felt as a weight" (Haight V: 252).

51. Robert Dale Owen (1801–1877), spiritualist and author of *Footfalls on the Boundary*

of Another World (1859) and *The Debatable Land Between This World and the Next* (1872). Prior to writing Eliot, Stowe had promised Owen that she would review his *Debatable Land* as well as attempt to get Eliot to peruse it: "I shall take some pains to get the book read by leading minds in England, particularly by Mrs. Lewes (*Adam Bede*), with whom I correspond" (Wilson 333).

52. The stress of preparing *Lady Byron Vindicated* (1870) induced an illness in Stowe that her sister Isabella termed a "great nervous exhaustion" (Hedrick 367). Stowe's remedy was to visit New York and take up Dr. George Taylor's Swedish Movement Cure. As a result of Taylor's own interest in spiritualism, Stowe attended four séances held by Katie Fox Jencken, a professional New York medium. For more on Stowe and Katie Fox, see Sarah L. Taylor's *Fox-Taylor Automatic Writing* (1–3).

53. Berg Collection, NYPL.

54. "But peaceful was the night / Wherein the Prince of Light / His reign of peace upon the earth began. / The winds, with wonder whist, / Smoothly the waters kissed, / Whispering new joys to the mild Ocean, / Who now hath quite forgot to rave, / While birds of calm sit brooding on the charmed wave." John Milton, "On the Morning of Christ's Nativity," *The Complete Poems of John Milton: The Harvard Classics*, ed. Charles W. Eliot (Danbury, CT: Grolier Enterprises Corp., 1980), 7–15.

55. A conversation between Edward Casaubon and the young surgeon, Mr. Lydgate, in chapter 42 of *Middlemarch* in which Lydgate reveals to Casaubon that he is going to die (310).

56. According to *Webster's*, a "Chinese Mandarin" is synonymous with a "pedantic official" — specifically, "a person of position and influence especially in intellectual or literary circles." Thus, this Boston couple treats each other like stuffy administrators. *Webster's Third New International Dictionary*, vers. 2.5 (Springfield, MA: Merriam-Webster, Inc., 2000).

57. The anonymous and undated typescript of this letter held at the Berg Collection transcribes this word as "jollitride," but I maintain it is "jollitude." It is worth noting that this particular typescript normalizes and alters much of Stowe's original throughout.

58. ‹here›

59. James Anthony Froude (1818–1894), English historian and early member of the High Church movement at Oxford. In 1872, Froude went on a lecture tour of America.

60. Juan Ponce de Leon (1460–1521), an explorer who first came to the Americas as part of Columbus's second voyage in 1493 and who is credited for naming modern-day Florida.

61. While this note from Eliot to Calvin Stowe is lost, in July 1872, Calvin wrote a letter to Eliot on his theology and love of *Faust*. See Calvin Stowe, letter to Mary Ann Evans [George Eliot], 31 July 1872, Berg Collection, NYPL.

62. ‹has›

63. Berg Collection, NYPL.

64. From February to September 1876, *Blackwood's Magazine* in England and *Harper's* in America carried simultaneous installments of Eliot's last novel, *Daniel Deronda*.

65. Scott, Edgeworth, and Disraeli are all nineteenth-century British novelists. Sir Walter Scott (1771–1832) created a Jewish heroine, Rebecca, for his romance *Ivanhoe* (1819); Maria Edgeworth (1767–1849) portrayed Jews in a number of fictional works, but *Harrington* (1817) is a novel that overtly exaggerates anti-Semitism for its own ends; and Benjamin Disraeli (1804–1881) was both a sensation novelist and the only Jewish Prime Minister of England.

66. These are two early eighteenth-century Jewish histories, Johann Jacob Schudt's *Jewish Curiosities* (1714), a chronicle of the Frankfurt Jews after the 1711 ghetto fire, and Johann Andreas Eisenmenger's *Jewry Unmasked* (1711), an anti-Semitic work. Both Schudt and Eisenmenger worked to convert Jews to Christianity.

67. ‹being›

68. Chapter 13 of *Daniel Deronda* details Mallinger Grandcourt's aggressive courting of one of the novel's two heroines, Gwendolen Harleth. In a riding scene in which the two verbally spar about whether Gwendolen should risk getting hurt by taking a leap with her horse, Grandcourt says to Gwendolen, "I should like to have the right always to take care of you," and she replies, "Oh, I am not sure that I want to be taken care of: if I chose to risk breaking my neck, I should like to be at liberty to do it" (133). It is after this reply that Grandcourt responds, "Damn her!," although he thinks the line rather than saying it out loud.

69. ‹clergyman›

70. Chapter 13 also presents a scene between Gwendolen Harleth and her uncle, the Rector Gascoigne, in which the uncle bullies his niece into accepting Grandcourt as a brilliant match for a girl of great beauty but no wealth. Gascoigne is fully aware that Grandcourt has fathered children with his mistress — but assumes that his niece could not know of such things.

71. Stowe refers here to the practice in England of bestowing ecclesiastical sinecures upon certain well-bred gentlemen, especially second sons who could not inherit their father's estate. A "sinecure" literally means "without care" and included a yearly allowance and the use of a residence without any real expectation of having to perform much in the way of work.

72. A French idiom meaning "bad taste" or "bad breeding."

73. ‹I was some›

74. Mordecai Cohen is a Jewish prophet and mentor to Deronda as well as the brother of Mirah Cohen, one of the novel's two heroines who ultimately marries Deronda.

75. ‹as›

76. ‹far more›

77. ‹by›

78. Originally, the diamonds were a gift from Grandcourt to his mistress, Lydia Glasher — the woman Grandcourt keeps but does not marry. When Glasher discovers that Grandcourt is going to marry someone else, she devises a way to tell Gwendolen of her existence and of how Grandcourt's son would be disinherited should they marry. In the end, Gwendolen marries Grandcourt anyway, and after their wedding, as per Grand-

court's demand, Glasher sends Gwendolen the diamonds — but with a note Grandcourt does not know about. The note reads, in part, "These diamonds, which were once given with ardent love to Lydia Glasher, she passes on to you. You have broken your word to her [. . .]. Perhaps you think of being happy, as she once was, and of having beautiful children such as hers, who will thrust hers aside. God is too just for that [. . .]. The willing wrong you have done me will be your curse" (358–359).

79. "For thus saith the high and lofty One that inhabiteth eternity, whose name is Holy; I dwell in the high and holy place, with him also that is of a contrite and humble spirit, to revive the spirit of the humble, and to revive the heart of the contrite ones" (*King James Bible*, Isa. 57:15).

80. "He giveth power to the faint; and to them that have no might he increaseth strength" (*King James Bible*, Isa. 40:29).

81. "And I will bring the blind by a way that they knew not; I will lead them in paths that they have not known: I will make darkness light before them, and crooked things straight. These things will I do unto them, and not forsake them" (*King James Bible*, Isa. 42:16).

82. Stowe means "Mr. Tyran's."

83. ‹name of›

84. There are two possible sources here: the first is from Luke: "But when Jesus perceived their thoughts, he answering said unto them, What reason ye in your hearts? Whether is easier, to say, Thy sins be forgiven thee; or to say, Rise up and walk? But that ye may know that the Son of man hath power upon earth to forgive sins, (he said unto the sick of the palsy), I say unto thee, Arise, and take up thy couch, and go into thine house" (*King James Bible*, Luke 5:22–24); while the other comes from Acts: "Then Peter said, Silver and gold have I none; but such as I have give I thee: In the name of Jesus Christ of Nazareth rise up and walk" (*King James Bible*, Acts 3:6).

85. In a letter from May 1876, Eliot asks Stowe, "I wonder whether you ever suffered much from false writing [. . .] in the newspapers. I dare say that pro-slavery prints did not spare you. But I should be glad to think that there was less impudent romancing about you as a *citoyenne* of the States than there appears to be about me as a stranger. But it is difficult for us English who have not spent any time in the United States to know the rank that is given to the various newspapers" (Haight VI: 246).

86. In 1871, Stowe's son Frederick William (1840–1871?)—a decorated Civil War soldier — disappeared in San Francisco after sailing around the Horn. Fred was an alcoholic, and Stowe and her husband never learned whether he drank himself to death, committed suicide, or simply decided to vanish. In turn, Stowe's son Charles Edward (1850–1934) married Susie Monroe and became a minister, first in Maine and, later, back in Hartford, where his parents lived. Charles Stowe is the author of the *Life of Harriet Beecher Stowe, Compiled from Her Letters and Journals* (1889), in which many inaccurate copies of Stowe's letters first appeared.

87. In Eliot's previous letter dated 6 May 1876, she writes, "When we come back from our journeying I shall be interesting myself in the MS.s and proofs of my husband's third volume of his Problems, which will then go to press" (Haight VI: 246–247). Eliot

refers here to Lewes's *Problems of Life and Mind*, a five-volume work written between 1874 and 1879.

Works Cited

Cognard-Black, Jennifer. *Narrative in the Professional Age: Transatlantic Readings of Harriet Beecher Stowe, George Eliot, and Elizabeth Stuart Phelps*. NY: Routledge, 2004.

Coultrap-McQuin, Susan. *Doing Literary Business: American Women Writers in the Nineteenth Century*. Chapel Hill: U of North Carolina P, 1990.

Douglas, Ann. *The Feminization of American Culture*. NY: Anchor Books, Doubleday, 1977.

Eliot, George. *Daniel Deronda*. 1876. Ed. Terence Cave. London and NY: Penguin Books, 1995.

———. *Middlemarch*. 1872. Ed. Gordon Haight. Cambridge, MA: The Riverside Press, 1956.

Fields, Annie. *Life and Letters of Harriet Beecher Stowe*. Boston and NY: Houghton, Mifflin, and Co., 1898.

Haight, Gordon, ed. *The George Eliot Letters*. 9 vols. New Haven: Yale U P, 1955.

Hedrick, Joan. *Harriet Beecher Stowe: A Life*. NY: Oxford U P, 1994.

Kaminsky, Alice R. *George Henry Lewes as Literary Critic*. Syracuse: Syracuse U P, 1968.

Lewes, George Henry. "Dickens in Relation to Criticism." *Fortnightly Review* 17 (1872): 141–154.

Morse, John T. Jr. *Life and Letters of Oliver Wendell Holmes*. 1896. 2 vols. NY and London: Chelsea House, 1980.

Mott, Frank Luther. *Golden Multitudes: The Story of Best Sellers in the United States*. NY: Macmillan, 1947.

Springer, Marlene. "Stowe and Eliot: An Epistolary Friendship." *Biography* 9.1 (Winter 1986): 59–81.

Stowe, Charles Edward. *The Life of Harriet Beecher Stowe Compiled from her Letters and Journals*. 1889. Detroit: Gale Research Co., 1967.

Stowe, Harriet Beecher. *Uncle Tom's Cabin; or, Life among the Lowly*. 1852. Ed. Ann Douglas. NY: Penguin Books, 1986.

Taylor, Sarah L., ed. *Fox-Taylor Automatic Writing, 1869–1892: Unabridged Record*. Boston: Bruce Humphries, 1936.

Tompkins, Jane. *Sensational Designs: The Cultural Work of American Fiction, 1790–1860*. NY: Oxford U P, 1985.

Wilson, Forrest. *Crusader in Crinoline: The Life of Harriet Beecher Stowe*. Philadelphia: J. B. Lippincott, 1941.

Wolfit, Margaret. "The Toast to the Immortal Memory." *George Eliot Fellowship Review* 20 (1989): 60–62.

Chapter 2

FRANCES SMITH FOSTER

Frances Ellen Watkins Harper (1825 – 1911)

Frances E. W. Harper's professional reputation was first established as an abolitionist lecturer and writer. Her poetry and prose appeared regularly in antislavery publications such as the *North Star*, the *Liberator*, the *Anti-Slavery Bugle*, the *Provincial Freeman*, and the *National Anti-Slavery Standard*. William Still verifies her prominence in that movement by devoting an entire chapter of his history, *The Underground Rail Road* (1872), to Harper's life and by including excerpts from about thirty of her letters.

Though Frances E. W. Harper is most frequently remembered as an abolitionist, Harper's interests and her audiences, even before emancipation, were more diverse than this single issue. In recognition of her leadership as a featured writer or contributing editor to the *Repository of Religion and Literature and Science and Art*, the *Anglo-African Magazine*, the *Christian Recorder*, and other African-American periodicals, *The Afro-American Press and Its Editors* (1891) deemed Harper "the journalistic mother, so to speak, of many brilliant young women who have entered upon her line of work" (Penn 422). Among those African-American journalists to whom Harper was mentor and friend were Mary Shadd Cary, Ida B. Wells, Victoria Earle, and Kate D. Chapman. Furthermore, as a national officer of the Women's Christian Temperance Union, a leader in the women's suffrage movement, and an ardent pacifist, Frances E. W. Harper shared the podium with luminaries such as Elizabeth Cady Stanton, Susan B. Anthony, and Frances E. Willard and published regularly in journals dedicated to these causes. In short, Frances Harper's life and letters were inextricably woven with various nineteenth-century social reform movements. For more than sixty years, she was an international figure with extensive networks among the literati and political leaders.

Not only was Frances E. W. Harper a popular writer and a political arbiter, she was also one of the first African-American women to make her living as a wordsmith who published texts intended to make history as well as to recover or to revise it. Thus it is particularly striking that there are few extant letters in which Harper writes about writing. Whether it be in terms of aesthetics and authorial purposes or in terms of the more mundane but certainly relevant business correspondence of a professional author, one finds hardly any letters that speak directly about Harper's literary experiences or theories. Perhaps even more curious is the fact that in what appears to be the only extant private letter in which Harper wrote specifically about the kinds of literature she espoused, she says, "If our talents are to be recognized, we must write less of issues that are particular and more of feelings that are general. We are blessed with hearts and brains that encompass more than ourselves in our present plight [. . .]. We must look to the future which, God willing, will be better than the present or the past, and delve into the heart of the world" (Redding 39).[1] Since Harper's writing career was devoted to championing specific causes, this statement seems more than a little odd. When one considers that this letter was addressed to Thomas Hamilton, the editor of the *Anglo-African Magazine,* which proudly presented itself as published by, for, and about African Americans, it seems even more odd. Moreover, the "present plight" to which Harper referred was the Civil War, a topic that few, if any, nineteenth-century American writers could ignore and a topic upon which Harper focused in two novels, an epic, and countless shorter poems.

For a woman who published thousands of words, who inspired and mentored many writers during a professional writing career of more than six decades, the sixty-five words about writing seem meager indeed — until one factors in several historical and social realities. To understand her comments to Hamilton, two words, "extant" and "appears," need emphasis. "Extant" suggests that what we possess is not necessarily all there was or is. Indeed, evidence is clear that the personal papers of African-American writers available to researchers or the general public are only a small part of the body of materials generated over the past centuries. Put simply, the vast majority of the writings by African Americans before now have been misplaced, hidden, or destroyed. "Appears" is also important because the excerpt from Harper's letter is a quotation published by the eminent historian J. Saunders Redding who, in 1939, claimed that the letter was privately owned. Though these words often have been cited, after twenty years of researching Harper's life and works, I have yet to find the actual document or another scholar who has seen the original letter.

Such epistolary lacuna is not unique to Frances E. W. Harper. Most nine-teenth-century African-American women's writings were neither protected nor preserved. Sometimes this disappearance was by fate, as was the case with some of Harper's professional correspondence that was destroyed in a fire in her publisher's offices. In other cases, the absence of personal papers is a result of economic or educational disadvantages or racial discrimination. Untold num-bers of pages have been lost by family members who were ignorant of their value or whose proffered donations were rejected by historical societies, state libraries, and university archivists that did not value African-American materials. All too frequently letters and other personal papers did not survive the relocating and hazards of fortune within African-American families and organizations that did treasure women's writings. Some that were collected in archives of his-torically black colleges and universities were damaged or remain inaccessible because such institutions have had little money and inadequate space to catalog and preserve their holdings.

When studying the lives and letters of most African-American women writ-ers, a paucity of personal information is the norm. Moreover, there is another significant factor — deliberate censoring or protective silencing — that stems di-rectly from racism. In defense against allegations that black women are immoral and ignorant, that their manners and mores deviate from white, middle-class theories of gentility and decorum, African-American women writers and their correspondents have regularly practiced a politics of respectability that requires careful monitoring of their public words and rigorous protection of their in-timate communications from the curious or the casual eye. As a result, when letters, diaries, and journals by nineteenth-century African-American women writers do exist, the heirs or literary executors rarely allow publication or cita-tion without close editing and many omissions.[2]

This anthology represents one of the tangible and tangled problems that histor-ical discrimination and social exclusion can produce. The editors rightly wanted to include letters about writing from major women writers representing two na-tions and multiple cultures. And yet, had they defined this project rigidly, they would have found it nearly impossible to be inclusive. By understanding "letters" as forms of communication and particularly by recalling that in the nineteenth century the boundaries between private and public correspondence were perme-able, by recognizing that fiction, poetry, and essays were ways of communicating personal and true ideas in much the same manner as epistles, there is plenty of evidence that Frances E. W. Harper was a prolific and professional writer who communicated her theories and methods to others through "correspondence." In many newspaper columns and other media, Harper's creed that literature that expressed the ideas and ideals of African Americans could be both aesthetically pleasing and socially dynamic is clearly evident. As one of her poems states, her goal as a writer was to "make the songs for the people."[3] And there is ample evidence that African Americans knew and appreciated Harper's literary aims and attitudes.

Thinking of Frances E. W. Harper in the context of her era and of her race as well as her gender gives greater insight into the words quoted from her 1861 letter that "we must write less of issues that are particular and more of feelings that are general." Most of the surviving letters by Frances E. W. Harper were written to an individual but then circulated within communities and published in periodicals. Sometimes the published letter was prefaced by comments from "a friend," sometimes it was addressed to the editor who was, oftentimes, Harper's colleague or acquaintance. Harper also wrote as a regular correspondent to some papers, describing her travels, experiences, and opinions and soliciting help from or addressing her remarks to a general public whom she addressed as "dear reader."

The selections that follow come from Harper's fiction, journalism, and poetry as well as her published letters, and they show that Harper used generic forms interchangeably and repeatedly in public and private correspondences. For example, on 4 June 1860, Charles Sumner[4] gave a speech called "The Barbarism of Slavery" on the floor of the United States Senate. On 26 June, Harper sent Sumner a letter that consisted of one sentence and a poem that began "Thank God that thou hast spoken." On 17 July, the poem and an extract of another letter were published in the *National Anti-Slavery Standard*, and on 20 July, the poem appeared in the *Liberator* under the title "To Charles Sumner." In Harper's *Poems* (1871), the poem bears the title "Lines to Charles Sumner," and nearly fifty years later, in 1903, Frances E. W. Harper sent the same poem in a letter to the Reverend Francis Grimke.[5] In an earlier letter to Grimke, Harper had requested copies of his published sermons. In her thank you for receiving the sermons, Harper wrote that publications such as Grimke's could "open the eyes of this generation to the duties and dangers of the hour," and she included her poem as elaboration. Obviously, for Frances E. W. Harper, poems and letters, sermons and other publications were equally or interchangeably useful as letters and lectures, as celebration and praise, as inspiration and guidance, as *utile* and *dulce*.

For the *Christian Recorder*, Frances E. W. Harper contributed a series that she called "Fancy Sketches" and sometimes "Fancy Etchings,"[6] which is another example of her blending of art and work, public and private letters. In one "Fancy Etchings" column, Harper's narrative persona, Jenny, tells Aunt Jane that she wants her elder to "write a book, a good book, full of hard, earnest thoughts. A book that will make people better and happier because they read it."[7] Strikingly similar words are uttered in Harper's 1892 novel, *Iola Leroy*, by Dr. Latimer, who tells Iola she should "write a good, strong book which would be helpful" to her community. Iola responds first that one needs "both leisure and money" as well as "patience, perseverance, courage, and the hand of an artist to weave it into the literature of the country" but then agrees that "out of the race must come its own thinkers and writers" (262–263). Iola's words convey the same theory of literary obligations as in the conclusion of Harper's serialized novel *Minnie's Sacrifice* (1869) and in another "Fancy Etchings" column wherein Jenny says that especially the people whose daily lives are difficult should have "flowers of poetry" scattered around their paths.[8]

The selections that follow are thus different from those in other sections of this volume. They are not, strictly speaking, personal letters about writing from a writer to an individual correspondent. They are, however, communications from a writer who thought carefully and clearly about art and its relationship to action. They are letters to an entire nation that show more than tell what Frances E. W. Harper envisioned as the proper roles and responsibilities of writers in nineteenth-century America.

Letter 1. Frances Ellen Watkins [Harper] to Charles Sumner, Finley, Ohio, 26 June 1860[9]

Honored Sir,

Will you permit me a sister of the outcast race to present you this simple tribute, as one might lay an humble flower upon a costly shrine?

Thank God that thou has[t] spoken
Words earnest, true and brave
The lightening of thy lips has smote
The fetters of the slave.

I thought the shadows deepened
Round the pathway of the slave
As one by one his faithful friends
Were dropping in the grave.

When other hands grew feeble
And loosed their hold on life
Thy voice rang like a clarion
In freedom's noble strife

Thy words were not soft echoed
Thy tones no syren[10] song,
They fell as battle axes
Upon our giant wrong.

God grant thy words of power
May fall as precious seeds
That yet may leaf and blossom
In high and holy deeds.

May the God of Justice and Freedom ever bless and defend you, and keep you "beneath the hollow of his hand and as a apple of his eye."

Yours with much respect and gratitude.
Frances Ellen Watkins

Letter 2. Frances Ellen Watkins [Harper], 7 July 1860[11]

Mr. Sumner's Speech

Was there not something grand in that masterly exposition of "The Barbarism of Slavery"? No softening down of *slave* States into *capital* States; no unholy and craven pledges, if the bond-men should attempt to break their chains, on which the rust of centuries has gathered, that he and Massachusetts stand ready to quench their aspirations by bayonets and blood; no singing in the guilty ears of the slave master that Carolina, with half, or more than half, of her children in chains, is more developed than Great Britain, whose air has so little affinity with our intense despotism that it melts every fetter and dissolves every chain; no brutal flings at the alleged inferiority of the negro, no insults to our feebleness. Again we may say Thank God that he has spoken![12]

Letter 3. Frances Ellen Watkins Harper, 20 February 1873[13]

"Fancy Etchings" By Mrs. Harper
"Aunt Jane? Aunt Jane!"
I lifted up my eyes as a fresh young voice sang out my name in tones of pleasurable excitement, and before me stood my niece; her face aglow with one of those beautiful enthusiasms which ever lend a charm to the plainest face.
"What is it, darling?"

"Why Aunty, I want you to immortalize yourself. I want you to write a book, a good book, full of hard, earnest thoughts. A book that will make people better and happier because they read it. I wish I had your power of utterance, and I would write such a book. I am just from College and I mean to do something for my race."

I said, "What do you mean to do?" for her words had awakened my interest.

"I hardly know what I shall succeed in doing, but I want to be a living loving force, not a mere intellectual force, eager about and excited only for my own welfare; but a moral and spiritual force. A woman who can and will do something for woman, especially for our own women be-cause they will need me most."

"I am glad, very glad, Jenny, that you have concluded to make something out of your young life. I am always delighted when I see young people full of enthusiasm and lofty aspirations. Our women have been treated as the 'fag'[14] end women of the country, but now that advantages are thrown open to you, which were denied to us older women, I hope that you will prove that your minds are widening with the cycles of the sun. Jenny, darling, permit me to say to you, set your mark high; aim at perfection, and if you would succeed yourself, always be ready to acknowledge the success of others, and do not place the culture of your intellect before the development of your soul. The culture of the intellect may bring you money and applause, but the right training of your soul will give you character and influence; but really Jenny you did not ask me for a sermon and I will stop moralizing."

"Oh! no dear Aunty, I love to hear you talk. You often regret your limited knowledge of books; but you are a book yourself, and I am passionately fond of reading you."

"Thank you, darling, you are quite complimentary to me this morning, but I suppose you like to say pleasant things to Aunty."

"But Aunty if they are pleasant, they are true. If some of us younger women have more learning, you have more knowledge; and if we know more of books, you know more of life; and one knowledge should supplement the other. I felt rather provoked, when Thomas Pemroy who was discussing with you on some disputed point, asked you in such a tone of conceited superiority, 'Don't you know any better than that?' and I thought that you felt a little sensitive when Mary Talbot took the liberty to correct a mispronounced word of yours in the presence of several persons."

"Of course I did not feel as if she were treating me very politely, but I attributed it to her lack of social training. Of course I don't suppose that any of us like as if our words were mice, and that a critic sat beside us like a watchful cat, ever ready to pounce upon a mishap or slipshod word. I think an undue cultivation becomes a kill joy to genial conversation, and a repressive force to society."

"I think Aunty, that conversation ought to be made of the finest and most excellent of all arts. Have you not met with some people with whom you feel it easy to converse? They seem to un-lock your heart and loosen your lips. Then there are others who do not talk to you; they make speeches at you; they step through their sentences as if their words were eggs and they were afraid of hatching them, and they convey to your mind an idea of a self-consciousness that annoys you."

"Yes, I have met with just such people; but how I do enjoy those genial souls, whose fine social tact and generous appreciation, unloosen your lips and make you feel at home with them. I often desire these people with tact, more than I do the people with mere talent; but when both are combined, I think it creates a delightful companionship. But Jenny we have wandered from our original subject, what do you intend doing in the future."

"Well Aunty I will tell you when I come again. It is a pleasant little secret, but it will keep; and I must go now for I have an engagement at eleven o'clock, and it is now half past ten, so good-bye Aunty."

"Good-bye Jenny, come again soon, and unfold Aunty's willing ear, all the wise schemes and loving plans you have for the good of our people, and in the meantime rest assured of my hearty sympathy for the cause in which you are interested."

Letter 4. Frances Ellen Watkins Harper, 24 April 1873[15]

"Fancy Etchings"

"[. . .] Aunty I want to be a poet, to earn and take my place among the poets of the nineteenth century; but with all the glowing enthusiasms that light up my life I cannot help thinking, that more valuable than the soarings of genius are the tender nestlings of love. Genius may charm the intellect, but love will refresh the spirit."

"I am glad, Jenny, that you feel so, for I think the intellect that will best help our race must be heart supplied: but do you think by being a poet you can best serve our people?"

"I think, Aunty, the best way to serve humanity, is by looking within ourselves, and becoming acquainted with our powers and capacities. The fact is we should all go to work and make the most of ourselves, and we cannot do that without helping others."

"And so having sounded the depths of your inner life you have come to the conclusion that you have a talent or genius for poetry."

"Aunty, do you remember that poem I wrote some months since which you and others admired so? To me that poem was a revelation, I learned from it that I had power to create, and it gave me faith in myself, and I think faith in one's self is an element, of success. Perhaps you think this is egotism."

"Oh no, I do not think that consciousness of one's ability to perform certain things, is egotism. If a woman is beautiful it is not vanity for her to know what the looking glass constantly reveals. A knowledge of powers and capacities should be an incentive to growth and not a stimulus for vain glory; but Jenny, what do you expect to accomplish among our people by being a poet?"

"Aunty I want to learn myself and be able to teach others to strive to make the highest ideal, the most truly real of our lives[.]"

"But, Jenny, will not such an endeavor be love's labor lost? what time will our people have in their weary working every day life to listen to your songs?"

"It is just because our lives are apt to be so hard and dry, that I would scatter flowers of poetry around our paths; and would if I could amid life's sad discords introduce the most entrancing strains of melody. I would teach men and women to love noble deeds by setting them to the music, of fitly spoken words. The first throb of interest that a person feels in the recital of a noble deed, a deed of high and holy worth, the first glow of admiration for suffering virtue, or thrill of joy in the triumph of goodness forms a dividing line between the sensuous and material and the spiritual and progressive. I think poetry is one of the great agents of culture, civilization and refinement. What grander poetry can you find than among the ancient Hebrews; and to-day the Aryan race with all the splendor of its attainments and the magnificence of its culture; still lights the lamp of its devotion at Semitic altars. Ages have passed since the blind beggar of Chios[16] was denied a pension, in his native place, but his poetry is still green in the world's memory."

Letter 5. Frances Ellen Watkins Harper, 1 May 1873[17]

"Fancy Etchings"

"What does uncle Glumby think about your being a poet?"

"He says, it is all moonshine, that poetry is like the measles, it generally breaks out in the young; and that in a few years I will be over, what he calls, my new fancy."

"Have you ever read him any of your poems."

"Yes, Aunty, and that to my sorrow."

"How so, Jenny."

"Oh! he is so unappreciative, I don't believe he hardly knows one piece of poetry from the other. Aunty, you do not know how provoking it is, after you have racked your brain, for thoughts, to have some one listen to you with an indifferent air, and when you are finished, to say with a yawn — that sounds well; but I think that I have seen something like it before. Do you remember that poem I wrote on the 'Shadows of Morning'?"

"Yes, and I thought it was very fine. What did uncle Glumby think?"

"Why, Aunty, I don't believe you'd find out if you guessed for an hour. I was so provoked, I could have cried and I thought, I would never read any of my verses to him again as long as I lived. When I had finished and sat waiting for his opinion he peered at me through his spectacles and asked, 'Can you cook a beef steak?'"

"Ha!, ha! ha! That is just like my dear, prosy, matter of fact, brother; my niece, builds her beautiful air castles and he stands at the threshold and cries, 'beef! beef! beef!!!' . . ."

Letter 6. Frances Ellen Watkins Harper, 25 September 1869[18]

Minnie's Sacrifice[19]

And now, in conclusion, may I not ask the indulgence of my readers for a few moments, simply to say that Louis and Minnie are only ideal beings touched here and there with a coloring from real life?

But while I confess (not wishing to mis-represent the most lawless of the Ku-Klux) that Minnie has only lived and died in my imagination, may I not modestly ask that the lesson of Minnie shall have its place among the educational ideas for the advancement of our race?

The greatest want of our people, if I understand our wants aright, is not simply wealth, nor genius, nor mere intelligence, but live men, and earnest, lovely women, whose lives shall represent not a "stagnant mass, but a living force."

We have wealth among us, but how much of it is ever spent in building up the future of the race? In encouraging talent, and developing genius? We have intelligence, but how much do we add to the reservoir of the world's thought? We have genius among us, but how much can it rely upon the colored race for support?

Take even the *Christian Recorder;* where are the graduates from colleges and high school whose pens and brains lend beauty, strength, grace and culture to its pages?

If, when their school days are over, the last composition shall have been given at the examination, will not the disused faculties revenge themselves by rusting? If I could say it without being officious and intrusive, I would say to some who are about to graduate this year, do not feel that your education is finished, when the diploma of your institution is in your hands. Look upon the knowledge you have gained only as a stepping stone to a future, which you are determined shall grandly contrast with the past.

While some of the authors of the present day have been weaving their stories about white men marrying beautiful quadroon girls, who, in so doing were lost to us socially, I conceived of one of that same class to whom I gave a higher, holier destiny; a life of lofty self-sacrifice and beautiful self-consecration, finished at the post of duty, and rounded off with the fiery crown of martyrdom, a circlet which ever changes into a diadem of glory.

The lesson of Minnie's sacrifice is this, that it is braver to suffer with one's own branch of the human race, — to feel, that the weaker and the more despised they are, the closer we will cling to them, for the sake of helping them, than to attempt to creep out of all identity with them in their feebleness, for the sake of mere personal advantages, and to do this at the expense of self-respect, and a true manhood, and a truly dignified womanhood, that with whatever gifts we possess, whether they be genius, culture, wealth or social position, we can best serve the interests of our race by a generous and loving diffusion, than by a narrow and selfish isolation which, after all, is only one type of the barbarous and antisocial state.

Letter 7. Frances Ellen Watkins Harper to Francis J. Grimke, Philadelphia, 30 March 1903[20]

Dear Mr. Grimkie

Respected friend permit me to thank you for the strong brave words you have spoken in your pamphlet of sermons and to ask if you can furnish me with one or two of those pamphlets and at what price can they be obtained? I like your idea of suggesting a day of fasting. What sight would be more impressive than a race upon its knees, appealing from the injustice of man to the everlasting justice of God. Well although the shadows of the fast are still projected into the life of the race, there is sunshine still mingled with the shadows when you and others are able to present our cause as you can at the present times. May God bless you and strengthen you to do valiant[21] work for those whose feebleness should be their best defence, their weakness an ensign of protection.

Remember me to Mrs. Grimkie.
Yours respectfully
Frances E. W. Harper

Letter 8. Frances Ellen Watkins Harper to Francis J. Grimke, [1903?][22]

Dear Sir:

I received your sermons on lynching for which accept my thanks for your rememerance of me. And also permit me to emphasize my gratitude to you especially for your manly refusal to accept the verdict of the mob, in the cases of lynching. [. . .] Do these sermons have a circulation outside of our people? Could there not be some contrivance planned by which your sermons would reach larger audiences than they do now. Could not the council plan for their circulation, and the women's clubs induced to scatter them among the white people in different localities [. . .]? Perhaps after New Year's day I will get a few from you to distribute. The first Thursday in next month I expect a paper on personal religion. Please if you are selling them send me the price. Please remember me to Mrs. Grimke. And if you have one more that you can spare send it to me. If at any time there is any movement to circulate these sermons, although my means are limited, count on me as a subscriber. Oh my friend when we have among us such men as you, who can handle our cause as you can, we have reached the place where we can "Thank God and take courage." And instead of only looking "Gloomily to the past,["] we should learn to look more hopefully to the future. Oh there is a field before us which will might fill an angel s hand, and thrill an angels heart. Is there not an amount of unused power among us? A lack of Christly consecration to the attainment of life highest excellence and beauty. Oh that God may ever help you to help others, and teach you to teach others I am an old woman, whose span of life may soon, very soon be done. I belong to a generation whose ranks are thinner and whose grave are thicker, but upon you my younger brother has not God himself laid a burden of loving service. Oh thanks, many thanks to you for sending the sermons, and pardon my delay in acknowledging them. [. . .]

F. E. W. Harper

That seamless robe shall yet enfold
    The children of the sun
Till rich and poor, and bond and free
    In Christ shall all be one
And for his sake from pride and hate
    Our spirits shall be free
Till through our souls shall sound the words
    Ye did "it unto me."[23]

Frances E. W. Harper.

Letter 9. Frances Ellen Watkins Harper to Francis J. Grimke,
Philadelphia, 27 June 1903[24]

My dear friend and brother:

You do not know how grateful and pleased I am to receive your welcome
and timely sermons. Oh if they could only be scattered broadcast through the
whole country, to open the eyes of this generation to the duties and dangers of
the hour, and create within them an earnest desire to create and develop within
the race the most precious thing that a man or woman can possess, and that is
good character. "And who will harm us if we follow that which is good." I do
not think there has been an hour since the surrender that there has been more
need of the wisest counsels, the warmest hearts, the holiest influences, and the
most Christ-like endeavors. When the race produces many men like you, so
able to understand, and so ready to bestow such instruction as is contained in
your sermons, we may thank God and take courage, and look beyond the present pain with hope for a better and brighter future, in which love shall conquer
hate, and both branches of the human family in this country realize that their
interests and duties all lie in one direction, and that we cannot violate the one
without dissevering the other. Please accept these lines[25] which I send you as
the expiring flicker of a lamp whose earthly light is well nigh spent, whose span
of life may very soon be done. May God bless you and your wife, and keep you
both as the apple of His eye and beneath the hollow of his hand.

Yours gratefully,
Frances E. W. Harper

Notes

1. This excerpt comes from an 1861 letter to Thomas Hamilton, editor of the *Weekly Anglo-African* and of the *Anglo-African Magazine*, a periodical for which Harper was listed as a regular correspondent. The quotation here is from the earliest source, J. Saunders Redding's *To Make a Poet Black*. Redding writes that this letter is privately owned.

2. See Gloria T. Hull, "Researching Alice Dunbar-Nelson: A Personal and Literary Perspective."

3. From her poem "Songs for the People" published in *Poems* (Philadelphia: George S. Ferguson, 1896), 69–70.

4. Charles Sumner (1811–1874), an outspoken abolitionist who represented Massachusetts in the U.S. Senate from 1851 until his death.

5. Francis J. Grimke (1850–1925), a former slave who studied at Howard University and Princeton Seminary before becoming minister at the Fifteenth Street Presbyterian Church in Washington, DC, where he distinguished himself as a preacher and a civil rights activist.

6. The "Fancy Etchings/Fancy Sketches" columns appeared in 1873–1874; however, Harper's connection with the *Christian Recorder* resulted in nearly a half century of serialized novels, poems, essays, and letters from her and regular announcements of her travels and lectures.

7. 20 February 1873.

8. 24 April 1873.

9. Sumner Papers (bmsAm1[45-2]), Houghton Library, Harvard University, Cambridge.

10. An alternate spelling for "siren," which means seductive or beguiling.

11. Extract of a letter published in the *National Anti-Slavery Standard*.

12. Here follows the poem that was sent to Charles Sumner dated 26 June.

13. Harper's "Fancy Etchings" columns were published nationally in the *Christian Recorder*, edited by the African Methodist Episcopal Church. It was a major source of news for African Americans and often published poetry, stories, and essays by major and aspiring writers.

14. The remnants or very end of something.

15. Extract of a "Fancy Etchings" column, published in the *Christian Recorder*.

16. Chios is a Greek island and home to the poet Homer.

17. Another "Fancy Etchings" column, published in the *Christian Recorder*.

18. Part of *Minnie's Sacrifice*, a serialized novel that appeared in the *Christian Recorder* from 12 June 1869 through 25 September 1869.

19. These are the final paragraphs of *Minnie's Sacrifice*.

20. Frances J. Grimke Papers, Moorland-Spingarn Research Center, Howard U.

21. ‹wash›

22. Moorland-Spingarn Research Center, Howard U.

23. Included as a postscript.

24. Moorland-Spingarn Research Center, Howard U.

25. From a poem that begins "Thank God that thou hast spoken," which had been sent to Charles Sumner in a letter and published in several places as "Lines to Charles Sumner."

Works Cited

Harper, Frances E. W. *Iola Leroy; Or Shadows Uplifted*. 1892. NY: Oxford U P, 1988.

———. *Minnie's Sacrifice*. 1869. *Minnie's Sacrifice, Sowing and Reaping, Trial and Triumph: Three Rediscovered Novels by Frances E. W. Harper*. Ed. Frances Smith Foster. Boston: Beacon P, 1994. 1–92.

Hull, Gloria T. "Researching Alice Dunbar-Nelson: A Personal and Literary Perspective." *But Some of Us Are Brave: Black Women's Studies*. Eds. Gloria T. Hull, Patricia Bell Scott, and Barbara Smith. NY: The Feminist P, 1982. 189–195.

Penn, I. Garland. *The Afro-American Press and Its Editors*. 1891. NY: Ayer, 1988.

Redding, J. Saunders. *To Make a Poet Black*. 1939. Ithaca: Cornell U P, 1988.

Still, William. *The Underground Rail Road: A Record of Facts, Authentic Narratives, Letters &c., Narrating the Hardships, Hair-breadth Escapes, and Death Struggles of the Slaves in Their Efforts for Freedom, as Related by Themselves and Others or Witnessed by the Author*. Philadelphia: Porter & Coates, 1872.

Chapter 3

SHARON M. HARRIS

Rebecca Harding Davis (1831 – 1910)

Although born in a small town in Alabama, Rebecca Harding Davis lived in Wheeling, (West) Virginia, from the age of six until her marriage to L. Clarke Davis in 1863, settling thereafter in Philadelphia. It was the environment of Wheeling, a cotton and iron manufactory town, which gave Davis the background for her most famous story, "Life in the Iron-Mills" (1861). Considered one of the pioneers of mid-century realism, Davis became a regular contributor to the major U.S. literary periodicals of the day—including the *Atlantic Monthly, Harper's, Scribner's, Galaxy,* and *North American Review*—and to popular magazines such as *Peterson's, Youth's Companion,* and *St. Nicholas.* The 1860s were prolific years for her as a writer and immensely complicated years for her personally: she published more than a dozen stories in the *Atlantic,* married at the age of thirty-two, serialized and then published in book form three novels (*Margret Howth, Dallas Galbraith,* and *Waiting for the Verdict*) and serialized a novella ("David Gaunt"), gave birth to three children (Richard Harding Davis, Charles Belmont Davis, and Nora Davis), suffered a severe illness after the birth of her first child, and became a contributing editor for the *New York Daily Tribune.* But the 1860s were only the beginning of Davis's lifelong career as a remarkably talented and prolific author. She continued to publish her work until shortly before her death at age seventy-nine. She published fiction and nonfiction on such diverse topics as the effects of industrial capitalism, race relations in the postwar United States, women's need for economic independence, the abuse of the mentally ill, the need for changes in the laws that limited women's rights in marriage, and the devastating effects of U.S. imperialism in the 1890s.

The Davis family was a literary dynasty as well. Davis maintained her standing as a major writer throughout her life. Her husband was a highly regarded journalist, editing the *Philadelphia Inquirer* and later the *Philadelphia Ledger*. Her eldest son, Richard, became a popular novelist and journalist (and the male model for the popular Gibson Girl portraits), and her younger son, Charles, wrote fiction and nonfiction, including an epistolary biography of his brother, *Adventures and Letters of Richard Harding Davis* (1917). Only Nora declined the writing profession, although she seems to have moved in notable social circles.[1]

Davis was also involved in and vocal about several reform movements of the nineteenth century. Not surprisingly, considering her views on women's need for economic and legal independence, she supported suffrage; she was also ardent in her belief in the need for the abolition of slavery, temperance laws, and individual acts of charity (though she did not support the rise of the large charitable institutions because she felt they removed the personal interaction necessary for true charity). Through these activities and her writing career, Davis came to know many of the most renowned writers and political leaders of the nineteenth century. Her autobiography, *Bits of Gossip* (1904), recounts the many people — famous and unknown, honorable and disreputable, from the North and the South — whom she knew during her lifetime. Her voice of protest never failed her, and in the last years of her life she wrote fifteen articles on topics relating to national and cultural agendas. One such essay, "One Woman's Question" (1907), was particularly striking in its denigration of the corruption that seemed to be pervading U.S. society — not just in its governing bodies, which garnered much public attention, but in individual instances of vulgarity and dishonesty. She saw such instances as "the symptoms of a creeping paralysis which threatens us almost unnoticed," maintaining to the end her refusal to ignore the reality of American life and to insist on the potential for a more honorable and democratic future (133). Davis died on 29 September 1910, in Mount Kisco, New York, on a visit to her son Richard's home.

Davis did not write in her letters, or in the fragments of her diary that are extant, any philosophical commentaries about writing or about herself as a writer. Instead, her attitudes about writing and her identity as an author are revealed in the letters she exchanged with her editors and publishers. The letters selected for this volume reflect her negotiations with publishers to have her work appear as she wished; and in presenting her arguments about her choices as a writer, she reveals what she valued about her own work — realism, honesty, and respect for the choices (large and small) she had made in crafting her work. Like most women authors in the mid-nineteenth century, she struggled to maintain control of her published works through every detail of content, spelling, and illustrations and yet honor the concept of the genteel publisher (still popular when Davis began her writing career) who had great control over an author's work but presented himself or herself as a friend and benefactor. Her first editor, James T. Fields of the *Atlantic Monthly*, still practiced the model of the genteel publisher. As a new author, she cautiously negotiated her vision with his editorial desires.

Within a few years, the genteel editor/publisher was giving way to a more business-oriented figure and—equally important—Davis was then an experienced and highly regarded author. Thus her correspondence with editors such as F. P. Church and William Conant Church of the *Galaxy* and with publishers at Charles Scribner's Sons maintains a nineteenth-century sense of female propriety but also reflects the fact that Davis had learned the art of negotiating for the integrity of her written product. She often used a tone of seeming humility with an editor—might her work be of interest to his magazine? Or "you must not think me cross"—that, in fact, could turn bitingly critical of any changes made to her writing. She was her own harshest critic, sometimes revealing to her editors her sense that her work was not what it should be—most often because of the pressures of time. She fought for the right to have a significant lead time before a serial began publication, so she could craft the story as well as possible. Additionally, she was often the major contributor to the Davis household finances, which sometimes forced her to write more quickly than she would have liked and for popular magazines as well as the established literary periodicals. We cannot forget that as a woman writer, she had neither an office nor privacy when she was writing.[2]

Her most productive years—the 1860s—were also the years in which she was establishing her family. Shortly after the birth of her first child, Davis revealed the hectic nature of her daily life in a letter to her friend Annie Adams Fields, wife of James T. Fields and an unofficial associate editor who often read and critiqued authors' manuscripts and then made recommendations on publication: "But talk of running three periodicals like steam engines? Why a baby uses up twice the motive power! Think what a woman is worth by night when all day she has been in momentary expectation of seeing that infant hope of the world brought in choked by a pin or strangled on a coal or whatever else its fingers can lay hands on—A woman too who has a husband that has taken to fancy work at tools for exercise and whittles and files away all regard for wife or family—Look upon us as virtually divorced by means of this last hobby—My place is *quite* filled by 'bits of wood with a beau-ti-ful grain' etc. etc."[3]

One exception to Davis's pattern of not writing lengthy letters about her craft comes in the form of a detailed and heartfelt commentary she wrote to her oldest son, Richard Harding Davis, in 1887 when he was beginning his writing career. She articulates her artistic values to Richard, especially the need to practice one's craft before seeking fame. It was a theme she used more than once in short stories, too, such as "Marcia," in which she asserted that false ideas about the art of writing were misleading young people into assuming they could go to a large city such as Philadelphia or New York, learn the ways of the publishing houses, and find great success. If she joked late in life that her style was not as popular as it once had been, she recognized the value of her writing as a well-aged wine. Ever the realist and anti-Romantic, she condemned the "popular belief in the wings of genius, which can carry it over hard work" ("Marcia" 926). Both genius and hard work sustained Rebecca Harding Davis for more than fifty years as an author.

Letter 1. Rebecca Harding [Davis] to James T. Fields, Wheeling, 15 March 1861[4]

Mr. Fields.

Your kindness touches me. The more because it is so unexpected. I see that the novelty of the scene of the story[5] has made you over estimate it — another, most probably, would disappoint you — However I will try. I have nothing written now. I have been sick since you wrote — If the story is published in an English magazine, will you tell me which one? As to the money, thank you sincerely.

I receive the offer as frankly as you made it, but you must pardon me if I decline it. Money is enough a "needful commodity" with me to accept with a complacent smile whatever you think the articles are worth. But if I were writing with a hundred dollar bill before me in order to write on it "I have paid him" I am afraid the article would be broad and deep just $100 — and no money-dollarish [more?]. Pardon me. I am grateful all the same. In proof of it I will ask a favor of you instead of the money. If any of your exchanges notice the story will you send them to me? That is a trouble, is it not? I would like to see them, partly from selfish notions and partly because it would please my father and mother — I trust to your kindness, to give me the pleasure — provided any one likes the article as you do —

Respectfully
Rebecca B. Harding

Letter 2. Rebecca Harding [Davis] to James T. Fields,
Wheeling, 9 August [1861][6]

Mr. Fields

I am *very* glad — the story disappointed me and I was afraid you would not
like it.[7] It was so much like giving people broken bits of apple-rind to chew.

Divide it as you please certainly and alter the Teagarden[8] as you choose. Do
you like the other names?

About the other minor points (and I make[9] that they are *so* minor) The weather
is all right for our Indian summers; however I will alter it if it affects your calmer
New England temperaments. How would it do, Mr. Fields, for you to return me
all the ms but the first division, and suffer me to revise it, leaving out the separated words &c &c? you have the first copy, the only one, indeed, or I should not
trouble you so much. I think I can improve it now; although it has not laid away
even nine weeks: besides if I could send you each division as you need it, I could
make it more truly a story of to-day.[10] I say all but the first division, because I
hope you will begin its publication soon. Forgive me, but I am afraid if it was kept
long it would be as stale as uncorked champagne.

As to the money, I would be glad if you would send me the first $40 now and
the remainder each month as you propose, if quite convenient to you. At home
they think I might write under my name with this story, what do you advise?
You did not think I imitated Charlotte Bronte, did you? I would rather you had
sent it back than thought that, but tell me cordially if you did. I may have done
it unconsciously —

Yours sincerely
R. B. H.

Letter 3. Rebecca Harding [Davis] to James T. Fields,
Wheeling, 17 August [1861][11]

Mr. Fields

Your letter has just arrived. The mails between here and Pittsburgh have run
"clean daft" like everything else.[12] For that reason it would be better as you say
not to return the mss, we'll have to leave the weather and superfluous adjectives
to the misery of the readers.

I wish you would add "1860" to the date of the ledger — somewhere in the first
pages, will you please?[13] I forgot and another thing, can the division between

the 2nd and 3rd parts, as *I* made it, be a division for your arrangements? The sense demanded a break there, imperatively.

About the name, unless you very much prefer it, I don't like "Margret Howth" at all because she is the completest failure in the story, besides not being the nucleus of it. However if you do not see this, and really think it a more apt title, alter it, certainly. You know best about what is attractive, since I do not care, myself. I put that *all* into your hands —

"What is *today* fifty years hence?" "Par bleu!" as Gen. Pierce[14] says "Am I at work for future ages?" I am very glad it can appear in September — thank you — and I quite agree about my name not being given, although I don't think the public will wonder to any alarming extent —

I give you an address to which please enclose your letters in future, or for a while. If Gen. Lee[15] can pass Rosecranz's[16] force, it is probable he will scatter our Wheeling government, and our mask will be deranged. I do not think it likely, but it is well to be safe. Just now "New Virginia" and its capitol are in a state of panic and preparation not to be described.

Sincerely yours,
R. B. H.
Care of James B. Wilson, Esq
Washington
Washington co.
Penna —

May I send my regards to Mrs. Fields, and ask her to tell me if she likes the stories when she reads it? I mean *criticism*, not praise, seriously.

Letter 4. Rebecca Harding [Davis] to James T. Fields, [1861][17]

Mr. Fields.

First — thanks for yourself. I would like to say a good deal on "the study" but I suppose a Solomon of good taste would remind one that there is a time to keep silence. Thank you, which I do say sincerely.

I would like *Margret* restored.[18] I would also like the book called Margret Howth — you were right and I was wrong. Is it too late? Chapters — I suppose — I'll mark them.

Now for a favour. Will you publish the book anonymously? I cannot tell you the repugnance I feel to seeing my name in print when the time comes near. The book would sell as well — nobody knows *me* — and I very much wish it if you are willing —

Do not change the name if you dislike a change.

Another thing — my spelling calls out most rebelliously to your proof-reader to be let alone. Some "slang" I will restore right — he cannot be expected to understand slang, as for the rest I abide by your judgment. Out here we never open Webster — swear by *English* dictionaries and as I am a native of "out here" *mayn't* I spell honour with a u? Childish you think? Well spelling is my hobby. If it hurts your established rules, never mind, however —

For a week I have been trying to bring a story down to your limits have not had time to go up[19] for that likeness. I will send it tomorrow with the story — It is a desperate tragical concern — the story, I mean, not the face, but I *hope* you'll publish it — *I* like it being written honestly —

Always yours
RBH

Indeed I *was* glad about that dinner praise — It has put me in a good humour Perhaps though your Chacquot [?] was good and gave my story a rosy light

Letter 5. Rebecca Harding Davis to F. P. Church,
Philadelphia, 10 December [1867][20]

My dear Sir.[21]

Please don't forget to send either the *Mss* of "The Captain's Story"[22] or the number of *Mss* pages so that I can have an idea of how to proportion chapters — As for the alteration in the size of the page[23] — of course I understood the price was for the page as it was when the contract was made, I also understand, according to your letter, that this will not affect the gross amount to be paid.

I notice in the Prospectus that you say the publication of the story would begin in January — But you must adhere to our arrangement & begin it the middle of February or I am afraid there will be a break down. My reason for asking you to wait so long was that I always write slowly and I must have a number or two done in advance — If I knew there was no reserve for me to depend on — I would be sure to grow imbecile out of sheer nervousness — Besides I must have a start in case sickness of ourselves or the children should interrupt me — I will send what I have written — enough for the first number — this week — for Mr. Hennessey[24] — of course with the understanding that you won't start the train till I say "All right — "

I conjectured from the Prospectus that the shade of George Robins[25] was assisting you —

Mr. Davis says he sent an announcement of the story to all the Phila papers —

With his regards, I am
Truly yours
RH Davis

Letter 6. Rebecca Harding Davis to F. P. Church and William Conant Church, Philadelphia, 19 April [1868][26]

My Dear Messrs Church.

I was very sorry to learn from your letters of your entended change as your difficulty must follow unavoidably. With your sized page, you cannot finish two serials[27] before next year without giving up most of the magazine to them. I understand the trouble, and will most willingly do all I can to help you. Still, I would like you to perceive that the embarrassment to which I am so abruptly subjected is equally annoying, as it is by no will of mine, and will prove in every way a loss.

You recollect that it was not my intention to publish this story except in book form, after giving it care and time, and that it was only at your urgent request that I gave it to The Galaxy to publish serially. When the agreement was made with you, however, I adhered to it — That was, you remember, for a story of the length of "Archie Lovell" and in the plot and conduct of the novel, I have kept that in view. Mr. F. P. Church's arrangement — to comprise the remainder unpublished, into seven numbers of 30 pages each would take off over 60 pages at the last, when every page is of importance. It would be equivalent to asking Mr. Hennessy to cut off the heads of his figures because you wanted to alter the size of your page! You must allow me the feeling which the humblest workman has for his work. The loss in money would be about $500, besides delaying the time of issue as a book. You must not think me cross about it — I have no doubt that it was a prudent thing to start another serial after mine and to twice alter the arrangement of the magazine but it is hardly fair that *I* should pay the penalty.

I went over the outline of the unfinished part carefully yesterday, anxious to do all I could to help you which I will do — without injury to the story. But I cannot consent to omit a word which would affect its meaning or what I conceive to be its artistic development, for any injury to it is a permanent one to my reputation.

What I *can* do is to finish the story this year, provided that you give me not less than 35 pages in each number after May lst, including December. That would shorten it by about 35 pages. I cannot spare more. The book can be issued in November, as before arranged. That would be in time then for the fall trade sale, and the appearance of one number in The Galaxy afterwards would hurt neither the magazine nor book — It is usual — I believe in the publication of all serials.

If you cannot do this, the story must run into next year & the book be delayed in which case my loss would be equivalent to your own

I regret very much that the difficulty has arisen. If I had heard earlier of your wish to shorten the story it could have been done — but at this advanced stage, it is impossible to do more than I propose —

With Mr. Davis regards to both
Very truly RHDavis

Letter 7. Rebecca Harding Davis to Richard Harding Davis,
Philadelphia, January 1887[28]

Dear Boy:

What has become of *The Current*? It has not come yet. If it has suspended publication be sure and get your article back. You must not destroy a single page you write. You will find every idea of use to you hereafter.

Sometimes I am afraid you think I don't take interest enough in your immediate success now with the articles you send. But I've had thirty years experience and I know how much that sort of success depends on the articles suiting the *present* needs of the magazine, and also on the mood of the editor when he reads it.

Besides — except for your own disappointment — I know it would be better if you would not publish under your own name for a little while. Dr. Holland[29] — who had lots of literary shrewdness both as writer and publisher — used to say for a young man or woman to rush into print was sure ruin to their lasting fame. They either compromised their reputations by inferior work or they made a great hit and never played up to it, afterwards, in public opinion.

Now my dear old man this sounds like awfully cold comfort. But it is the wisest idea your mother has got. I confess I have *great* faith in you — and I try to judge you as if you were not my son. I think you are going to take a high place among American authors, but I do not think you are going to do it by articles like that you sent to *The Current*. The qualities which I think will bring it to you,

you don't seem to value at all. They are your dramatic eye. I mean your quick perception of character and of the way character shows itself in looks, tones, dress, etc., and in your keen sympathy — with all kinds of people —

Now, these are the requisites for a novelist. Added to that your humour.

You ought to make a novelist of the first class. But you must not expect to do it this week or next. A lasting, real success takes time, and patient, steady work. Read Boz's first sketches of "London Life" and compare them with "Sydney Carton" or "David Copperfield" and you will see what time and hard work will do to develop genius.[30]

I suppose you will wonder why I am moved to say all this? It is, I think, because of your saying "the article sent to St. Nicholas[31] was the best you would be able to do for years to come" and I saw you were going to make it a crucial test of your ability. That is, forgive me, nothing but nonsense. Whatever the article may be, you may write one infinitely superior to it next week or month. Just in proportion as you feel more deeply, or notice more keenly, and as you acquire the faculty of expressing your feelings or observations more delicately and powerfully which faculty must come into practice. It is not inspiration — it never was that — without practice, with any writer from Shakespeare down.

Understand me. I don't say, like Papa, stop writing. God forbid. I would almost as soon say stop breathing, for it is pretty much the same thing. But only to remember that you have not yet conquered your art. You are a journeyman not a master workman, so if you don't succeed, it does not count. The future is what I look to, for you. I had to stop my work to say all this, so good-bye dear old chum.

Yours,
Mother.

Letter 8. Rebecca Harding Davis to [Charles Scribner],
Philadelphia, 25 October [1892][32]

Dear Mr. Scribner

These are a half-dozen stories which I should like to see in a book. I know that they are not modern nor at all "up-to-date"

But are there not a few people still living who prefer a musty tang in their books as in their Madiera?[33]

Will you let me know what you think about them?

Cordially yours
Rebecca Harding Davis

Notes

1. The paucity of information we have on Davis's only daughter is due to the fact that Nora lived with her mother until Davis's death, so letters were not needed. Davis dedicated her novel, *Frances Waldeaux* (1897), to Nora. See Harris, *Rebecca Harding Davis and American Realism*.

2. Her husband sometimes wrote at home, but he had an office at his newspaper as well.

3. Rebecca Harding Davis, letter to Annie Fields, n.d., Richard Harding Davis Collection (#6109), Clifton Waller Barrett Library, Manuscripts Division, Special Collections, University of Virginia Library, Charlottesville; hereafter Richard Harding Davis Collection, U of Virginia.

4. Richard Harding Davis Collection, U of Virginia.

5. Davis is referring to "Life in the Iron-Mills," which would be published in the April 1861 issue of the *Atlantic Monthly*.

6. Richard Harding Davis Collection, U of Virginia.

7. Davis had sent Fields the manuscript for her first novel, *Margret Howth*.

8. The name of a character in *Margret Howth*.

9. ‹indecipherable word›

10. *The Story of To-Day* was Davis's intended title for the novel.

11. Richard Harding Davis Collection, U of Virginia.

12. During the Civil War, the trains carrying mail to Wheeling ran only sporadically.

13. The title character is a bookkeeper in the manufactory; with the date, Davis wants again to emphasize the timeliness of her story.

14. Probably General James Pierce (1810 – ?) of Erie County, Pennsylvania, where his mining of coal and establishment of a furnace business transformed him into a captain of industry.

15. General Robert E. Lee; Wheeling, as part of Virginia that stayed with the Union and renamed itself New Virginia (later West Virginia), housed Union troops and was a dangerous place.

16. William Starke Rosecrans (1819 – 1898) commanded the Union forces in the Wheeling region.

17. Richard Harding Davis Collection, U of Virginia.

18. The proofreader had made numerous changes to Davis's manuscript of *Margret Howth*, including changing the spelling of the title character's name to "Margaret." At one point she wrote to Fields, "Is the proof reader *quite* killed? That's one good thing. I hope he has no ghost." Rebecca Harding [Davis], letter to Annie Fields, 17 September [1861], Richard Harding Davis Collection, U of Virginia.

19. ‹indecipherable word›

20. William Conant Church Papers, Rare Book and Manuscripts Division, NYPL, Astor, Lenox, and Tilden Foundations, NY; hereafter William Conant Church Papers, NYPL.

21. F. P. Church was editor of the periodical the *Galaxy*.

22. This story is unidentified. It may have been a story or chapter title that was later changed.

23. After contracting for this story and for the serialization of *Waiting for the Verdict*, the publishers reduced the page size of their journal. Within the next couple of months, the Churches attempted to have Davis curtail the length of her novel, although they had originally encouraged her to write at whatever length was necessary to tell the story.

24. W. J. Hennessey designed the illustrations for the novel.

25. George Henry Robins (1778–1847), an extremely successful London auctioneer.

26. William Conant Church Papers, NYPL.

27. In addition to *Waiting for the Verdict*, the *Galaxy* had begun serializing *Archie Lovell*, a novel by the British author Amelia Edwards (1831–1892).

28. Quoted in Charles Belmont Davis's *Richard Harding Davis* (33–35). This letter is addressed to Davis's son, Richard Harding Davis, who was beginning his own writing career.

29. Dr. Josiah Gilbert Holland (1819–1881), both a physician and well-known author. See Davis's autobiography, *Bits of Gossip*, for her extensive comments on Holland.

30. A reference to characters in Charles Dickens's *A Tale of Two Cities* and *David Copperfield*.

31. *St. Nicholas* was a premier nineteenth-century periodical for children, edited by Mary Mapes Dodge (1831–1905). Davis had published in the magazine several times during her career.

32. Charles Scribner's Sons, Author Files, Princeton University Library.

33. The stories were collected as *Silhouettes of American Life* (1892).

Works Cited

Davis, Charles Belmont. *Adventures and Letters of Richard Harding Davis.* NY: Charles Scribner's Sons, 1917.

Davis, Rebecca Harding. *Bits of Gossip.* 1904. Rpt. *Rebecca Harding Davis: Writing Cultural Autobiography.* Eds. Janice Milner Lasseter and Sharon M. Harris. Nashville: Vanderbilt U P, 2001. 21–130.

———. *Dallas Galbraith.* Philadelphia: Lippincott, 1868.

———. "David Gaunt." *Atlantic Monthly* 10 (September–October 1862): 257–271, 403–421.

———. *Frances Waldeaux.* New York: Harper and Bros., 1897.

———. "Life in the Iron-Mills." *Atlantic Monthly* 7 (April 1861): 430–451.

———. "Marcia." *Harper's Magazine* 53 (1876): 925–928.

———. *Margret Howth: A Story of To-Day.* Boston: Ticknor & Fields, 1862.

———. "One Woman's Question." *The Independent* 63 (18 July 1907): 132–133.

———. *Silhouettes of American Life.* NY: Scribner's, 1892.

———. *Waiting for the Verdict.* NY: Sheldon, 1868.

Harris, Sharon M. *Rebecca Harding Davis and American Realism.* Philadelphia: U of Pennsylvania P, 1991.

Chapter 4

SUSAN S. WILLIAMS

Mary Abigail Dodge [Gail Hamilton] (1833–1896)

Mary Abigail Dodge, who published under the name Gail Hamilton, was a well-known essayist, editor, and humorist who could best be described, in Judith Fetterley's words, as a "cultural critic-at-large" (424). She is now primarily remembered for her protofeminist essays, most notably those collected in *Country Living and Country Thinking* (1862) and *Woman's Wrongs: A Counter-Irritant* (1868). These essays link her with other "disobedient" women writers who engaged in conscious revisions of received literary forms (Walker 28–31). More broadly, Dodge is a significant figure in the history of authorship in America. As a single woman, she supported herself solely through her writing and editing, working both to define the terms of her art and to make sure that she was adequately compensated for that art. In this respect, we might add her to what Naomi Sofer has termed the "transitional generation" of American women writers. This generation, which was most active between 1860 and 1880, "blended elements of the antebellum domestic model with aspects of the emerging high-art model of authorship," while also theorizing the importance of material support for literary production (33). As a cultural critic, Dodge took familiar, domestic subjects (one of her most famous essays is entitled "My Garden") and invested them with a mock high-art significance. (In another essay guests eating cherries become a "study for a sculptor," particularly when viewed by her brother "Halicarnassus" [Coultrap-McQuin *Selected Writings* 51].) At the same time, Dodge understood her writing to be a business, beginning with her early contributions to Gamaliel Bailey's *National Era*, for which she was paid $50, and extending to the later part of her career. "One ought not to *write* for money," she wrote in

1895, "but I consider it a first duty after one has written to exact the highest possible price" (Dodge II: 1065).

The letters included here document Dodge's commitment both to the quality of her art and to adequate material support for it. It is not surprising that some of Dodge's most prolonged discussions about writing occur in her letters; she was an inveterate correspondent who described letters as "the cream of social intercourse" (Hamilton *Twelve Miles* 181). As the metaphor suggests, she recognized both their richness and their decadence. Dodge understood that letter writing was an inherently social activity, one that implied a kind of ongoing conversation with her correspondents. The selection below attempts to capture this conversational spirit by transcribing several letters both to and from Dodge.

Even as Dodge considered letters "social intercourse," however, she also valued their privacy. Indeed, in some cases she had extensive correspondence with "dear friends," as she terms Grace Greenwood, whom she had never met. After several years of correspondence with Henry James Sr., for example, Dodge still declined his invitation for an actual visit. "The more you see me the more you won't know me," she wrote. "I sit in my room and write to you. It is my very own self speaking to you, without embarrassment or distraction. There isn't any world" (Dodge I: 407).

Although Dodge found her "own self" writing to men as well as women (she also had an extended correspondence with poet John Greenleaf Whittier), on literary matters she was particularly eager to correspond with fellow women writers. For that reason, I have included letters to and from four of these women: Greenwood, Lydia Sigourney, Fanny Fern, and Sophia Peabody Hawthorne. In the 1860s, when Dodge was coming into her own as an author, Sigourney and Fern were already well-established celebrities. Their letters to Dodge suggest the importance of literary mentoring for women joining what Sigourney calls the "fraternity of authors," a mentoring that Dodge also directly requests from Greenwood when she asks for her advice on publishing. Like Greenwood, Sophia Hawthorne was as much a friend and colleague of Dodge's as a literary "mother": a relationship that enabled Dodge and Hawthorne to support each other in their efforts to petition the publishers Ticknor and Fields for fair pay.

On one level, Dodge's letters reflect her belief in the efficacy of writing for its own sake. She expressed this view most succinctly in her 1862 essay "Men and Women," in which she defined authorship as "the great safety-valve of society," one that allowed women to find an outlet for the "pent-up mind" (Coultrap-McQuin *Selected Writings* 100–102). Her early correspondence, represented below in the letters to Sigourney and from Greenwood, shows Dodge's aspirations toward high art and a tradition of accomplished writing (Sigourney compares her to Washington Irving). As Dodge's career progressed, however, she increasingly understood that such an autotelic model of writing depended on an equally strong contractual model that defined writing as "public property" that produced "reserved rights" for authors.[1]

This emphasis on reserved rights became particularly strong after 1867, when Dodge read an article in the *Congregationalist and Boston Recorder* on "The Pay of Authors." This article made an open secret of pay practices by reporting that the "ordinary remuneration" to authors was ten percent of the retail price of the book. Dodge was being paid only fifteen cents a copy, or 6 ⅔ to 7 ½ percent, on her books. Having corroborated the article's percentage with other writers, she requested that her publishers, the highly regarded Ticknor and Fields, pay her the market rate, first through letters to Fields himself and eventually through an arbitration panel. She eventually received $1,250 from Ticknor and Fields in backpay, along with a promise that she would receive a ten percent royalty on all future sales. In 1870, she published *A Battle of the Books*, an account of how she learned, as she put it, to "deal with publishers, not like women and idiots, but as business men with business men" (Coultrap-McQuin *Selected Writings* 194).

Dodge's staunchest ally during this dispute was Sophia Hawthorne, widow of Nathaniel. Dodge had been introduced to the Hawthornes in 1863 by James T. Fields, their mutual publisher. They warmed to each other immediately, and after Hawthorne's death in 1864, Dodge frequently visited Sophia and her children in Concord. During one such visit in the summer of 1868, Dodge told Sophia about her dispute with Ticknor and Fields. Sophia, who was already facing financial difficulties, realized that she, too, was not receiving fair compensation for her husband's books (Stewart 45–47). The intensity of the women's dispute with Ticknor and Fields is clear in their correspondence from that period. As these letters attest, Sophia was particularly angry that Ticknor and Fields had taken advantage of her husband's childlike trust. In this respect, she and Dodge read Nathaniel Hawthorne himself as a feminized writer who was suffering from the sexism of a "gentleman publisher."[2] In the end, Sophia too resolved the matter, with Ticknor and Fields agreeing to give her a fixed percentage of the retail price on all of her husband's books as well as on her own edited volume, *Passages from the American Note-books of Nathaniel Hawthorne* (1868).

Taken together, the letters included here show Dodge's allegiance to artistic integrity and to understanding herself — and her female peers — as professionals who deserved fair compensation. For her, these allegiances were not ultimately antithetical. She saw the literary market not as a necessary evil but as a productive agent, one that enabled the "fraternity of authors" to gain a public voice. By writing under the pen name Gail Hamilton (taken from her hometown of Hamilton, Massachusetts), she endeavored to distance that celebrity status from her private life. It is significant that Fanny Fern and Grace Greenwood—the public pen names for Sarah Payson Willis Parton and Sara Jane Clarke, respectively—wrote to "Gail Hamilton" rather than to "Mary Abigail Dodge," while Sigourney and Hawthorne wrote to Dodge under her real name. The instability of the superscription captures the complexity of Dodge's literary persona, which "dodged" (a pun used by many of her friends) between concealment and exposure. As such, these letters also demonstrate the liminal nature of letters themselves: a genre sufficiently capacious to allow one's "very own self" to speak "without embarrassment or distraction," while also enabling a public person—Gail Hamilton—to pursue her legal rights as an author.

Letter 1. Mary Abigail Dodge to Grace Greenwood [Sara Jane Clarke], Hartford, Connecticut, 15 April 1857[3]

You dear Grace Greenwood:[4]

I think you are just as splendid and kind and dear and delightful as you can be. I have just received your letter. If you had not answered mine at all I should not have blamed you in the least; I know your time must be so occupied, and I have no claim upon you, but you have written me, and such a kind letter. I understand what *nous venons*[5] means on a mother's lips. When I was a little girl and used to ask my mother for anything, "I will see about it," was always equivalent to a downright affirmative.

Suppose you were a little bit of a writer—a *very* little bit of one, without a reputation, without much experience, but with the *cacoethes scribendi*[6] strong upon you, what should you do? That is the question.

I have been writing a little for about a year, chiefly for the "National Era" and "Independent."[7] I shall probably continue to do so this year, but that does not use up half my writing material, and I don't know what to do with the rest of it. Is there any good-sense, respectable newspaper that you would like to write for, supposing you were in my place. Perhaps you may think I am too fastidious for a tyro,[8] but I think it is better to have your standard too high than too low. I am poor enough, to be sure, and generally in debt, and would be glad to get money for writing; but I would rather write for a *good* paper without pay, than a foolish one *with*. If I become a good writer I shall be rich enough one day. Dr. Bailey, of the "Era," made a regular bargain with me, and he expressed himself more than satisfied. He has treated me very generously.

I will send you the only article of mine that I have on hand (out of my scrapbook), and you can judge a little from it. I will follow your advice in anything unless you advise me not to write at all. Write I must. It is absolutely essential to my happiness.

My dear friend, — mine though I never saw you, and dear whether you will or not, — don't write to me again till you can almost as well as not. If you do not write to me again, I shall know you are blessing some one else; and shall not bate one jot or tittle of the regard, the love, I now bear you.

Very truly yours, Gail Hamilton.

On looking, I find two pieces and send them both. You will see that the rhymes are in answer to one of Jenny Marsh's poems.[9]

Letter 2. Lydia H. Sigourney[10] to Mary Abigail Dodge, Hartford, Connecticut, 21 March 1863[11]

My dear Miss[12] Dodge, —

I have been for some time intending to welcome you into our fraternity of authors, and express the pleasure derived from the spirit and style of your writings. They abound in what is so rare among us, that quiet and delightful humor, which with the exception of our lamented Washington Irving,[13] and a few other instances, is almost a deficient department in American literature. Without derogation from your classical or logical powers, this seems to me your forte, to which I hope you will give due scope, under the guidance of true feminine tastes. Among your graver essays, that on the "Complaint of Friends," in the October no. of the "Atlantic Monthly," I particularly admire.[14] I am not quite certain of quoting its title accurately, as some person who was as much pleased with it as myself, has abstracted it from my library-table.

I have just been re-perusing your "Country Living and Thinking," and am your debtor for sundry impulsive and salubrious cachinations,[15] for I count laughter as medicinal to advancing years.

I do not write you as an absolute stranger, recollecting to have seen you in my visits to the High School in this city,[16] while you were an instructor there, and being acquainted with some who were then under your charge.

With good wishes, truly your friend, L. H. Sigourney

Letter 3. Mary Abigail Dodge to Sophia Hawthorne,
Hamilton, [Massachusetts,]14 July 1863[17]

My dear Mrs. Hawthorne

I hope and trust you have all been wondering at least as often as three times
a day, in family conclave, why I have not written — because if you haven't it indicates a most remarkable and, I think I may say culpable indifference to my
whereabouts and welfare. Any way I shall achieve the anxiety which you ought
to feel by informing you that I have been on an exploring expedition to the North
Pole and am but just returned.[18] Mr. Fields, inflamed with love for the glories of
the mountains sent for me in a great flurry and I went to the Alpine House and
the glen house — to Jefferson and Bethel — taking Mt. Washington in flank and
war broadside and enfilading — in using technical terms I always fling about
right and left.[19] I know what I mean, and if the words are not the right ones, so
much the worse for them — and I dipped into all the cascades and talked about
"views" with artists in the most reckless manner, hasarding criticisms and suggesting points and enjoyed it all high mightily. And coming home a gentleman
introduced himself to me as a Dodge — which is a strong objection to any body
in my estimation and *wanted* me to go to Labrador. His yacht takes out Bradford
the marine painter.[20] I suppose you know all about him but I didn't till I was
told — to be gone six or eight weeks and see icebergs and savages and Louisberg
and be sea-sick and everything.[21] If I had only known it a little sooner I would
have gone but being now engaged three deep till October I believe I must turn a
deaf ear to him. But you will see that I have been in a state of modified whirlpool
since I left you and have not had till now a quiet moment to tell you how very
very much I enjoyed my pilgrimage to Concord — and how much I enjoy it now
thinking it over. The walks and the talks and the pictures — do you know the
kinks in my brain have all turned themselves into beautiful curved lines since
I was at Concord. That is some of them have — perhaps on trial a few of them
might be found to be a little kinky yet. I find one thing that I am in possession
of a photograph of Mr. Hawthorne. Not[22] any one of yours — nor any that have
gone hang in the shop-windows — one that I took myself — or rather one that
took itself. This letter is to you but I depend upon your going straightway and
reading at least this part of it to Mr. Hawthorne because he will be so delightfully
annoyed and impatient and I think it is very demoralising for a man of genius to
be so happily situated as he is. A little irritation is necessary to promote healthy
circulation. And since none of his family seems inclined to take that part upon
themselves why I modestly offer my services. What I was going to say was that in

my photograph Mr. Hawthorne sits like a great dream in the doorway of darkness glowing out, phosphorescent. I hope you know what it all means. What a remarkable derangement of things there is in this world! I would give the whole of it for the sake of looking romantic and Mr. Hawthorne agonises to bring himself down to commonplace — and I look as romantic as a healthy pumpkin and he cannot open his eyes without seeming the very Spirit of Imagination.

I suppose there is a little gentle trepidation at Wayside to-day over the apostate Julian but I have no doubt everything will come to a happy issue. In just four year lacking a few weeks Una will be dancing on the green in all possible glories of gossamer and silk and Rose will be sitting down to regular siege attacks upon such batteries of strawberries and cake as her soul loves for of course even she will go to Julian's class-day. I wonder if the names of those who pass examination will be published.[23]

I am going to be impertinent again. I came home from Greenland by way of Boston and waiting in Mr. Field's lair he gave me the advance sheets of A. M. to read Civil Dinners and I read it![24] and had to buy a bottle of cherry brandy to get home on after it! It was written by a former consul of ours in England. I don't know anything about him personally and I don't suppose you do. He has written a very many good things but this is the tippest-toppest best of all from turret to foundation stone. There is something so perfectly hypocritical in his fun. He takes you aside in the gate to speak with you quietly and smites you under the fifth rib, and I felt as if I could have pounded him for indignant delight. The conclusion is the most provokingly ridiculously funny thing you ever saw — pray get the Magazine early and read it.

When I am rich enough to have a new house built and plenty of servants built in it to take care of us, I shall have a lake and a boat made for Una and a metropolis for the Roseate dolls. Three shall be no end of edge-tools for a Julian department. You shall be surrounded with perpetual Flaxmans and unfailing past board. There shall be a stone tower built on the top in which we will lock up the Prince of the Powers of Darkness and what a grand time we will have. Meanwhile I hope you will take as much pleasure as possible in the pleasure you have given me and meanwhile perhaps — who knows? — I may have a chance to rescue the Lady Una from some dragon monstrous, horrible and vast or in some way, even before my ship comes home from sea, prove to you how very gratefully and truly I am

Yours, M. A. Dodge.

This is not the *handsome* letter I am going to write you some time just to show you I can. That won't come till my pen is mended!

Letter 4. Fanny Fern [Sarah Willis Parton][25] to Mary Abigail Dodge,
24 January 1868[26]

Miss Dodge.
otherwise,
My dear Gail Hamilton

   A book is in prospect. The title is to be, Eminent Women of our time. You and
I are to figure in it. *I* am to do *you*! Who is to take me the gods know. Meantime
I desire to know at what age you cut your first tooth, and w[h]ere. Also whether
you had the measles before the mumps, or the mumps before the measles. Also,
any other interesting items about yourself, which you can furnish me at your
earliest convenience. It will be a labor of love with me, because I rejoice every
day in your existence. In short — you are one of the women I believe in. So don't
be stingy of the facts. Horace Greeley, Theodore Tilton, my husband, and others
are all to "do" somebody.[27] It is intended, that the book shall be handsomely got
up, in every respect. Will you please send me an early response.

Yours very truly,
Fanny Fern Parton, 303 East Eighteenth St., New York

Letter 5. Sophia Hawthorne to Mary Abigail Dodge, 20 August 1868[28]

My dear Mary,

   Your letters are invaluable to me. I like your clear trenchant style of writing
about business, and you are so clear headed about figures too, it is as refreshing
as a breeze from ice bergs when the thermometer is at 90. I enclose you a piece
of Mr. Hillard's last letter of yesterday. Judge Hoar said that the tax on manufac-
turing articles would no doubt be soon taken off — and in that case should not
I hold to 15 per cent?[29] Do you see all the contracts Mr. Fields tells Mr. Hillard
were *verbal*. I do not believe Mr. Hawthorne ever consented to change to ten
per cent, because he would have told me and besides, you see, he had 15 per cent
for the very last book he gave them! Those that were at ten per cent were books
bought of other publishers, written before the Scarlet Letter, which was the first
book Mr. Hawthorne gave them.[30] After that they wished to be sole publishers
of all, and so bought the rest.
   So that it is as plain as possible that the only contract ever made between Mr.
Hawthorne and T and F was for fifteen per cent. It was for the first book unto
the last — with the exception of the small books, and Mosses and T. T. Tales.

They have, however, mixed up with these bought books the Wonder Book and Tanglewood Tales, for which I know perfectly well that Mr. Hawthorne made no deduction.[31] And now they say he made a *verbal* agreement with Mr. Ticknor, who is dead!! and cannot say any thing. But they show no papers. And Mr. Hawthorne never had a single paper given him or signed by them from first to last. Ah — they took advantage of his delicacy and confidence. They knew he would continue to trust and to be silent. This dog day kills me, and I cannot write but I will take your notes and reply seriatim[32] some day. Meantime I thank you greatly & beg you to continue your criticisms.

Ever your true friend, Sophia Hawthorne

Letter 6. Mary Abigail Dodge to Sophia Hawthorne, 24 August 1868[33]

My dear Mrs. Hawthorne

I am very glad if my letters have done you *any* good. If they could help you out of your perplexities I should be still more glad. I don't precisely know what to do now. Did Judge Hoar advise you to hold to 15 per cent? I suppose really few publishers, in fact perhaps none, pay 15 per cent now. But T. & F. made that contract with Mr. H. and I don't see why they should not be held to it even if they do lose money by it. They make enough out of others. Besides as the bargain was fairly made what right have they to cry out against it? I never heard that the discovery that a contract was unfavorable to your self was any reason for violating it. If they had bought a house and found afterwards that they paid too much, they could not have helped themselves. They would have had to keep the house just the same. Why should they be allowed to retreat from their contract with you the moment it bore hard on them? Not that there is any proof that it did bear hard. I am not sure that they would not make money as it was. Only of course not so much. But whether they did or not is of no consequence.

I think the preponderance of evidence is on your side. Their letter to you admits the 15 per cent in most cases — and on the very last book. They have no proof of any change that the contract made with Mr. Hillard was to benefit you is disproved by the figures I sent you — and I should think that contract ought to be invalidated and might be on the ground of having been made on false representations. Certainly a verbal contract without witnesses between two dead men seems to me to be as near nothing as anything in law can be — and I am surprised that Mr. Hillard should seriously bring it forward. If anything can surpass it in worthlessness it is Mr. Fields' assertion of its existence.

You say very justly that Mr. Ticknor cannot be wholly responsible for the carelessness of accounts since the accounts have been equally neglected since his death[34] but I admire the prudence, not to say the generosity, which lays it to his charge.

I dare say that for a time the use of price in the book was no benefit to the publishers. The cost [of] material was so high that they may have made no more money but mental ease is as necessary to a writer as paper and ink to a publisher and the cost of that does up with the use of prices. That cost Mr. Hawthorne as much as Mr. Fields and he needed an increase in price just as much as Mr. Fields instead of which his part went down. I am very strongly inclined to believe you ought to refuse anything but the original contracts. If they were in your favor why should T. & F. refuse to restore them? If you have referees I think you should have them but if you have nobody to argue your case but Mr. Hillard you will lose because he is on the other side to begin with. Have you the nerve to do it yourself? You ought to have a self-possessed advocate. Don't be in a hurry, at any rate, to accept ten per cent. Nothing that I say of Mr. Hillard makes against his being a charming companion, an invaluable friend, an honorable man. It is only his management of this case which I mistrust and he is so involved in it that I question if he can look at it quite clearly. In the verbal contracts I have not the smallest faith. Mr. Fields told me that they did by Longfellow just as they do by me & now Mr. H. says they argue to you that they only pay Longfellow ten per cent. They pay me 6 2/3 and 7 1/2 . They also are willing to pay you 10 p.c. then why not pay me the same? My dear friend this is hateful but we are not assoiled by what we are forced to do.

Letter 7. Mary Abigail Dodge to Sophia Hawthorne,
Hamilton, [Massachusetts,] 2 September 1868[35]

My dear Mrs. Hawthorne:

It needs the wisdom of Solomon and not such a poor little naif as I to meet Messrs. T. and F. for indeed their ways are past finding out. Apart from any question of honesty, their business seems to be conducted with a carelessness so immeasurable that figures have quite lost their historic stability. Their logic also appears out at elbows. You affirm that you have no proof that Mr. Hawthorne's accounts were properly kept. They reply that they have the best of evidence inasmuch as they have carefully examined the papers. I do not know much about business, but it certainly seems to me that the party who ought to have the written proof in his possession is the attorney's employer and not the firm to which the attorney happened to belong. You are the person to be satisfied, not they.

What they adduce as evidence — elegant extracts from Mr. Hawthorne' letters — are utterly worthless. They might just as well bring forward extracts from my letters to show that they have done right by me. Mr. Hawthorne and you and I were thoroughly satisfied with what we supposed to be true, not with what we now fear is false. We were satisfied and delighted with the money we got, not with the money they held back. The[36] extracts indeed confirm your assertions. In 1853 Mr. Hawthorne acknowledges the reception of the account. Naturally if there had been any subsequent account, they would have its acknowledgment also. But you have said all along that there[37] was an account[38] in 1853. In 1856 he speaks of a satisfactory summary. What sort of a business paper is that? It might have been some such general statement as he made himself about the $20,000 — very satisfying and comforting but without exactness or legal value. Their assertion that they are quite content with these friendly and familiar assurances of Mr. Hawthorne's as evidences that he had nothing to complain of is quite feminine in its simplicity. For my part I am altogether tired of the friendly and familiar style of doing business and should be well content to exchange it for a little hostile and formal accuracy. About this attorneyship of course I know nothing, but I should suppose that between man and man, there must be some proper mode of transacting business so that one could at any time, or at least at certain set time, know whether or not everything was going on correctly. And I should suppose that any mode of conducting business which did not make provision for such investigation was an improper one.

About the $700 charge, they say that such a mistake could not have occurred without quick detection and they should not be likely to keep in their employ any person[39] liable to make such errors. I know that they did make an error in one of my accounts of about twenty-two dollars which I happened to see and to point out. They rectified it. Another error they made of about twenty dollars which I never spoke to them about and which if they ever detected, they never paid me. Another case I know of in which they had over-charged, which they reluctantly & rather roughly re-examined, and, in which they found and admitted they were wrong. In these three cases the errors were all in their own favor. They did not detect them themselves, one they never detected and I never heard that the clerk who made them was dismissed. So that the question at once arises, how large must a mistake be in order to be discovered by T. & F. It may be, by my experience, more than 20$, without attracting their attention, but $700 they think they should infallibly notice. I believe banks and monied institutions generally are rather proud of discovering discrepancies only as large as five dollars but the magnificent house of T. & F. have no such microscopic meanness of vision and recognise nothing less than double eagles.

Have you their letter explaining the overcharge by saying that the book-keeper made out some one else's charge instead of yours? If you have, keep it to produce if best. Their last explanation may be the true one but two are suspicious. When they sent the bill to you were not the items given, $500 to Mr. Hillard etc. If not what did they say about it and what date did they assign to the $500 or $700? I should not think there was any necessity for a misunderstanding.

They change ground again about the copyrights. First they said the change from 10 and 15 per cent to 12 cents was to your advantage *because* the aggregate of the latter was greater than the aggregate of the former. You denied and disproved that. Now they say the reason of the advantage is that they, by economising where only they could economise, vis: in paying you, were able to throw larger editions upon the market and therefore really brought you more money. This may be true or the other might be true but they cannot both be true. You cannot at the same time and by the same contract be receiving more copyright on the same fourteen books than by the old arrangement, and also be receiving less copyright and so enabling them to make more books. If the new contract gave you more copyright than the old arrangement, as they showed by figures in the first letter, they could not be economising in copyright as they assert in the second letter. It is this shifting about perpetually that makes the difficulty. They stick to nothing. If they are honest, they are most unskillful. These different and contradictory reasons for a fact make the fact itself doubtful.

Messrs. T. & F's figures are but bruised reeds to lean upon. Whenever we have sufficient data to go upon we find them wrong. Of course then when we cannot pass judgment our selves we suspect them to be wrong. But take their own showing. Their exhibit is

Cost to them of a set of works[40] 11.27
Price received by them 12.26
Profit left to them .99
Out of which they must pay a copyright of 1.68
So that they lose on every set sold — as I make it — .69

Now I pray to know if this is the ordinary meat on which our Caesar feeds that he is grown so great. If so, surely the house of T. and F. thrives on its losses as much as other men on their profits. I am filled with admiration at the genius which robes itself in purple and fine linen and fares sumptuously every day on sixty nine cents less than nothing!

It is far easier to pick flaws in their dealing than to decide what is best for you to do about it. You say shall they not be held to their written and signed assertions. But where are such? There are absolutely no contracts existing except the one with which you are dissatisfied. I do not see but that you must accept what they choose to offer or you can let the present contract be and withhold the future works. If they insist on holding you by the[41] new contract, you probably have no power to force them to give it up since the contract was legally made. And it is possible that the new contract may not in the future be bad for you. From their readiness to go to ten per cent I am inclined to think that they have gotout of the fixed-sum way all the good it has for them and that in the future 12 cents on a volume may be better for you than 10 per cent. But this I do not know. I should ask Judge Hoar, I think.

You must not say that Mr. Ticknor sent a full statement of Mr. Hawthorne's account, etc. All you know is that you never received it. All your other comments on the letter seem to me just and well put. The contra dance of those $50 & $100 is amusing. First one is 50 & the other 100. Then one is 100 & the other 50. Then both are 100. It is a type of their dealings. They are either from dishonesty or mismanagement utterly untrustworthy. I cannot say it is the former — indeed I cannot believe that they are so bad as their manner seems to indicate — but the results to us may be just as fatal — and certainly their reckoning is the most remarkable I ever heard of in business. As to whether it would be best for you to make a ten per cent contract for a few years I do not at all know — or even whether they would be willing to make such a contract. It depends so almost entirely upon things concerning which publishers know so much more than authors that it is difficult to tell what is best. That is why it is so important for publishers to be honorable men. They have these things in their own hands and it is next to impossible to help yourself. Why not apply to other publishers and see what they will do? I don't know of any better way to ascertain a little where you are. You need not be in a hurry to answer T. & F's letter. You could state as much of the case as you choose to Lee and Sheppard, or you need state nothing if you prefer it but simply say that you are contemplating a change of publishers and ask them what they would be willing to do. I think however that I should do it as a private matter. There is also Little & Brown. One of their men, Mr. Bartlett, is said to know more about the inside matters of publishing than any man in Boston. Why not consult him?[42] I should want to know what I could do elsewhere before making a new contract. I have so much company and so many engagements I cannot well leave home now and really I do not think it would be so well for me to go. You are doing better with me here then you would with me there.

Yours.

Notes

1. These terms are included in a letter reprinted in Fern, "Gail Hamilton," 204–205.

2. For a discussion of the tradition of the gentleman publisher and Dodge's critique of it, see Coultrap-McQuin, *Doing Literary Business*, 105–136.

3. Published in Dodge, *Gail Hamilton's Life in Letters* I: 139–140.

4. Grace Greenwood, pseudonym of Sara Jane Clark Lippincott (1823–1904), a journalist and travel writer who also founded a children's magazine, the *Little Pilgrim*. Like Dodge, she was admired by Nathaniel Hawthorne.

5. French for "we will see."

6. A Latin phrase meaning "writer's itch." It is also the title of a story published by Catharine Maria Sedgwick in the *Atlantic Souvenir* in 1830; see Fetterley.

7. The *National Era* was a weekly abolitionist paper founded in 1847 by Gamaliel Bailey — best known for serializing *Uncle Tom's Cabin*. Dodge later served as a governess for Bailey's children. The *Independent* was a Protestant religious magazine edited by Theodore Tilton.

8. Amateur or novice.

9. Jenny Marsh Parker (1836–1913), a writer from Rochester, New York, who contributed frequently to magazines such as the *Atlantic* and the *Outlook*.

10. Lydia Sigourney (1791–1865) had a fifty-year publishing career and was among the best-known nineteenth-century poets in the United States. For Dodge to have received a letter from such a well-established writer would have been a great compliment.

11. Mary Abigail Dodge Papers, Peabody Essex Museum, Salem, Massachusetts; hereafter Peabody Essex Museum.

12. ‹H›

13. Washington Irving (1783–1859), famous for his *Sketch Book* (1822) and travel writings.

14. Hamilton, "A Complaint of Friends." In this essay about the mysteries of friendship, Dodge returns to the metaphor of a safety valve: "You must open the safety-valve once in a while, even if the steam does whiz and shriek, or there will be an explosion, which is fatal" (359).

15. Loud or immoderate laughter.

16. The Hartford High School for Boys, where Dodge taught from 1855 to 1858.

17. Berg Collection, NYPL.

18. Dodge's "North Pole" was a trip to the mountains of New Hampshire.

19. The Alpine House in Gorham, New Hampshire, was a popular mid-century tourist destination in the White Mountains. The Glen House was at the foot of Mt. Washington and was accessible by the Mt. Washington Road, completed in 1862. For another account of this trip, see Dodge's letter to Mr. Wood, also written 14 July 1863, in Dodge's *Life in Letters* (I: 355–357).

20. William Bradford (1823–1892), an American marine painter who was known for his depictions of Arctic shipwrecks.

21. Labrador, in Newfoundland, Nova Scotia, featured Fort Louisburg, which had been built by the French beginning in 1713. It is now part of Cape Breton Island, Nova Scotia.

22. ‹of›

23. Una, Julian, and Rose were the three Hawthorne children, born in 1844, 1846, and 1851, respectively. "Class-day" was the orientation event at Harvard, where Julian began studying in 1863. The Wayside was the name of the Hawthornes' home in Concord, Massachusetts; they had purchased it from the Alcott family in 1852.

24. Dodge refers to Nathaniel Hawthorne's "Civic Banquets," published in the *Atlantic Monthly* 12 (August 1863): 195–212. Dodge also had an article in this issue entitled "Side-Glances at Harvard Class Day."

25. Fanny Fern (Sarah Payson Willis Parton) (1811–1872), a syndicated journalist who had particular success with her collection of essays, *Fern Leaves from Fanny's Portfolio* (1853) and her autobiographical novel, *Ruth Hall* (1854). A version of this letter was included in the essay that Fern wrote about Hamilton in *Eminent Women of the Age* (1868).

26. Peabody Essex Museum.

27. Horace Greeley (1811–1872), editor of the New York *Tribune*; Theodore Tilton (1835–1907) worked for the New York *Observer* and then edited the *Independent*, a Congregationalist weekly; James Parton (1822–1891), a biographer and historian whom Fern had married in 1857.

28. Peabody Essex Museum.

29. George Hillard (1808–1879), a Massachusetts politician and author of the enormously popular *Six Months in Italy* (1853). Ebenezer Rockwood Hoar (1816–1895), a Concord lawyer and Hawthorne family friend who served as a judge on the Massachusetts Common Pleas Court and the Massachusetts Supreme Court. He was also United States Attorney General.

30. *The Scarlet Letter* was published by Ticknor and Fields in 1850. See Fields, *Yesterdays with Authors*, 48–52.

31. Hawthorne's *Mosses from an Old Manse* (1846) and *Twice-Told Tales* (1837) were compilations of his short stories that had helped put him on the literary map; *A Wonder Book* (1852) and *Tanglewood Tales* (1853) were collections of short stories for children.

32. Following in a series.

33. Berg Collection, NYPL.

34. William Davis Ticknor died in 1864; the publishing firm he helped establish continued to be called Ticknor and Fields until 1868, at which point it became Fields, Osgood, and Company.

35. Berg Collection, NYPL.

36. ‹accounts›

37. ‹has been no›

38. ‹since›

39. ‹likely›

40. ‹12.26›
41. ‹old›
42. John Bartlett (1820–1895), the compiler of the well-known *Familiar Quotations* (1855), had joined Little, Brown in 1863, becoming a senior partner in 1878.

Works Cited

Coultrap-McQuin, Susan. *Doing Literary Business: American Women Writers in the Nineteenth Century.* Chapel Hill: U of North Carolina P, 1990.

——, ed. *Gail Hamilton: Selected Writings.* New Brunswick, NJ: Rutgers U P, 1992.

Dodge, H. Augusta, ed. *Gail Hamilton's Life in Letters.* 2 vols. Boston: Lee and Shepard, 1901.

Fern, Fanny. "Gail Hamilton." *Eminent Women of the Age; Being Narratives of the Lives and Deeds of the Most Prominent Women of the Present Generation.* Hartford: S. M. Betts, 1868. 202–220.

Fetterley, Judith. "Mary Abigail Dodge [Gail Hamilton]." *Provisions: A Reader from 19th-Century American Women.* Ed. Judith Fetterley. Bloomington: Indiana U P, 1985. 421–445.

Fields, James T. *Yesterdays with Authors.* Boston: James R. Osgood, 1872.

Hamilton, Gail. "A Complaint of Friends." *Atlantic Monthly* 10 (September 1862): 359–368.

——. *Twelve Miles from a Lemon.* NY: Harper and Bros., 1871.

Hawthorne, Nathaniel. *The Letters, 1867–1864.* Ed. Thomas Woodson, James A. Rubino, L. Neal Smith, and Norman Holmes Pearson. Columbus: Ohio State U P, 1987.

"The Pay of Authors." *The Congregationalist and Boston Recorder.* 10 October 1867: 184.

Sofer, Naomi Z. "'Carry[ing] a Yankee Girl to Glory': Redefining Female Authorship in the Postbellum United States." *American Literature* 75 (March 2003): 31–60.

Stewart, Randall. "Mrs. Hawthorne's Financial Difficulties." *More Books* 21 (February 1946): 43–52.

Walker, Nancy. *The Disobedient Writer: Women and Narrative Tradition.* Austin: U of Texas P, 1995.

Chapter 5

JENNIFER PHEGLEY

Mary Elizabeth Braddon (1835 – 1915)

Mary Elizabeth Braddon was one of the most popular and prolific writers of the nineteenth century, though she was also one of the most controversial. In 1865 Henry James crowned Braddon "the founder of the sensation novel," a title that brought with it more ridicule than accolades.[1] Sensation novels were a genre of fiction that exposed the lurid underbelly of Victorian middle-class society by depicting criminal activities such as forgery, bigamy, and murder perpetrated by seemingly respectable citizens who were often women. Braddon, a major purveyor of this genre, was an obvious target for critics who defined good literature as moralistic and realistic and saw sensation fiction as a dangerous manifestation of immorality and outrageous situations. While the three best-selling English novels of the nineteenth century were sensational — Wilkie Collins's *The Woman in White* (1860), Ellen Price Wood's *East Lynne* (1861), and Braddon's *Lady Audley's Secret* (1862) — Braddon received the brunt of the critical uproar over the genre. The critical focus on Braddon was partly due to her precarious personal life, which alienated her from "polite" society. Braddon violated Victorian codes of proper femininity as an actress, writer, and mistress who was thrust into the spotlight when her books started selling in the thousands. Braddon's unsavory critical reputation was compounded when she took on the highly public position as editor of her own literary magazine.

At the height of Braddon's popularity and power, she began a correspondence with Charles Kent (1823 – 1902), a journalist and reviewer who took Braddon's work seriously and viewed it favorably. While Braddon would ultimately attain longevity and respectability as a novelist, Kent was one of the first critics to defend her early controversial work in the press, and he thus became a lifelong friend and ally. Reproduced here are eighteen letters Braddon wrote to Kent during the 1860s, 70s, and 80s.

Mary Braddon was born in London on 4 October 1835 to Fanny and Henry Braddon. Braddon's father was a solicitor whose business endeavors were not as successful or as honest as her mother would have liked. As a result of Henry Braddon's adultery and financial failure, he separated from his wife and family when Mary was a child. From the age of five, Mary and her older sister Margaret were brought up in a single-parent household (their brother Edward was sent to boarding school and shuttled between his mother and father on holidays). Financial difficulties caused the family to move frequently, though Fanny made sure that her daughter received whatever education was available and affordable and that she was brought up in a respectable middle-class home. When, at the age of seventeen, Braddon decided to support herself and her mother by taking up a career as an actress, her relatives must have been shocked.[2] To protect her family name, she adopted the stage name Mary Seyton, and to further mitigate any damage to her reputation, she was diligently chaperoned by her mother as she embarked on an eight-year career as an actress.

During this time she also began writing, hoping to have her own plays performed on the stage. Though she was unable to break through as a playwright, Braddon found a patron in the eccentric and wealthy John Gilby, a man she probably met at one of her performances. With Gilby's professional ties and financial support, Braddon was able to break into the publishing industry. Under Gilby's guidance, Braddon turned her attention more fully to authorship, writing a volume of poems entitled *Garibaldi*. However, Gilby was a harsh taskmaster who, it seems, stifled Braddon's creativity. Braddon found writing the long epic poem he requested a tedious task and soon discovered a more amenable direction for her work when she began writing a serial novel on the side. The novel, *Three Times Dead*, was published in the *Beverley Recorder* in 1860. While this tale of murder, blackmail, and detection was not an immediate success, it intrigued publisher John Maxwell enough that he reprinted it under the title of *The Trail of the Serpent* a year later. In this guise the novel sold rapidly, spurred on, no doubt, by the success of *Lady Audley's Secret*, which was simultaneously being serialized (from 6 July to 28 September 1861) in Maxwell's magazine *Robin Goodfellow*.[3]

Braddon quickly became a frequent contributor to Maxwell's publications, and in 1861, he hired Braddon's mother, who had previously contributed to magazines for extra income, to edit the *Halfpenny Journal*. Braddon became the chief fiction writer for the magazine. Her writing also dominated Maxwell's two-penny weekly magazine the *Welcome Guest*. Once established with these journals, Braddon began angling to get her novels published in Maxwell's more prestigious shilling monthly, *Temple Bar*. Maxwell serialized her next novel, *Aurora Floyd*, in that periodical from January 1862 to January 1863 and kept her happy with the promise of editorial work when a position came open. Meanwhile, Braddon worked behind the scenes as subeditor under Anna Maria Hall of *St. James's Magazine*, a position Maxwell insisted would provide her with excellent training. However, Maxwell would not fulfill his promise to make her an editor until 1866. By then, Braddon's relationship with Maxwell had become more personally — and scandalously — involved. Indeed, as early as 1861 Braddon's relationship with Maxwell had caused a complete break with Gilby, who apparently saw her as more than a business interest and became furious about her increasing reliance on Maxwell.

It seems that Gilby's suspicions about Maxwell were well founded. On 19 March 1862 Braddon gave birth to the first of six children she would have with him. Braddon and her mother had moved in with Maxwell despite the fact that he was legally married to another woman with whom he had five children. Maxwell was estranged from his wife, who was apparently insane and living either in an asylum or in Ireland with family members. Their socially unacceptable relationship became even more scandalous in 1864 when Maxwell leaked false news of their marriage to the press, hoping to put an end to the gossip they had aroused. However, this news only stoked the fire as counter-reports issued by Maxwell's brother-in-law revealed that his first wife was, indeed, still living. It was not until 1874 that they were finally able to marry as a result of the death of Maxwell's wife. Braddon's sensational life and her sensational story lines were inextricably linked in the minds of her critics, who barraged her with bad reviews throughout the 1860s.

Once Braddon established her own magazine, she was able to defend herself and her brand of fiction against the stream of hyperbolic critical attacks, which included accusations of personal immorality and plagiarism. Braddon's battle against her critics in her magazine, *Belgravia*, may actually have been modeled on the kind of support she received from Charles Kent, who used his position as editor (beginning in 1845) and owner (from 1850 to 1871) of the liberal newspaper the *Sun* to make a case for Braddon's talents as a writer. Kent first came to Braddon's attention in September 1865 when he responded to W. Fraser Rae's anonymous and venomous assault on her entire body of work in the *North British Review*.[4] In a September 1865 article, "Sensation Novelists: Miss Braddon," Rae contended that "the impartial critic is compelled . . . to unite with the moralist in regarding [Braddon's novels] as mischievous in their tendency and as one of the abominations of the age. Into uncontaminated minds they will instil false views of human conduct" by leading readers "to conclude that the chief end of man is to commit murder, and his highest merit to escape punishment; that women are born to attempt to commit murders, and to succeed in committing bigamy" (203, 202). Rae — along with the majority of elite critics — focused on Braddon's gender and on her creation of unsavory women characters who transgressed gender and class boundaries.

When it came to her female characters, Braddon's personal life often became a subtext that interfered with assessments of her professional work. Rae implied that a proper middle-class woman would not create such characters: "An authoress who could make one of her sex play [such a role], is evidently acquainted with a very low type of female character, or else incapable of depicting what she knows to be true" (190). Rae was appalled that "the unthinking crowd . . . regarded [Braddon] as a woman of genius" (180). This "false" conception, along with Braddon's "bewitching" popularity, led Rae to famously conclude that Braddon had "succeeded in making the literature of the Kitchen the favourite reading of the Drawing room" (204). Kent came to Braddon's defense, though he did not yet know her, by calling Rae's review "extremely unfair" in its "coarse, and almost vulgar ungraciousness!" Kent maintained that Braddon had a "wide and brilliant reputation" that would not be destroyed by such "a highly elaborated panegyric on her genius as a Novelist" (Wolff *Sensational Victorian* 197 – 198). Likewise, in a review of *Sir Jasper's Tenant* in the 17 October 1865 issue of the *Sun*, Kent praised Braddon for her "extraordinary industry" and "remarkable" intellectual achievement (Wolff *Sensational Victorian* 198 – 199). Kent was stalwart in his contention that Braddon was a top-notch writer who deserved recognition for her literary skills.

Kent's book reviews made the *Sun* one of the first newspapers to regularly review fiction, a tradition he carried on when he edited the Catholic journal the *Weekly Register* from 1874 to 1880. Kent's support of Braddon lasted throughout his career, during which he was a frequent contributor to Charles Dickens's magazines *Household Words* and *All the Year Round*. Kent associated not only with Dickens but also with Leigh Hunt, Charles Reade, Robert Browning, George Meredith, Matthew Arnold, and Braddon's own literary mentor, Edward Bulwer-Lytton. He also published a book of poems, *Aletheia, or, The Doom of Mythology and Other Poems* in 1850; contributed a series of poems on English poets to the *New Monthly Magazine,* which were published in 1862 as *Dreamland; or Poets in their Haunts*; and released another edition of poems in 1870. He was known in later years for editing well-known writers such as Robert Burns (1874), Charles Lamb (1875), and Bulwer-Lytton (1883); for writing remembrances of writers such as Charles Dickens (1884) and Leigh Hunt (1888); and for contributing to the *Dictionary of National Biography.*

Braddon's correspondence with Kent is important because it reveals an alternative critical assessment of her work and indicates the importance she placed upon refuting her negative reputation. It also provides insight into Braddon's own handling of her public relations in her magazine. Braddon and Maxwell launched *Belgravia* in November 1866 with the intention not only of having a steady vehicle for the publication of her fiction but also a public forum in which to counter the negative critical attention she was garnering. George Augustus Sala was one of Braddon's chief Belgravian soldiers. In "The Cant of Modern Criticism" (November 1867) and "On the Sensational in Literature and Art" (February 1868), Sala vigorously defended Braddon, sensationalism, and women readers against the assaults of what he characterized as biased and jealous critics, thereby launching an offensive that ran throughout the first five years of the magazine. Braddon was able to use her own magazine to sustain a critical discourse that was friendly to her work, thus extending the service that Kent had provided for free.

Much like her other, better-known correspondent Edward Bulwer-Lytton, Kent also provided a sounding board for Braddon's professional anxieties and doubts. But, unlike she did with Bulwer-Lytton, whose letters from Braddon have been collected and published by Robert Lee Wolff,[5] Braddon did not seem to feel the need to please Kent. Therefore, her letters are more frank despite the fact that the early ones are primarily written in thanks for his ardent support. Her confidence in Kent's opinion may account for her desertion of the cautious explanations about the intentions of her work and the adulation she expresses in her letters to Bulwer-Lytton. In her letters to Kent, Braddon abandons the role of "devoted disciple" and instead emerges as an independent writer who is sure of her own talent and literary identity.

In 1876 *Belgravia* was sold to Chatto and Windus, and Braddon gave up her editorial seat. By this time the furor over sensation fiction had died down and Braddon had, remarkably, emerged unscathed. Braddon remained a prominent literary figure throughout the rest of the century, editing a Christmas annual, the *Mistletoe Bough*, from 1878 to 1887 and continuing to write prolifically. In the 1880s and 90s she wrote several historical novels, which she considered to be her greatest works. In 1913 she saw her early novel, *Aurora Floyd*, made into a film. By the time of her death in 1915, Braddon had become one of the era's most prolific and respected novelists. She had published as many as ninety books (the last published posthumously in 1916), edited two periodicals, and written numerous poems, essays, short stories, and plays. Writers such as Arnold Bennett, Ford Maddox Ford, Henry James, and Alfred, Lord Tennyson commented on her talent and influence. By the time she was interviewed in the *Pall Mall*

Magazine in 1911, she was a literary icon whose home and office were presented with veneration in the magazine's lavish photographs. In this interview, Braddon assesses her prolific and successful career by claiming that her primary goal was always "to tell a good story and to keep the interest from flagging till the last page. No writer can do much more than this; a great many of them, I fear, do much less" (Holland 707). Braddon certainly was able to "tell a good story," and she did so both with and without stirring up critical controversy throughout her long, prolific career.

Letter 1. Mary Elizabeth Braddon to Charles Kent,
26 Mecklenburgh Square, 12 September 1865[6]

My Dear Sir,

The Post has this moment brought me "The Sun" for this evening in which I discover your most kind, most disinterested, and able defence of me against the furious onslaught of "The North British Review." I had heard of the latter, but I have been and indeed am still too busy with the finish of my "Sir Jasper's Tenant"[7] to send for the Review or to trouble my head with an attack at once so virulent and malignant. I have been informed that the criticism in question is written by a novelist whose failure to excite public attention should at least have made him more charitable to a fellow labourer.[8] Pray allow me to assure you that I feel myself utterly unable to express my sense of obligation for your generosity towards my work; and I hope you will do me the justice to believe that I place the highest value upon your good opinion and hope yet to prove myself worthy of your most kindly encouragement.

I am, my dear sir,
Gratefully Yours
M. E. Braddon

Letter 2. Mary Elizabeth Braddon to Charles Kent, [4 October 1865][9]

Dear Sir,

I was absent from home when the copy of "The Sun" arrived, and since my return I have from day to day deferred the very pleasing duty of offering you my thanks for the last proof of your unfailing kindness.

In all sincerity I thank you, dear Sir, for your hearty and chivalrous championship, and I have the pleasure to subscribe myself once more

Gratefully Yours,
M. E. Braddon

Letter 3. Mary Elizabeth Braddon to Charles Kent,
26 Mecklenburgh Sq. W. C. [4 September 1866]

My Dear Sir,

The "Sun" kindly sent to me here arrived while I was away at St. Leonard's on Sea, and was *not* forwarded. I have just returned to find the packet awaiting me — and once more I have occasion to offer you my best thanks, which are none the less heartily given because your opinion of my *earliest 'atrocity'* is not altogether favorable.[10] You see a "Sigismund Smith" must needs go through his apprenticeship before he blossoms into the legitimate 3 Vols.[11]

I enclose a copy of "Saunders's Newsletter" just to show you a favourable review[12] of that first attempt but not in any way to *reproach* a critic whose friendship & generous opinion has been so unfailing that I am quite satisfied to bow my head submissively when he is compelled to blame.

Once again with sincere thanks, I subscribe myself my dear sir.
Very faithfully Yours,
M. E. Braddon

Letter 4. Mary Elizabeth Braddon to Charles Kent, [11 October 1866]

My Dear Sir,

A thousand thanks for your more than kind letter — and a second thousand or so for the two paragraphs in "The Sun."

I really do *not know* how to thank you heartily enough for so much kindness. The first gentleman of the press I ever met was Mr. Richard Martin, of the Sun. I only saw him once, but he kindly promised that if I ever needed a good word in your journal he would obtain it for me. A year or so after that I wrote to ask a favour for a friend — but alas, his kindly heart had ceased to beat! A gentleman whose name, I think, was Greene wrote me a most cordial letter & granted my request for love of his friend, poor Mr. Martin. And now *you* almost crush me with the kindness you heap on my unworthy head.

So, you see, however checkered my career may have been, "The Sun" has shone on me through it all. May it never cease so to shine — and may I become more worthy —

Ever, my dear sir, gratefully yours,
M. E. Braddon

Letter 5. Mary Elizabeth Braddon to Charles Kent, [26 November 1866]

My dear Mr. Kent,

I can scarcely tell you how deeply I regret the cause which will deprive me of the great pleasure I had anticipated in seeing you on Tuesday next. There will be many present on that occasion, for whose kindly encouragement I have every reason to be grateful — but there will be no one to whom I owe more gratitude than I do to you for your unfailing & most hearty championship. I trust when you receive this you will be on the high road to recovery, and may perhaps be able to join us, your refusal notwithstanding.

Very Truly Yours,
M. E. Braddon
Saturday night

Letter 6. Mary Elizabeth Braddon to Charles Kent, [n.d.][13]

My Dear Mr. Kent,

We do not at present contemplate giving more than our long serial in "Belgravia", as we find that by giving novelettes in three numbers we shall have more field for variety. However I shall have much pleasure in getting Mr. Asherstone's[14] novel carefully read by a much better critic than myself — as I have just at present neither time nor *eyesight* for the task — and I will send you a candid and critical opinion if that will be any satisfaction to your friend.[15]

I think I owe that gentleman some very kind hints upon small details in "Aurora Floyd," communicated in a gracious & kindly letter written more than three years ago. I lost the letter & by that means was deprived of the pleasure of expressing my thanks. Will you now be so good as to be my proxy in this matter — when next you see — or write to Mr. Asherstone.

I took advantage of his corrections lately when revising "A. F." for the two shilling edition.

I daresay you have heard our annoyances with regard to "Belgravia" & the very unfair attempt of Messrs. Hogg to interfere with the [project?].[16] Will you kindly give us a lift in society if you hear the matter discussed, as we hope to come out so strongly as to "*ecraser l'infame*,"[17] who has done his best to crush us.

Please pardon a hurried scrawl and with all thanks for yr. kind letter,
Believe me Always Sincerely Yours,
M. E. Braddon

Letter 7. Mary Elizabeth Braddon to Charles Kent, 28 February [1867]

Dear Mr. Kent,

I have to thank you again for your kindness in giving me so prompt a notice of my magazine.[18] I fear I must have seemed ungrateful for not[19] acknowledging the copy of the "Sun" ere this — but you have been so good to me that I have really begun to accept your kindness almost as a matter of course.

May I be bold enough to put in a word for a person whose cause has been warmly pleaded by an old friend of mine, and entreat that if you have not already reviewed — and should purpose reviewing a novel entitled "Saint Alice"[20] you will mercifully say a good word for it, if it deserves such indulgence,

And oblige your already deeply indebted[21],
M. E. Braddon.

Letter 8. Mary Elizabeth Braddon to Charles Kent, 14 March [1867]

Dear Mr. Kent,

I really am almost ashamed to address you after this long delay, but I trust you will readily believe that, among the many causes of my seeming neglect *ingratitude* has no part.

The last two or three weeks have been for us a perpetual scramble, and this morning I avail myself of the first really quiet half hour I have enjoyed since the receipt of the two newspapers so kindly sent me. One containing your flattering review of Lady Lisle,[22] the other your notice of "Belgravia."

My household is in the act of "moving," and I have no doubt you well know the misery involved in that one word. Every day brings some new trouble. And my literary work scarcely begins till late at night.

Once more with all thanks & apologies,

I remain, dear Mr. Kent,
Very faithfully Yours
M. E. Braddon

Letter 9. Mary Elizabeth Braddon to Charles Kent, 27 October [1876]

My Dear Mr. Kent,

I am so very sorry that you should have happened to call here on a day when I was out — as it would have given me very great pleasure to see you here. I hope it is truly a pleasure deferred, & that not for long.

I have been daily intending to answer yr. last kind letter[23] — but so many small matters have occupied every hour of my life that I have waited for a *quiet* hour in vain.

Yesterday I had a great shock from a pair of run away horses which I fully thought were taking me & mine to instant death — but thank god *we* were all saved at the cost of the near horse which fell against a lamp-post & stopped the carriage. All was occasioned by the steam roller working at mid-day.

My husband and I would be much pleased if you could name yr. own day for dining with us — next week — or at any time most convenient to yourself.

"Joshua Haggard" is the 31st novel[24] — & I trust — should you do us the honour to read it — you will find some slight improvement in the quality of the work since the old days when you were so hearty a champion of my literary claims.

Yrs. always true,
Mary Maxwell

Letter 10. Mary Elizabeth Braddon to Charles Kent, [31?] December, [1876]

Dear Mr. Kent,

You heap favours upon me so fast that I am bowed beneath the load. First yr. charming letter which reached me on Friday evening & next yr. glowing criticism which my husband read to me directly I awoke on Saturday morning.[25] Yes, I think you have hit the right nail on the head — you being the only critic who has noticed the point — & that the moral of Joshua Haggard's life is more or less an argument for a celibate clergy. A man who has the souls of his fellow men in his keeping should keep his own soul unclouded by passion — should inhabit a loftier region than the low earthly world of his flock.

Once more a thousand thanks for a most thoughtful, & only too appreciative review.

I hope that now you are returned we may very soon have the pleasure of seeing you here, & that I may be able to thank you in person. With kind regards from "Max" & myself

Very truly Yrs.
Mary Maxwell

Letter 11. Mary Elizabeth Braddon to Charles Kent, 5 October [18]77

Dear Mr. Kent,

You are more than kind to take such trouble on our account; & whatever the result my gratitude to you will be warm & sincere.

Saturday will be a grand night, & I should delight in being present at the first performance of that most interesting play,[26] yet what a vein of sadness must be in every mind at the thought that he, who so loved dramatic success, cannot assist at his own triumph.

Yrs. with a thousand Thanks,
M. E. M.

Letter 12. Mary Elizabeth Braddon to Charles Kent,
40 Albion Street, Broadstairs, 25 Feb [1878]

Dear Mr. Kent,

Once again — as in so many years past — have I to acknowledge with sincerest gratitude your much unchanging & inexhaustible kindness, & that power of appreciating the most trivial beauties in one's workmanship, which so few critics possess, or at any rate care to exercise. You are always staunch, true, and kind — & I feel assured, if I wrote a book you could not find it in your heart to praise, you would let the offending volumes pass unnoticed, for you could not find it in your heart to blame.

Yes, I quite agree with you. My High Church curate is a cur — & yet I meant him to be all that is staunch & noble. Only he went askew somehow in the working out.[27] I am now finishing a simple — easy going — love story with a frank high spirited girlish heroine whom I venture to think you will like when I submit her to your kindly jurisdiction.[28]

We are here for a week or so with children who have been ill, & who are in need of strengthening breezes. I trust you are well, & with less cause for anxiety than when I last had the pleasure of seeing you.

Believe me
Always gratefully Yrs.
M. Maxwell

Letter 13. Mary Elizabeth Braddon to Charles Kent, [6 October 1879]
Monday Morning

My Dear Mr. Kent,

It is I who am ungrateful — it is I who am blameworthy. All this week just past I have been intending to write & thank you heartily for yr. last boon: the splendid review in the Register: but a constant succession of duties, engagements, the ever-lasting scramble of daily life, etc., etc. have conspired to prevent me. Pray come & see us some Sunday afternoon that I may have time to tell you how deeply I feel my large debt to yr. unfailing kindness.

I now have only time to say that constant as that goodness has been — & ungrateful as I may often seem — I have *not* grown to regard yr. favours as a matter of course.

I trust you & yr. family are well — & that you have been able to find time for a pleasant holiday this year,

Believe me
Most sincerely Yrs.
Mary Maxwell

P. S. I am going — if I live — to write a novel next year which I think you will like — It will be called 'Daphne.' It will be intensely sentimental, & will end in tragedy.[29] This in confidence — I have said as much to no one else.

Letter 14. Mary Elizabeth Braddon to Charles Kent, 9 October [1880]
Saturday night

Dear Mr. Kent,

Just when I had heard you were ill & feared that for a time I might not see the touch of the well-known hand which has ever been so active in my interest I received the ever-welcome Catholic Register[30] with another splendid notice, [heartening?] all the old generous spirit & delicacy of thought.[31] That which pleased me much better even than the kindly criticism was the thought that you could hardly be so much an invalid as my informant of a day or two before had said, more especially as the [cover?] was directed by yr own hand.

I shall be very grateful for a line from you to say how you are, & should be still better pleased were you able & inclined to name any evening in the coming week when you could dine with us quietly here, & give us the pleasure of an evening's talk. My husband joins with me in this desire, as well as in most anxious concern for yr. health.

Believe me, Dear Mr. Kent
Yrs. always gratefully & sincerely
Mary Maxwell

Letter 15. Mary Elizabeth Braddon to Charles Kent, 28 October [1880]

Dear Mr. Kent,

I am heartily rejoiced at getting yr. own assurance that yr. illness is a thing of the past, & I trust with God's mercy it may be long ere the future bring you any recurrence of suffering. I only heard of yr. being ill just before I wrote to you or you may be assured we should have taken some means to inform ourselves of yr. progress towards recovery.

I envy you yr. visit to Knebworth & the delight of long hours of talk with Lord Lytton, whose conversation has all the charm wh. comes from a richly stored memory & most poetic mind. I hope he will honour me by coming to see us when he is next in London, & at leisure — if ever *that* can be in a life so full as his.

If you cannot name a day — saving always Tuesday and Friday — for dining with us *en famille* next week will you come to our Sunday Yorkshire tea — sharp seven — on November 14th, when I expect some very nice amusing people. No full dress — quite a friendly affair.

Believe me, as always
Most sincerely Yrs.,
Mary Maxwell

Letter 16. Mary Elizabeth Braddon to Charles Kent,
Bank Cottage, 20 May [1881]

Dear Mr. Kent,

How good you are! I see now that you are one of those staunch & sterling souls who can be indulgent even to the failings of a friend — more than a "little kind" to her faults. No, my dear sir, I have *not* tried to astonish the British public as the great sorceress. I have seen Ristori play the part — and — tho' it is more years ago than I care to say, I well remember how grand & glorious she was — with a touch of the Demoniac — in that impersonation.[32]

When, encouraged by the generous advice of that great Master of his Art whom I revere as the first cause of all I have ever done in literature, I put my hand to the plough, there was no looking back at the more fascinating profession wh. I surrendered.[33] I dearly love the drama & there is one particular line of comedy wh. had at the time — twenty years ago — an intense charm for me — but those days are long past — & I have no longer any ambition beyond the walls of my study.

The Medea whose name deceived you is *Miss Brandon.*

I hope you are well, & enjoying the intellectual pleasures of the London season — new plays, recitations, concerts, etc., etc, etc. We have been here since Easter, & my poor husband has been very unwell during a considerable portion of the time. I have also had my beloved son laid up with sore throat. Thank God both are now better.

We go back to Richmond, all being well, on the 2nd June, after wh. date I hope you will speedily name a day for dining with us, so that we may have a long talk.

[34], Believe me,
Dear Mr. Kent
with most cordial regards, in wh. my husband joins,
Ever sincerely Yrs.
Mary Maxwell

This is one of the loveliest places in the world. I wish you were here to admire it.

Letter 17. Mary Elizabeth Braddon to Charles Kent, 13 July [1881]

Dear Mr. Kent,

The Journal for next Xmas is all in type[35] — the illustrations in the engraver's hands — & a great deal of the text revised. I would, however, gladly hold over Mrs. Kent's little story for 1882 shd. I think it strong enough for an annual wh. has to fight so many "blood & thunder" rivals. But, charmingly as Mrs. Kent's story is written, it appears to me, from its chief interest turning upon the very natural juvenile misapprehension about Mr. "Right" to be better fitted for a somewhat juvenile periodical than for the Misletoe Bough. I trust that neither you nor Mrs. Kent will be offended at the perfect frankness with which I am writing about a story which I read from the first line to the last with much interest. Lord Lytton is to honour us with his company next Monday 18th July at a two o'clock luncheon, & it would give both my husband & myself great pleasure if you can find time & inclination to join our circle.

With very kind regards
Most Sincerely Yrs.,
Mary Maxwell

Letter 18. Mary Elizabeth Braddon to Charles Kent, 16 November [n.y.]

Dear Mr. Kent,

Your thoughtful kindness has afforded me a great pleasure — &, — although I do not know how to reach you save thro' yr. former address, as you may be on the wing—I cannot wait to thank you till our little dinner here with Father [Bagsh——?] —which I hope however is to take place soon.

I am delighted with "England & the English," which I read all yesterday evening.[36] Tonight I shall enjoy yr. prefatory memoirs to the handy edition of Elia. Need I say that I love that sweet, witty, & most eloquent writer? I think his essay upon Borrowers & Lenders one of the most exquisite specimens of witty writing in our language. Even Bulwer owed him much, & Dickens, at his best, comes nearest Lamb. Au revoir, dear Mr. Kent, I shall thank you a little more warmly when we meet.

Yrs. Very truly,
M. E. Maxwell

Notes

1. Although James generally displays a positive regard for Braddon —affirming that she is an "artist" with a "knowing style" and "shrewd" observational skills—he claims that her fellow sensationalist Wilkie Collins deserves "a more respectable name" (593).

2. Jennifer Carnell explores Braddon's career as an actress in detail in her biography.

3. When that periodical folded, Maxwell reserialized the popular novel in his new *Sixpenny Magazine* from January to December 1862. When the novel was published in three volumes in 1862, it went through eight editions in three months (Carnell 147).

4. The *North British Review* article epitomized the assault launched against Braddon in the press in earlier reviews such as the one by Henry Mansel in the *Quarterly Review* (April 1863).

5. See Wolff, "Devoted Disciple: The Letters of Mary Elizabeth Braddon to Sir Edward Bulwer-Lytton, 1862–1873."

6. All of the following letters were collected by Robert Lee Wolff and are housed in the Wolff Collection at the Harry Ransom Humanities Research Center at the University of Texas at Austin; hereafter Harry Ransom Center, U of Texas. In *Sensational Victorian*, Wolff mistakenly cites the date of this letter as 13 September 1865. Not only does the original letter say 12 September 1865, but within the letter Braddon refers to an article that appeared on the twelfth.

7. *Sir Jasper's Tenant* was serialized in *Temple Bar* from February to December 1865. It was published in three volumes by Maxwell in 1865.

8. Wolff notes that Braddon may have mistakenly assumed that the reviewer was Frederick Greenwood, an unsuccessful novelist who was friends with her former patron, John Gilby. Greenwood did later attack her in a series of reviews in the *Pall Mall Gazette*.

9. Dates in brackets are assigned by Wolff either on the letter itself or in *Sensational Victorian*.

10. Braddon refers to Kent's assessment of *The Trail of the Serpent*. This novel, originally published by W. & M. Clark as *Three Times Dead* (1860), was reissued by Maxwell under the new title in March 1861 and was serialized in the *Halfpenny Journal* 1 August 1864 – 6 February 1865.

11. Braddon jokingly compares herself to the hack sensation writer she created for *The Doctor's Wife* (1864) and later renamed Sigismund Smyth in *The Lady's Mile* (1866). For a discussion of Smith as Braddon's "alter ego," see Lyn Pykett's introduction to *The Doctor's Wife*.

12. Braddon enclosed a laudatory review of *The Trail of the Serpent* published in the 29 August 1866 issue of *Saunders's News Letter and Daily Advertiser.* This journal had also defended Braddon against Rae's attack in the *North British Review* on 24 October 1865 (Wolff *Sensational Victorian* 450).

13. This letter was likely written sometime between November 1866 and March 1867 when the Hogg ordeal, explained in note 16 below, was resolved.

14. Possibly writer Edwin Atherstone (1788 – 1872).

15. Jennifer Carnell cites this letter as evidence that Braddon did not conduct day-to-day editorial duties for *Belgravia*. Instead, she explains that Charles Smith Cheltnam apparently dealt with incoming manuscripts. While it is clear that Cheltnam played a role in editing *Belgravia*, it is difficult to determine how extensive that role really was. It may have been convenient for Braddon to use Cheltnam as an excuse so that she would not have to reject a friend's submission.

16. Carnell explains that Maxwell was furious about a *Belgravia* knock-off intended to profit off of Braddon's name. The periodical was called *Belgravia: A Magazine of Fashion and Amusements.* Maxwell apparently won a lawsuit against the imposter's proprietor, Mr. Hogg, and after only five issues, he had the magazine put out of business (Wolff *Sensational Victorian* 175).

17. French phrase meaning "crush the scoundrel."

18. Kent apparently reviewed *Belgravia* in the *Sun* sometime between the magazine's launch in November 1866 and the time this letter was written.

19. ‹answering›

20. *Saint Alice, who, However Was No Saint* (1867), a novel by Edward Campbell Tainsh.

21. ‹indecipherable word›

22. *Lady Lisle* was serialized in the *Welcome Guest* from May to September 1861 and published in volume form by Ward & Lock in 1862.

23. ‹s›

24. *Joshua Haggard's Daughter* was serialized in *Belgravia* from December 1875 through December 1876 and was published in three volumes by Maxwell in 1876.

25. Kent's review of *Joshua Haggard's Daughter* probably appeared the last week of December 1876 just as the serial was completed and the novel was issued. December 30 fell on a Saturday, so the letter was likely written the following day.

26. *The House of Darnley,* a play by Edward Bulwer-Lytton that was left unfinished at

his death in 1873. Braddon encouraged Bulwer-Lytton's son, Robert (pen name Owen Meredith), to complete it, and it was performed on 6 October 1877 at the Royal Court Theatre.

27. Kent reviewed *An Open Verdict*, which was published in 1878 after being serialized in various newspapers the year before. In the novel, a curate refuses to stand by his fiancé when she is accused of a murder he knows she did not commit (Wolff *Sensational Victorian* 277).

28. Her novel *Vixen* serialized in *All the Year Round* from October through June 1879.

29. Probably *Asphodel*, serialized in *All the Year Round* from July 1880 through March 1881 and published by Maxwell in 1881 (Wolff *Sensational Victorian* 285).

30. After the failure of the *Sun* in 1871, Kent edited the *Weekly Register and Catholic Standard* from 1874 until 1881.

31. Kent's review of *Just As I Am* appeared in the *Weekly Register and Catholic Standard* on 2 October 1880.

32. Adelaide Ristori, a famous Italian actress who played Medea in London and Paris in 1856.

33. As Carnell points out, Braddon is likely referring to her mentor, Edward Bulwer-Lytton (74).

34. ‹indecipherable phrase›

35. The *Mistletoe Bough*, which Braddon edited from 1878 to 1887.

36. Though this letter is undated, Braddon probably refers to Charles Kent's edited volume of Edward Bulwer-Lytton's *England and the English*. Between 1875 and 1883, Kent edited a twelve-volume collection of *Miscellaneous Works* by Bulwer-Lytton, and *England and the English* (published in 1833 by Richard Bentley) was the fifth volume of the Routledge edition. In 1875, Kent's thirty-eight volume centenary edition of Charles Lamb's works was also published by Routledge. This set included *Essays of Elia* (first published in 1823) and *The Last Essays of Elia* (originally published in 1833). Braddon also refers to Kent's memoir about Lamb.

Works Cited

Carnell, Jennifer. *The Literary Lives of Mary Elizabeth Braddon: A Study of Her Life and Work*. Hastings, East Sussex, UK: The Sensation Press, 2000.

Holland, Clive. "Fifty Years of Novel Writing: Miss Braddon at Home. A Chat with the Doyenne of English Novelists." *Pall Mall Magazine* (November 1911): 697–709.

[James, Henry.] "Miss Braddon." *The Nation* 1.9 (November 9, 1865): 593–594.

Pykett, Lyn. "Introduction." *The Doctor's Wife*. Mary Elizabeth Braddon. Oxford: Oxford U P, 1998. vii–xxv.

[Rae, W. Fraser.] "Sensation Novelists: Miss Braddon." *North British Review* 43 (September 1865): 180–205.

Wolff, Robert Lee. "Devoted Disciple: The Letters of Mary Elizabeth Braddon to
    Sir Edward Bulwer-Lytton, 1862–1873." *Harvard Library Bulletin* 22 (1974): 5–35,
    129–161.
———. *Sensational Victorian: The Life and Fiction of Mary Elizabeth Braddon.* NY:
    Garland, 1979.

Chapter 6

LINDA PETERSON

Mary Cholmondeley (1859 – 1925) and Rhoda Broughton (1840 – 1920)

Mary Cholmondeley and Rhoda Broughton were both daughters of Anglican clergyman. Both grew up and spent their early adult lives in isolated parsonages on the northern English-Welsh border (Broughton in Cheshire and Staffordshire, Cholmondeley in Shropshire); both moved in overlapping circles of the country gentry, though as children of impoverished "younger sons" rather than titled aristocrats; and both moved to London, where they continued their friendship after they became established novelists. A friend of the family and the elder by a generation, Broughton mentored the younger Cholmondeley, encouraging her career as a novelist and introducing her to Richard Bentley, the publisher of triple-decker novels and the periodical *Temple Bar*.

If biographical anecdotes are true, both Rhoda Broughton and Mary Cholmondeley turned to writing fiction after unhappy love affairs: Michael Sadleir postulated that the impetus for Broughton's novel writing was "the sublimation of an unhappy teenage romance," and Percy Lubbock quoted Cholmondeley as saying that it was "the repression of my youth, my unhappy love-affair," rather than sheer talent, that motivated her career.[1] Whether true or not, the two young women were motivated more significantly by the desire to join a women's literary tradition that had gained strength and status during the nineteenth century. After reading Anne Thackeray's *The Story of Elizabeth* (1863), written by an author her own age, Broughton began drafting her first novel, *Not Wisely But Too Well* (1867), which she placed in the *Dublin University Magazine* before revising it for Bentley. Taking Elizabeth Gaskell's *Life of Charlotte Brontë* as her model,

Cholmondeley compared herself and her three sisters to the Brontë siblings; she recalls in her memoir, *Under One Roof* (1918), how, like those "other eager young women" before them, "we often raced up and down the old schoolroom to get warm," while "our hands in our muffs, we had long discussions on books and people and Life."[2]

A women's literary tradition, as well as a cultural practice of experienced professional women helping younger aspirants to break into the ranks of authorship, provides the basis for the correspondence between Broughton and Cholmondeley. The earliest letters between these two friends and fellow writers seem to be lost, most likely because Broughton "destroyed during her last illness all the letters she had received."[3] A set of later letters, however, remains intact. It begins with a discussion of Cholmondeley's highly successful *künstlerroman*, *Red Pottage* (1899), and continues until Broughton's death in 1920, just as Cholmondeley was collecting stories for her final volume, *The Romance of His Life* (1921). I like to think that Broughton preserved these letters from the general destruction because they represent the successful transmission of literary talent, professional lore, and cross-generational friendship from an older to a younger woman writer—in effect, from literary mother to daughter.

The letters selected here focus on two important aspects of literary life: assessment of Cholmondeley's work, especially its ambitions and achievements; and professional negotiations in the late nineteenth- and early twentieth-century marketplace, especially about royalties and other financial matters. The artistic assessment was important to Mary Cholmondeley, who wrote in isolated circumstances until she was forty and who, after her mother's early death, relied on Rhoda Broughton and their publisher, Richard Bentley, for literary advice. The professional exchange was equally important. As memoirs and letters reveal, Broughton was forthright, even brash, in her dealings with editors and publishers; Cholmondeley was far more uncertain and reticent. Thus, for example, as represented in the first letter below, Broughton was perfectly willing to challenge Bentley about the reduced royalties for her novels of the 1890s, whereas Cholmondeley was too timid—and too proud—to write to Macmillan, the publisher who bought out Bentley and Son in the mid-1890s, about their interest in her new work.[4]

Of course, the letters are also about other things: family affairs, friends and authors of mutual acquaintance, incidents of daily life and local color. Cholmondeley frequently sent Broughton news of writers in their London circle. In August 1913, for example, she reported her worries about Howard Sturgis, a mutual friend and fellow author, to whom Cholmondeley had dedicated her collection, *The Lowest Rung* (1908). Sturgis had suffered an accident that required multiple stitches, only some of which had "come out and healed entirely." "Howard," Mary told Rhoda, had spent an "enjoyable fortnight" convalescing in the country, but "he needs a more drastic change than that, and he seems determined to delay it as long as possible" (29 August 1913).[5] Her concern for Sturgis's bodily and mental condition is echoed in later letters, suggesting that she and Broughton, both single women, played mother and nurse to many of their friends.

As Broughton grew older and withdrew from active public life, Cholmondeley wrote less about professional matters and more about family and friends, including amusing anecdotes of life at "The Cottage," Ufford, Suffolk, where Mary and her sister Victoria lived for long stretches during World War I. Most of Cholmondeley's letters of 1914 to 1918 record local details of war, including Victoria's nursing of wounded soldiers, her nephews' military service, the shortages of food and clothing, and eyewitness accounts of "bombs dropping in the dark," an enemy "plane sinking slowly in flames to his doom," and everyone "except myself" going out "to look at the wreck" (14 July 1917). But the letters also continue the exchanges about reading and writing fiction, dealing with publishers, and placing stories in periodicals. On 8 September 1917, as the war reached its turning point, Cholmondeley wrote happily to Broughton about a visit to her new publisher, John Murray, with whom she "settled various matters about a little book he is bringing out of mine after Christmas, not a novel."[6]

Throughout the correspondence, even when both women would have been deemed "elderly," there remains a sense of an older and a younger writer exchanging views, a consciousness of Broughton as the mentor, Cholmondeley as the apprentice. It was a kind and supportive mentoring relationship, without apparent difficulties. Although Broughton had received help from her uncle, Sheridan Le Fanu, as she launched her literary career, that mentoring relationship had hit sharp rocks when Rhoda submitted her second novel, *Cometh Up as a Flower* (1867), to Bentley and Son. Bentley's reader, Geraldine Jewsbury, "professed herself shocked by the coarseness and boldness of the novel," and rather than support his niece, Le Fanu backed off from his initial enthusiasm and blamed the author's naiveté for the novel's infelicities: "I ought to say that the author's boldness of style and description arises from an unfortunate ignorance of the actual force of some of what is set down and of the way in which the world — wiser in the knowledge of evil — might read it."[7] In contrast, Broughton never abandoned Cholmondeley or withdrew her support; indeed, the correspondence conveys a strong sense of encouragement not only for Mary's writing but also for her sister Victoria's painting and tactile arts.

The letter of 30 October 1899, sent soon after the publication of *Red Pottage*, suggests that Broughton's praise of this particular novel was unusually strong and much desired. *Red Pottage* was unlike its predecessors in that it departed from Cholmondeley's early sensation fiction (the genre she had inherited from Broughton) and derived instead from her personal experiences and credo as a writer. Thus when Broughton praised this novel, she was praising not only its craft, but also the writer herself and her newfound independence. Unfortunately, we do not have the actual letter that Broughton sent — only the response that Cholmondeley penned, which is the second letter below. But its content, which addresses specific points in Broughton's letter, tells us much about the original praise and criticism, as well as about the emotional quality of the relationship.

I have included, in full, the letter about *Red Pottage*, as well as one in which Bentley replies to Broughton about the state of the publishing market in the 1890s. That assessment of a market with a declining interest in fiction and, more specifically, a turning away from the triple-decker, provides a context for the professional exchanges that ensue in later letters. Both women, who had achieved success in the era of sensation fiction and had mastered the three-volume format, now had to adapt to the brave new worlds of *fin-de-siècle* and modernist publishing. If, as Gaye Tuchman and Nina E. Fortin have suggested, the publishing industry, and specifically Macmillan, was edging women out, then the letters between Broughton and Cholmondeley show one strategy for "staying in": join forces with a fellow woman writer and use your mutual knowledge to continue your literary careers.[8]

I have taken the correspondence between Cholmondeley and Broughton through 1919, when both were ill and near their ends — a phase symbolized, perhaps, by the dismantling of Cholmondeley's house in Kensington, London, as articulated in letter 9 below. The last letters detail illnesses, including Mary's collapse from the influenza that swept Europe after the war and Howard Sturgis's death in February 1920. Rhoda Broughton was not to live much longer, as she died on 5 June 1920 at age 80. Her last book, *A Fool in Her Folly*, was published posthumously that year. Cholmondeley's last book, *The Romance of His Life*, appeared the next year.

Letter 1. Richard Bentley to Rhoda Broughton, 16 February 1898[9]

Dear Miss Broughton

The values of copyrights have not yet recovered from the rude shock they had some three years when by the abolishing of the "Library Edition" of novels an avalanche of cheaply produced (& generally very inferior) works poured into the market.

As we are approaching the end of the year (March) we happened to be testing the effects upon the various books only a couple of days before your letter arrived and I will take from the figures before me the annual sales of two or three works of fiction by writers of considerable prominence.

	Four years in succession			
Novel				
copies	1287	1071	822	978
Novel				
copies	233	189	196	153
Novel				
copies	1338	1192	1196	1191
Novel				
copies	210	106	146	74
Novel				
copies	653	512	444	494
Novel				
copies	583	525	348	376

If it were permissible to give the names of the books or their writers you would recognize that they were both representative ones & also that the respective works had a permanent place in the esteem of the public.

Every book for the time has suffered in like manner & it is likely to be some time before the better ones regain their average sale.

If the story which is verging towards completion is of the same extent as Scylla or Faustina[10] we should, if it were regarded from an absolutely business point of view assess its present value at £300 (besides what might come from America) but as this would represent a diminution of £50 I find on the amount paid for the last story I should not like this to occur.

I propose therefore that the amount payable shd. be £350 arranged in the same way as last time.

If you would like us to offer the story on your behalf in the United States we will do so with pleasure.

It is too soon to find *precisely* when it could begin in Temple Bar[11] as we have not yet ascertained exactly the length of the stories in hand, but this will be ascertainable almost as soon as the manuscript is finished.

Believe me
Yours very truly
Richard Bentley

Letter 2. Mary Cholmondeley to Rhoda Broughton, 30 October 1899[12]

Dear and *kind* Rhoda

I think you could hardly realize the pleasure your letter has given, not only to me, but to my whole family. I have been asked to read it aloud several times, and by special request to "Dick Vernon"[13] during his after dinner cigarette. It reached even *his* idea of what[14] is fitting to be said about my book. He informs me solemnly at intervals that I am a gifted person!

How I wish I could have more readers like you, but alas! I know very well that I must not expect in others the sympathy and kindly feeling which you have brought to bear upon "Red Pottage." Thank you many *many* times. I value your letter much, and am proud of it. I suppose there is a good deal of me in Hester,[15] tho' I had hardly realized it.

I think the character is entirely opposed to mine, but of course I have put in my own feelings exactly about "writing", or at least a small portion of them.

I saw the pike caught,[16] when I was about seven years old. I was in the boat with my brother and an old keeper.

Alas! for my imbecility about the starling.[17] Others are pointing out my error to me, far less kindly than you, and it is not a minnow of a mistake, it is a *whale*!

I can't forgive myself. It is like breaking one's leg on one's own doorstep, on one's own bit of orange peel. I pray fervently for a second edition "to make my honour bright."

I am so glad it is mild to-day, for this evening Dick is going to take us to the play, *your* play. I have not been anywhere for so long that I am quite excited, and hope this is the beginning of being able to creep about a little once more.

Mr. Russell lunched with us last Friday and was quite delightful. Mr. Guthrie was also most amusing. This was our first Friday luncheon, and I enjoyed it immensely, but I was so tired afterwards that Victoria, under whose thumb I live, says she will not allow me to have another until I am stronger.

[18]affectionately and gratefully
Mary Cholmondeley.

Letter 3. Mary Cholmondeley to Rhoda Broughton, 21 November 1917[19]

Dearest Rhoda

I might with truth say again "We live in stirring times," as you always accuse me of having said when you bought a new coat. I am very glad Lloyd George has survived this stirring up of the political cauldron. He is the best we have got, tho' he is an impulsive ignorant creature [. . .].

Have you read "Summer" by Mrs. Wharton. I thought it very fine and restrained, never once allowing you to have a glimpse of any of the men and women in the story except through the eyes and slow mind of an ignorant[20] American village girl.

My little volume "Under One Roof'" will be out early in January to avoid the Christmas traffic in gift books. I rather tremble in my shoes as to what those two excellent men my brothers will think of it. They will I fear expect the 4 people dealt with[21] to be portrayed as perfect characters: and I greatly fear that what seems to *me* character drawing will seem to *them* disloyalty.

The cheap edition of Notwithstanding[22] is selling particularly well. I called on Murray the other day, and he said 2000 had been ordered that morning.

I hope this mild weather suits you. At any rate it saves coal doesn't it. I hear we shall probably come to compulsory rations before long. I still with amazement see people take bread at meals, break and have half of it.

Yrs every
Mary

Letter 4. Mary Cholmondeley to Rhoda Broughton, 22 July 1918[23]

My dear Rhoda

[. . .] We are getting too much rain here, but it is a fault on the right side. I am glad to say V. and Essex Benson[24] will come here at the end of this week, and my brother Reginald shortly afterwards. We move back to London after the Bank holiday.

Essex Benson has had the comfort of hearing that her fragile little daughter Stella has reached America safely.[25]

I am just finishing a short story of the most frivolous nature. It is called "The Stars in their Courses."[26] Don't you think I am rather a "dab" at titles! It is about an asthmatic old maid who lived in a cottage. Is not that an alluring subject [...]!

Yrs ever
Mary

Letter 5. Mary Cholmondeley to Rhoda Broughton, 18 February 1919[27]

My dear Rhoda

Victoria is so busy that I have suggested that I should write to you this week.

I swelled with pride when I read your praise of my "Stars." I had a twinge of vanity about Anne. I hoped I had indicated a character tho' my span was limited — I am delighted that you think I have succeeded with her — Now Howard[28] does not even mention Anne but praises Gertrude highly, who in my eyes hardly possesses any character at all. He says she must have been taken from life —

Between you and me I got a hundred for it (between England and U.S.A.) and never was money more urgently needed.[29] But please dont mention this sum. Victoria most unkindly is now pressing me to write another to meet this years deficit. But I feel dreadfully unable to use my imagination. As a cook of ours always said "you cant make somethink out of nothink," but that is what an unhappy profession has to do. My imagination has dropped dead into the great crevasse of the war [...].

Yrs ever
Mary

Letter 6. Mary Cholmondeley to Rhoda Broughton, 11 May 1919[30]

Dearest Rhoda

[...] V. works early and late with Essex at the Exhibition, but she is supported by good sales. A splendid corner cupboard has just sold for £17. Her cupboards are too beautiful, and I long to buy one myself.

She is *very* tired, but when the Exhibition closes out this end of this month her work will be over, for her workshops are already closed and wound up [...].

I had rather a piece of work in coming up to time with my story dated fifty years hence.[31] But it is now in the Editor's hands. This whole number of the Magazine is to be full of papers and stories placed fifty years hence. How delightful it will be if Galsworthy, Chesterton and my other colleagues all hit on the same idea [. . .].

Yrs ever
Mary

Letter 7. Mary Cholmondeley to Rhoda Broughton, 20 May 1919[32]

Dearest Rhoda

Victoria and I both read your kind and frank letter and then I burnt it. It was good of you to tell us the real reason, for otherwise we might have been a little hurt that we might not have the pleasure of a visit from you.[33]

It is a reason which comes home to us both, and especially to me as a householder. You once said you had hoped "Under One Roof" would have filled my exchequer for the time. Between ourselves — *strictly* between ourselves — it has, so far, brought me in £27. I am hoping it may presently produce another thirty. That will be all it will do. It had a good but not large sale, and my royalty was very small. I consider myself fortunate that it did not cost me money.

I think I told you that I had been bribed to write a short story, taking place fifty years hence. This I did with many groans, and the other day a proof sheet arrived with a polite request from the editor that I would "make it six inches shorter." My Plantagenet blood rebelled, but my cupidity gained the day. I cut down several offshoots of my little plan, and returned it —

It is exquisite here,[34] and the quiet after the rage and dust and clamour of London is a constant refreshment. Instead of struggling to get into a No. 9 I wander in a little wood of dancing green, and pick a bunch of cowslips and bluebells [. . .].

Ever yrs
Mary

Letter 8. Mary Cholmondeley to Rhoda Broughton, 27 June 1919[35]

Dearest Rhoda

[. . .] I know you like Autobiographies but I wonder whether you have approved of Mrs Humphry Ward's Recollections.[36] It is all so extraordinarily flat and painstaking, and she never seems to me to know what to omit. But what a useful happy life she must have had, and what perfect health and prosperity and wealth. I do envy her the health especially, and a sort of satisfaction she seems to have. But among all the strings of names of distinguished acquaintances why dont you and Mrs. Wharton and I come in?

I like Eleanor best of Mrs. Ward's novels, but far the best of all her work her translation of Amiel.[37] I have compared it with the original, and it appears to me first rate. Mr. Creighton always said of her she was a scholar not a novelist [. . .].

Yrs ever
Mary

PS: In a day or two I hope to send you my "Stars."

Letter 9. Mary Cholmondeley to Rhoda Broughton, 5 December 1919[38]

Dearest Rhoda

I rose from my bed this morning earlier than usual, and ordered luncheon half an hour later, in order to spend a quiet hour with you from 12 to 1. But alas! the rain rushed down, and I am not yet well enough to ignore weather. So I had to stay mournfully indoors.

We had our last dinner party in this house[39] last night [. . .]. We had no wine left in the cellar except our large bottle of champagne and 3 small ones. This was poured out to them.

This morning the rugs and curtains are being collected for the cleaner who calls tomorrow. Next our splendid mahogany dinner table for 16 will leap into the arms of[40] men, who will remove it to Redlynch, Reginald's new home. He has bought it. On Monday we begin to take up the carpets, as the "removers" tear them so [. . .].

I should like you to know but please dont repeat it that I have just sold the American serial rights of a short story for a little over £200. I have never in my life received such a sum for a short story. It is about a goldfish and I told my agent I felt sure it would not sell serially tho' it would go to fatten a volume of stories I hope to publish next year.[41] He tried it serially with this result. Isn't it a fortunate moment when our expenses are inevitably heavy.

I know that any luck that comes to V. and me rejoices your heart.

Yrs ever
M. C.

Notes

1. Michael Sadleir, "Melodrama of the Breaking Heart," quoted by Marilyn Wood, 1; Percy Lubbock, 92.

2. See Wood, 9–10, and Mary Cholmondeley, *Under One Roof*, 102–103: "Later on when I read Mrs. Gaskell's *Life of the Brontës*, I realized with surprise that other eager young women had walked up and down their old schoolroom, just as we had done, before we were born."

3. See Wood, 6, who quotes Marie Belloc Lowndes, *The Merry Wives of Westminster* (1946), as her source of information. Mary Cholmondeley turned over her literary papers to Percy Lubbock, whom she asked "to do what best may seem to me with such scattered pages"; after writing his brief memoir, Lubbock set aside her "papers, manuscripts, and journals," which now seem to be lost. See Lubbock, 9–11.

4. For an account of Cholmondeley's dealings with Bentley and Macmillan, and the transition from one publisher to the next, see Linda H. Peterson, "The Role of Periodicals in the (Re)making of Mary Cholmondeley as New Woman Writer."

5. This letter includes news of Percy Lubbock, then an aspiring writer, to whom Cholmondeley dedicated *The Romance of His Life* (1921). Lubbock wrote the only biographical memoir of Cholmondeley, which includes a brief chapter on Broughton (see Lubbock, 33–43).

6. The book was *Under One Roof*, a family memoir, about which she wrote in detail in a letter here (21 November 1917).

7. Jewsbury and Le Fanu are quoted in Wood (12) based on the Bentley archives, reports 1864–1866 and letter book 1866, in the British Library.

8. See Tuchman and Fortin's *Edging Women Out* (1989).

9. Delves-Broughton College (Bundle B, MF 79/1/4/1), Cheshire, England; hereafter Delves-Broughton College. All of the following letters come from Delves-Broughton College, Box M, at the Cheshire County Record Office, Cheshire, England. Records in the Cheshire Record Office are reproduced with the permission of the Cheshire County Council and the owner/depositor to whom copyright is reserved.

10. The titles of Broughton's novels, *Scylla or Charybdis?* (1895) and *Dear Faustina* (1897), both published by Richard Bentley and Son.

11. The magazine, *Temple Bar with which Is Incorporated Bentley's Miscellany*, in which many of Broughton and Cholmondeley's novels were serialized before appearing in book form.

12. Delves-Broughton College (Bundle C, MF 79/1/2/1).

13. A character in *Red Pottage* based on her brother, Richard, just returned from Australia.

14. ‹should›

15. Hester Gresley is the writer-heroine of *Red Pottage*; she is a sensitive, inspired, yet frail young woman who writes a remarkable, if misunderstood, book. Despite Cholmon-

deley's disclaimer, much in Hester's character derives from her own, though the heroine was named "Hester" in honor of a sister who died young.

16. As the incident is recounted in chapter 26, the attempt to reel in a large pike capsizes a fishing boat.

17. Because Hugh Scarlett, the male protagonist, is trapped in a love affair from which he cannot escape, in chapter 1 Cholmondeley compares him to a starling in a cage.

18. ‹Yrs ever›

19. Delves-Broughton College (Bundle C, MF 79/1/2/9).

20. ‹New English›

21. The memoir includes four portraits, of her father, mother, nurse "Ninny," and sister Hester.

22. Cholmondeley's novel, published in 1913.

23. Delves-Broughton College (Bundle C, MF 79/1/2/10).

24. Victoria and Caroline, known by her middle name, Essex, were Mary's sisters.

25. Stella Benson (1892–1933), Mary's niece, had published two novels, *I Pose* (1915) and *This is the End* (1917). After the war she moved to California, in part to find a warm climate that might improve her health, and she worked as a maid, bill collector, book agent, and then as a reader for the University of California Press, on which occupation she based *Living Alone* (1919).

26. The story was later collected in *The Romance of His Life and Other Romances*; it is about a painter's wife and assistant who adds telling details to the "masterpieces" she is supposed to copy—most notably, a goldfish imprisoned in a fishbowl in luxurious domestic surroundings.

27. Delves-Broughton College (Bundle C, MF 79/1/2/14).

28. Howard Sturgis.

29. The fee was negotiated by Cholmondeley's American agent, to whom she refers in a letter of 5 October 1918 as "no doubt haggling over terms" (Delves-Broughton College [Bundle C, MF 79/1/2/12]).

30. Delves-Broughton College (Bundle C, MF 79/1/2/16).

31. "Votes for Men: A Dialogue," *Cornhill Magazine* (1909, 747–755), a satirical piece that imagines a world in which women govern and men must plead for the vote.

32. Delves-Broughton College (Bundle C, MF 79/1/2/17).

33. Apparently, it was lack of ready money, as well as physical infirmity, that prevented Broughton's visit. Her biographer, Marilyn Wood, notes: "The last years of her life were not easy ones, both in terms of ill-health and restricted finances" (121).

34. Her cottage in Suffolk.

35. Delves-Broughton College (Bundle C, MF 79/1/2/18).

36. In 1918, Mary Ward (Mrs. Humphry Ward) published *A Writer's Recollections*.

37. In 1890, Mrs. Ward translated and published *Amiel's journal, being the Journal intime of Henri Frédéric Amiel*.

38. Delves-Broughton College (Bundle C, MF 79/1/2/22).

39. At 2 Leonard Place, Kensington, where Mary and her sister, Victoria, moved in 1903 shortly after their father's death.

40. ‹indecipherable word›

41. *The Romance of His Life* (1921). In a letter of 21 September 1919, Cholmondeley had asked Broughton's advice about the title: "I myself am thinking of bringing out a volume of stories in the spring. Do you think this is a good title — The Romance of his life and other romances — to shew that it is stories and not a novel" (Delves-Broughton College [Bundle C, MF 79/1/2/20]).

Works Cited

Broughton, Rhoda. *Dear Faustina*. London: Richard Bentley and Son, 1897.

———. *Scylla or Charybdis?* London: Richard Bentley and Son, 1895.

Cholmondeley, Mary. *The Lowest Rung, Together with The Hand on the Latch, St. Luke's Summer, and The Understudy*. London: John Murray, 1908.

———. *Notwithstanding*. London: John Murray, 1913.

———. *Red Pottage*. London: Edward Arnold, 1899.

———. *The Romance of His Life and Other Romances*. London: John Murray, 1921.

———. *Under One Roof*. London: John Murray, 1918.

Lubbock, Percy. *Mary Cholmondeley: A Sketch from Memory*. London: Jonathan Cape, 1928.

Peterson, Linda H. "The Role of Periodicals in the (Re)making of Mary Cholmondeley as New Woman Writer." *Media History* 7 (2001): 33–40.

Sadleir, Michael. "Melodrama of the Breaking Heart." *Times Literary Supplement* 30 (November 1940): 604.

Sturgis, Howard. *Belchamber*. Westminster: A. Constable and Co., 1904.

Tuchman, Gaye, and Nina E. Fortin. *Edging Women Out: Victorian Novelists, Publishers, and Social Change*. New Haven: Yale U P, 1989.

Ward, Mrs. Humphry, trans. *Amiel's journal, being the Journal in time of Henri Frédéric Amiel*. London: Macmillan, 1890.

Wood, Marilyn. *Rhoda Broughton (1840–1920): Profile of a Novelist*. Stamford: Paul Watkins, 1993.

Chapter 7

GEORGE V. GRIFFITH

Elizabeth Stuart Phelps (1844 – 1911)

In her autobiography, *Chapters from a Life* (1896), Elizabeth Stuart Phelps claimed that she was destined for a literary life. Born Mary Gray Phelps on 31 August 1844, she entered a Boston family of accomplished writers. When Phelps was four years old, her father was appointed Professor of Rhetoric at Andover Theological Seminary. Before him there were ministerial ancestors accustomed to writing and publishing their sermons. Her mother, before her death in 1852, had become the best-selling author of *The Sunny Side*, an account of a dutiful minister's wife, which sold 100,000 copies its first year alone. Phelps's identification with her writing mother is evident in her adopting her mother's name, Elizabeth Stuart, and in her following her mother in becoming, by age twenty, the author of a series of children's books, first the "Tiny" series followed by the Gypsy Breynton series.

No event propelled Phelps more toward the life of the writer than the Civil War. The war claimed the life of a close friend and put her in the company of others grieving for the loss of loved ones. By the end of 1864, she began writing *The Gates Ajar*, a book exceeded in its sales in the nineteenth century only by *Uncle Tom's Cabin*. *The Gates Ajar* (1868) records the journal of the fictional Mary Cabot, who mourns her brother's death in the war. Comforted by a minister's widow, Mary comes to believe that the gates of heaven remain open: heaven is a womanly utopia where the strengths of women flourish and where women are compensated for their earthly sufferings. The book found a vast female readership in postbellum America. Its success assured Phelps of her own vocation and gave her what would be her theme for the rest of her career: the potential and necessity of women to be self-determining.

Beginning in the late sixties and throughout the seventies, Phelps developed her protofeminist ideas in essays she published in the *Independent*, *Harper's New Monthly Magazine*, and *Woman's Journal*. The earliest were two provocatively titled pieces in *Harper's*: "What Shall They Do?" (September 1867) and "Why Shall They Do It?" (January 1868). Both articles addressed the issue of the sexual double standard regarding women's work and "the wide-spread evils of the 'woman's wages' system" ("What Shall They Do?" 521). Both enjoined women to enter the world of work outside the home, denouncing men who kept women out of the workplace. In "Why Shall They Do It?," Phelps argued that "the notion that women are to be taken care of . . . is degrading to the last degree" (219). Later articles promoted women's education and health, their rights, needs, and pleasures. An article in the *Independent* (October 1871) took on the cult of the "true woman," contrasting that stereotype with the "real woman." Above all, Phelps advocated women's economic self-sufficiency, reflecting the fact that, as she boasted in her autobiography, she herself had always been a working woman.

The heroines of her novels were also working women. In her novels of the 1870s and 80s, her female protagonists offered alternatives to the Angel of the House, many occupying traditional male roles. In *The Silent Partner* (1871), a woman inherits her father's factory and promotes change when she discovers the factory's bleak working conditions. The character also rejects the "silent partnership" of marriage, preferring her business life. The protagonist of *The Story of Avis* (1877), a promising young artist, accepts marriage only to discover that domestic life saps her talents and her professional hopes. Finally, *Dr. Zay* (1882) inverts traditional courtship stories with an invalid male pursuing the independent female physician of the title.

Although by the late seventies Phelps's health had deteriorated (she suffered from chronic insomnia, weak eyes, and a palsied hand), she continued to correspond and publish. Carol Farley Kessler reads Phelps's invalidism as the cost of supporting women's causes (52). Those causes came to include, among others, women's dress, a reform that Phelps and other protofeminists believed was necessary if women were to be independent. Phelps herself, meanwhile, was married in 1889 to Herbert Ward, a man seventeen years her junior. The marriage was not a happy one, and her later novels may reflect her changed status. The earlier ones all present women who prosper outside marriage and decline proposals. After *The Story of Avis*, however, female protagonists accept marriage, usually reluctantly, and often experience its shortcomings. In 1902, less than a decade before her death, Phelps pseudonymously published *Confessions of a Wife* and for years denied authorship. Kessler characterizes the book as "one of the most damning indictments of marriage ever conceived by a Victorian American woman writer" (104).

It was in the context of her earlier ideas about marriage, and while she was herself still unattached, that she initiated correspondence with George Eliot. On 26 February 1873, Phelps wrote to Eliot applauding *Middlemarch*, urging her to complete what Phelps saw as only the beginning of a more ambitious and revolutionary project. Phelps no doubt had just finished reading Eliot's novel, which ended its serial appearance in *Harper's Weekly* a little more than a week earlier on 15 February 1873. Eliot was at the peak of her fame in the English-speaking world, universally characterized in the American press as a "genius."

Eliot trailed American writers in the changing attitudes toward women in the last quarter of the century. Phelps's letter is thus the work of a "recruiter" intent on bringing to her cause a fellow woman writer whose powerful intellectual reputation would lend weight to that cause. She declares herself an advocate of John Stuart Mill, whose *Subjection of Women* (1869), she says, expressed her views, and in the first letter reproduced here, she urges Eliot to become "the apostle of the 'Woman Question.'" She apotheosizes "the Coming Woman," one who never accepts wifehood as her "*metier*," and one by whom society "is yet to be revolutionized."

Phelps's 1873 letter initiated a correspondence that lasted until August 1880, four months before Eliot's death. It is extraordinary that Eliot responded at all. Although Eliot worried frequently that her unanswered American correspondents might think her "churlish," she routinely did not answer unsolicited letters, hundreds of which she received from American women writers, "worshippers" as G. H. Lewes referred to them, who sent what in one instance Lewes labeled "twelve page effusions" (Haight VI: 130, 52). Her sometimes incendiary feelings about Americans should have been ignited by Phelps's closing sentence which, after acknowledging that she might have crossed the bounds of propriety in writing, reminded Eliot that "I am an American and it is the birthright of Americans to be 'agitators.'" To Eliot's occasional contempt for Americans might be added her never-more-than tepid response to the women's movement. Yet Phelps was made an exception to Eliot's customary behavior, less perhaps because of the American's protofeminist appeal than because Eliot was, in part, persuaded by one whom she called in response a "fellow worker" (Haight V: 388).

In an exchange of perhaps as many as fifteen letters over the next seven years, the two were cautious about speaking of Phelps's politics or the wide differences between them regarding religious belief. On women's health and their vocations as writers, however, they forged a bond of common concern, recognizing in particular the threat of silence to the writer posed by ill health. Only with Harriet Beecher Stowe did Eliot write as much to an American correspondent.[1] Many others went unanswered.

Phelps was singled out for almost the last time by Eliot after Lewes's death, when, in April 1879, Eliot replied to her letters of condolence after a six-month period of near silence. Phelps's own letters are missing, but it is clear from Eliot's reply that the American, undaunted by Eliot's secularity, offered the condolences of a Christian confident in the immortality of spirit. "Your first letter," Eliot wrote, "has made a gentle echo in my mind ever since I read it — I mean its ending, where you say that 'Death is not the worst sorrow.' That is what I need to keep within me as a ground of complete submission" (Haight VII: 133). Phelps was both then and earlier silent about the legal and moral status of Eliot's relationship with Lewes, although her salutations as the exchange warmed — from "My dear madam" to "My dear Mrs. Lewes" — permitted Eliot, perhaps correctly, to infer that in Phelps she had found acceptance. Eliot concluded this letter by telling Phelps that she was now devoting herself to the completion of her husband's work and to the establishment of a memorial to him. She ended by remarking that she had just written to Harriet Beecher Stowe, "and I could not lay aside my note-paper without easing my heart of its gratitude to another of kindred feeling who has long entered into the meaning of 'America' for my thought" (Haight VII: 134).

In August 1880 the last exchange occurred just four months before Eliot's death. Phelps's letter, which accompanied a presentation copy of *Sealed Orders* (1880), is also missing. After wishing her "a time of recovery and confirmed health," Eliot urged Phelps to find consolation for her troubles of body and spirit in her work as a writer: "It makes a large part of one's calm and comfort in this difficult world to think of the lots of those we know as free from any hard pangs either of sorrow or bodily pain. That you have a mind free enough to make a larger world for yourself by creating is a great blessing" (Haight VII: 317).

Phelps's protofeminist and Christian utopias, born of the idealism of an American agitator, were always places too impossible for Eliot's skeptical realism, with its roots in English empiricism. And Eliot's reputation and audience attained heights of high seriousness never reached by the middlebrow American. But each woman recognized in the other a fellow writer who could reach across gulfs of geography and belief to find common ground.

Andover, Massachusetts,
February 26. 1873.

My dear Madam:

That the honest re-
ognition of one's hard work,
is never unwelcome, I have
learned so well by my own
small experiences, that I
venture to add to "the
benediction of the air" you
breathe, an expression of the
feeling which I have about
"Middlemarch."
It is as pure as a lily, and
as strong as the hills.
You have written the
novel of the century — but that
is one matter; you have always
analyzed a woman — and

Letter from Elizabeth Stuart Phelps to Mary Ann Evans (George Eliot), 26 February 1873. Yale Collection of American Literature, Beinecke Rare Book and Manuscript Library.

Letter 1. Elizabeth Stuart Phelps to Mary Ann Evans [George Eliot], Andover, Massachusetts, 26 February 1873[2]

My dear Madam:

That the honest re-cognition of one's hard work, is never unwelcome, I have learned so well by my own small experiences, that I venture to add to "the bene-diction of the air" you breathe, an expression of the feeling which I have about "Middlemarch."

It is as pure as a lily, and as strong as the hills.

You have written the novel of the century — but that is one matter; you have almost analyzed a woman — and that is quite another.

I say "almost," because I believe it remains for you to finish what you have begun, and that Middlemarch itself is the hint and proposition for the study of another problem, with a great solution. One of our leading theologians said to me: "Dorothea should never have married." So faintly can theology compre-hend her! Rather, should she never accept wifehood as a *metier*.[3] The woman's personal identity is a vast undiscovered country with which society has yet to acquaint itself, and by which it is yet to be revolutionized.

I cannot tell you how earnestly I feel that it will require a *great novel* to pro-claim the royal lineage of the Coming Woman to the average mind, nor what a positive personal longing it has become to me, that *you* should write it — if for no other reason to prevent my writing a small one!

I will spare you any explanation of my "views"; when I say that your own Mr. Stuart Mill partly expresses them in the "Subjection of Women,"[4] you will understand that I would fain add to your laurels, those of being the Apostle of the "Woman Question."

If I overstep the rights, to which, a letter intended only to express my personal interest in you and your work, should limit me — why, you will remember that I am an American, and that it is the birthright of Americans to be "agitators," and so, pardon me, I am sure?

I am, Madam,
most respectfully and sincerely yours,
Elizabeth Stuart Phelps.

Letter 2. Elizabeth Stuart Phelps to Mary Ann Evans [George Eliot],
East Gloucester, Massachusetts, 27 July 1875[5]

My dear Mrs. Lewes:

I am quite conscious that in my endeavor last year to learn from you *exactly*
how to treat in my lectures the biographical aspects of the author, I blundered so
far as to be misunderstood, if not indeed to give you positive offence.[6] And yet
I trust so far to your quick perceptions and kind heart as to venture once more
to ask a favor of you — the last time that I shall trouble you, I hope, in this way.

If I am found by my physicians strong enough, I am to read these long-delayed
lectures early in October next; the whole course being upon George Eliot.[7]

Now I make a "point" in one lecture, where, in reading such passages from
your letter as[8] I felt authorized to use, I want to lift the letter in my hand, that
the boys and girls may see it at the audience-distance. The whole *motif* of one of
my pet sentences hangs upon the act — and you can fancy my dismay at going
one day to my travelling-bag where I had packed your two letters with valuable
money papers for safe keeping, to find that my little travelling-flask of brandy
had leaked out and ruined them both. I think I would rather have lost the money!
But there they are — illegible; and the best chemical advice gives me no hope of
restoring them. Here then is my bold request: I enclose a copy of the extracts
which I so much want.[9] If you felt quite willing to rewrite them and send them
back to me, I shall gratefully appreciate it. If you do not, I am sure that you will
not. My address will be for a month or more, as above.

I was at Mrs. Stowe's pretty Florida home this winter, for a little; I like to hear
one great woman speak of another as she spoke of you. I am, Madam,

Yours sincerely,
Elizabeth Stuart Phelps.

I took the liberty of sending you the little volume of my verses just out,[10]
though I do not think largely of them myself, nor expect others to.

Letter 3. Elizabeth Stuart Phelps to Mary Ann Evans [George Eliot],
Andover, Massachusetts, 1 December 1876

My dear Mrs. Lewes:

I have delayed writing to you about Deronda, until my lectures in Boston
were over, and I could tell you something of those at the same time, thus impos-
ing but one letter upon you.

Do you remember anything about that matter? How the lectures were to be given before the College of Boston University, the new, and so far successful co-educational experiment; that I was so fortunate or unfortunate as to be the first woman chosen in our day — perhaps using day in the exegetical Hebrew sense! — to lecture before a College:[11] At all events those wise and pretty [12] are so far away that as we Yankees say, they "don't count."

The miserable victim selected for this sacrifice, determined to conquer or die under your great banner.

After three sick years in the worst of physical conditions, the lectures came off, at last, a few weeks since; and I write to tell you how great the interest seems to have been in my *subject*. Hundreds were turned away from the little College Classroom, for whom there was no admittance; and outside of the University, the interest felt in the matter by the Boston people to whom that institution is as yet an unguessed connundrum, was very kind. This I attribute to my subject, since I have never lectured in public, and have little fitness to attract an audience.

I think you would have been pleased with this interest; and especially with the earnest faces of the boys and girls who listened without moving an eyelash. The *girls* had read you most; and most appreciatively.

If I ever publish my lectures, which is uncertain for I'm barely able to put them into shape for the press, I shall do myself the honor of sending them to you.[13] Knowing me to be a believing Christian, you will foresee the points in which I should mourn over your later works. But I told them you were the novelist of this century, — and therefore, for us, of all time; for I'm a devout modernist. I dwelt at some length upon your *combination of great traits*, one or more of which are usually sufficient to make the artist in fiction. But I believe if Middlemarch had held the Christian truth of Adam Bede, it would have been *artistically* a greater book than it is, inasmuch as faith is philosophically broader than doubt and[14] art[15] to be perfect, must worship.

I said a good deal to them also, about your making the novel a reflective, rather than an emotive thing.

The lectures were four in number. The first gave just enough of a resume of the history of fiction to make them partly understand what conditions the artist of to-day must meet, and what a public he enters; with the slight biographical material with which you yourself had so kindly favored me, to introduce your name.

The second; treated somewhat of the mechanisms of novels; and of your *Plots*.

The third; of your *Characterization*, and *Style*.

The fourth; of your *Purpose*.

The invitations to repeat the lectures, which come in, all indicate that people are thirsty for *anything* about George Eliot.

And for Daniel Deronda — you do not need us to tell you that you have made another great book; but not as great as Middlemarch, on the whole.

Deronda is an ideal man; I have known his equal — nay, in some sense his superior, for my Deronda possessed the *cohesive* nature which is sprung of an energetic Christian faith; that makes fervor of tolerance and gives[16] to all chivalrous purpose the security of a beautiful torrent.

But Deronda is great, white, sad; lovely as the Sphinx; the counterpart of Dorothea.

Deronda and Dorothea should[17] marry[18] in some state of existence and devote their lives to the elevation of — perhaps the London poor.

I see you smile at me! I have heard that your smile is surpassingly sweet, however, and I'm not afraid of it.

Only give us another book — more — more! Give us one more Christian book, I pray you, for the sake of Christ, and for the sake of Womanhood, before the night cometh wherein you cannot work.

But before that twilight ever falls, may years upon years of the blessed sun be yours.

Something is the matter with my hand; I am hardly strong enough to write today. You will pardon the evidences of that — as well as my earnestness, I know, and the liberty I take to express it to you, and believe me to be dear Madam

Most sincerely yours,
Elizabeth Stuart Phelps —

P. S. Will you not come and make us a visit this summer? Please? I have a tiny cottage on Gloucester Harbor in this State, where I keep old maid's Paradise while the rest of the family, who are all mountain lovers, flee to the hills. There I spend the summer, with my maid, my dog, and my friends.[19] Come and try it! And when you are tired of me, you can travel, and so easily home again, that you won't know you've crossed the sea. Won't you *think* about it?

My Gloucester house is but a few miles from one of the most charming homes in America — that of my friend Mrs. James T. Fields of Boston, whom I think you have met.[20] She spends her summer on the shore. Will not *that* tempt you if my little shell cannot?

Letter 4. Elizabeth Stuart Phelps to Mary Ann Evans [George Eliot],
Andover, Massachusetts, 27 May 1877

My dear Mrs. Lewes:

I have just finished giving my lectures on George Eliot before the girls' school
in this town[21] — admitting my neighbors only to the last one. It has been an
uncommonly trying audience — the last one I mean — and one of studious habit
and cool impulse.[22] I have refused almost all of the invitations, which have been
abundant enough to have pleased you to have delivered the lectures again. This
instance with one or two before some appallingly critical but extremely kind
audiences of Boston ladies in their Clubs, Societies, Etc. — have been all since
the occasion in the Boston University.

Both here and in town, I think you would have felt gratified to see the enthusiastic reception which my *subject* met with.

"A *course* of lectures — on George Eliot?" "We are so glad to have *her*. We have
got used to the rest" — and so on. I never took more pleasure in a piece of work,
because I never did one in which I was so far compelled to forget myself. The
interest is so overwhelmingly in yourself, not in the lecturer, that it has been like
breathing a rarified air — exciting to me.

I wish I could have seen you this summer but my sympathies are with Mr.
Lewes about the sea-voyage and its effects on disordered hearts. Please tell Mr.
Lewes that his History of Philosophy is one of my old and valued friends.[23]

I cannot hope that you can remember me often, in your heavily mortgaged
life, but when you can, or if you can, a word from you is not only a great personal
pleasure but a permanent intellectual stimulant — as I need hardly say. It would
have been worth more than it is worth while to say, if I could have seen you
this year, and have had a critical word from you on the little new book, which,
after many years of enforced silence (from illness) I am now struggling with.[24]
I do not hope much for it now; I am physically too far spent even to do what
it is a bitter comfort to hope I might have done, if the success of[25] "The Gates
Ajar" had not driven a *very* young woman who wanted money, into rapid and
unstudious work, before the evil days came when work must be quietly put out
of the imagination like other forms of suicide. I shall take the liberty of asking
my English publishers to send you a copy in the Autumn, of this compromise

with fate.[26] Pray excuse the disordered hand. It is partly crippled by six months' wrestling with my novel.

I am looking for your next book as the next pleasure of my life.

Believe me to be, dear Mrs. Lewes,
Most sincerely your friend,
E. S. Phelps.

Do you *never* send an unseen friend your picture? I am half tempted to enclose a photograph to try and put you under some kind of imaginary bonds to exchange with me!

Notes

1. Some of Stowe and Eliot's correspondence is included in this volume; for additional examples, see Springer.

2. Phelps's letters to George Eliot, with one exception, are in the George Eliot collection at Beinecke Lib., Yale U. The exception, a letter of 27 July 1875, is housed in the Berg Collection, NYPL. Gordon S. Haight chose to include it in his edition of the Eliot correspondence.

3. A French word meaning vocation, trade, or business.

4. See John Stuart Mill's *The Subjection of Women* (1869).

5. Berg Collection, NYPL.

6. These sentences refer to the two missing letters of 1874 regarding Phelps's request for biographical information and Eliot's reply.

7. The lectures were not given at Boston University until 3 November 1876. An account of them is in "Miss Phelps Lectures," *Boston University Beacon*, 15 November 1876, 28–29.

8. ‹you›

9. These extracts of Eliot's missing 1874 letters exist in a single sheet in Phelps's hand at Beinecke Lib., Yale U. Eliot recopied them and included them in her reply of 13 August 1875.

10. *Poetic Studies* (1875). The book is not listed in the Eliot/Lewes library. See William Baker, *The Libraries of George Eliot and George Henry Lewes*. British Columbia: Literary Studies, No. 24, 1981.

11. The first Massachusetts school to award baccalaureate degrees to women, Boston University, had become coeducational three years earlier in 1873.

12. ‹indecipherable word›

13. The lectures were never published.

14. ‹any›

15. ‹must recognize religion›

16. ‹unity›

17. ‹have›

18. ‹ied and›

19. In the summer of 1876, Phelps built a house on Eastern Point of Wonson's Cove near Gloucester. She turned her experience of living there independently into two works of fiction — *Old Maid's Paradise* (1879) and *Burglar's Paradise* (1886) — which mocked those who scoffed at woman's independence; see Lori Duin Kelly's biography, 58–63.

20. James and Annie Fields visited the Priory, Eliot's London home, on 16 and 30 May 1869.

21. Either Abbott Academy or Mrs. Edwards' School for Young Ladies; Phelps herself was schooled at both.

22. Here, the following sentence appears as a footnote at the bottom of the page, signaled by an asterisk: *For we are a village of schools, academies, and professional institutions.

23. George Henry Lewes, *Biographical History of Philosophy*, 4 vols. London: 1843, 1845; *History of Philosophy*, 2 vols. London: 1867.

24. *The Story of Avis.*

25. ‹a young girls'›

26. Eliot told Phelps that she was unaccustomed to reading the presentation copies of books frequently sent her by American writers. "In general — perhaps I may have told you — it is my rule not to read contemporary fiction, and I have had to say so in many cases to country-women of yours," she wrote. "But you are an exceptional woman to my feeling," she went on, "and I read your 'Avis'. Only let this be *entre nous*" (Haight VI: 417). Before finishing *The Story of Avis*, however, Eliot loaned her copy to Edith Simcox on 17 November 1877 (Haight IX: 202).

Works Cited

Haight, Gordon, ed. *The George Eliot Letters.* 9 vols. New Haven: Yale U P, 1955.

Kelly, Lori Duin. *The Life and Works of Elizabeth Stuart Phelps, Victorian Feminist Writer.* Troy: Whitston, 1983.

Kessler, Carol Farley. *Elizabeth Stuart Phelps.* Boston: Twayne, 1982.

Phelps, Elizabeth Stuart. *Chapters from a Life.* Boston: Houghton, Mifflin, and Co., 1896.

———. "What Shall They Do?" *Harper's New Monthly Magazine* 35 (September 1867): 519–523.

———. "Why Shall They Do It?" *Harper's New Monthly Magazine* 36 (January 1868): 218–223.

Springer, Marlene. "Stowe and Eliot: An Epistolary Friendship." *Biography* 9.1 (Winter 1986): 59–81.

Chapter 8

PATRICIA LORIMER LUNDBERG

Mary St. Leger Kingsley Harrison
[Lucas Malet] (1852 – 1931)

Lucas Malet (Mary St. Leger Kingsley Harrison), remarkable for her literary productivity, wrote seventeen successful novels, several essays, and short stories. Her most important works are *The Wages of Sin* (1891), *The Gateless Barrier* (1900), *The History of Sir Richard Calmady* (1901), *The Far Horizon* (1906), *Adrian Savage* (1911), *The Survivors* (1923), and *The Dogs of Want* (1924). Two of her novels influenced her friends Thomas Hardy and Henry James, and in turn, two other novels were acclaimed as books of the season, in 1891 by C. E. Oldham for *The Wages of Sin* and in October 1901 by the *Bookman* for *The History of Sir Richard Calmady*. Compared favorably with George Meredith, Henry James, and George Eliot, Malet's work spanned Victorian, *fin-de-siècle*, Edwardian, and modernist periods, and she made important contributions to realism, naturalism, aestheticism, gothic, and modernist experimental writing as well as to gender politics and lesbian studies. Yet despite such success, Malet died in penury in 1931, her novels largely forgotten. Her essays, interviews, and letters help elucidate Malet's artistic theory; and her feisty defense of "deviant" art helps secure her legacy as a major writer and sheds light on the difficult reception women writers faced during Malet's time.

Second daughter of Anglican Divine and well-known Victorian author Charles Kingsley, Mary St. Leger was born on 4 June 1852. Educated at home in Eversley and not permitted novels but history, philosophy, and science, she lived a lonely childhood. She studied visual arts at the London Slade School of Art and began lifelong friendships with Arts and Crafts artists William DeMorgan and Edward

Poynter. And yet, despite her talent, she gave up notions of a career and married her father's curate, William Harrison, in 1876. A childless and unhappy marriage ensued, and Mary began writing under the name "Lucas Malet." Even as writing plunged her into bouts of illness and invalidism, she remained dedicated to her art; under the darkening cloud of her husband's dissatisfaction with her subjects, the couple split, unofficially, in 1891. Afterward, Malet happily wrote for a living. Though by her own admission a slow writer and even a bit "lazy" about the "exertion of composition," Malet wrote steadily until her death from cancer in 1931 (Dolman 147).

Malet's subjects range widely. She transitioned from novels and essays about female or male renunciation of self—with secular saints and celibate ascetics seeking to transcend life's temptations—to novels focusing on thwarted artistic ambitions and illicit love, stultifying marriages, and sexually bold or erratic characters. Superb at characterization, she created mothers and sensualists as well as strong-willed, independent, and mannish virgins. In *Calmady*, a Madonna-like mother saves her rake of a son from a sadistic seductress, and a character in love with his own mother asks her to marry him. In other novels, women driven mad by repression commit suicide or make themselves ridiculous in their inarticulate desire. A specialty of Malet's was triangulated love affairs—heterosexual and lesbian, licit and illicit, requited and unrequited—and her women characters reject marriage for creative artistry. In *The Survivors*, writing itself is bisexual: "the teller of tales and maker of stories is a bi-sexual creature, hermaphrodite—he who begets she who conceives, all in one" (292). Malet's modernist novels, framed in Freudian psychology, brood about aging and poverty and seek love beyond passion. She was equally at ease writing realism or naturalism and working in aesthetic and gothic traditions. And much of her work was feminist; she believed women writers were "Amazons."

Contemporary critics considered her a major writer, praising her craftsmanship and skill at characterization, but they often showed bias about the gendered ambiguity of her looks and strong personality. She was a fashionably attired and extroverted, intelligent woman, but critics wrote of her "masculine" look and wit. She herself was quoted on the Kingsley family's "ambiguous sexuality," noting that "Nature had jumbled things up altogether in the construction of her whole family" and that "she had one grave and fundamental quarrel with Fate. It turned her out a woman, and not a man" (Dickens 522). Malet's courage about her own gender identity presages bold depictions of sexually complex characters. Scandalously, Malet wore makeup, smoked cigars, and preferred Zola, Balzac, and French decadent writers over what she considered insipid English writing. Though criticized, Malet lived the life she advised in an interview: "Everyone can have what he wants in this world [. . .] if he only has the courage to take it when it comes. It doesn't do to hesitate. And if you're afraid — why, it's all over with you" (Dickens 523).

Other interviews reflect on Malet's artistic method. While deep into an "orgie of writing" ("Lucas Malet: An American") in 1898, Malet expressed preference for "a story which grows under my pen. All mine are absolutely in skeleton when they are begun. I, of course, develop them as I write and I may introduce new characters and intensify the power of others" (Smith). Her method was to write a book three times: "first the sketch [. . .] a tolerably full outline of the great scenes and of the characters. Then comes a time of misery and confusion, when you are extending and filling in the sketch — completing the book in the rough. And then, at last, you have your reward in the exquisite pleasure of writing the final form [. . .], which is the shorter version because you know [. . .] a great deal more about your characters than you ultimately find it necessary to tell your readers" (Archer 167).

The range of literature broached in this interview proved how well-read Malet had become after she was first permitted to read novels at twenty, and she never forgot her debt to literary foremothers and forefathers.[1] With insights gleaned from Malet's interviews, one can sense the complicated nature of her artistry and its reception. In her 1888 "The Progress of Women in Literature," Malet noted her debt to literary foremother George Eliot, arguing that "the enormous granite masses of *Middlemarch* and *Daniel Deronda* [. . .] are unquestionably the strongest, weightiest utterances we have got [. . .] from any woman. Ponderous almost always, often absolutely dull, defective in construction, [and] marred by lapses of taste, [. . .] they still rise supreme" (297 – 298). And in yet another forum, Malet praised her literary fathers: "Balzac, Gautier, Flaubert, and De Maupassant [. . .] Bourget, an occasional Zola, Daudet, and the at once perfect and detestable Loti in the French, and (in translations) Turgenieff, Tolstoi, and Dostoieffsky [. . .]. Our own Dickens I can always read and rejoice over. He seems to be the greatest creator of character we have in English fiction" (Dolman 149).

Few Malet speeches about writing survive, though two date from the height of her fame in 1901. One, to the New Vagabond Club, is reproduced below; the other was given when Malet presided as chairwoman over the tenth annual Women Writers Club dinner at the Criterion. In these two speeches, she railed against the literary double standard and a fickle public that penalizes writers of slow, careful craftsmanship. Covering the Women Writers Club dinner, the *British Weekly* paraphrased Malet speaking "on the dangers which at present menace literature [. . .] a half-educated public, without taste or culture, and with a voracity and strength of digestion which are nothing less than appalling. This public asks to be amused at the least possible intellectual cost. It wants to be made clever without mental effort, virtuous without spiritual effort" (np).

Among Malet's surviving letters, seven on her writing life are included here. Much of her correspondence was destroyed by Gabrielle Vallings, who had promised Malet never to permit anyone to write her life. Malet herself objected in 1900 to Ernest Hodder Williams, editor of the *Bookman*, that, "I am old fashioned, and do not admit the right of the public to be acquainted with the private life of any person either obscure or famous" (qtd. in Lundberg 109). Until the publication of *An Inward Necessity*, few letters had been recovered or published, and the ones in *Inward* encapsulate not only her artistic theories but also her philosophy of life. A few letters from the 1880s to her brother-in-law Clifford Harrison were conflated in his memoir, *Stray Records*. These range from appreciation of Fielding's and Sterne's realism, to the clarity of Matthew Arnold and the "warm muddle" of Coleridge, Carlyle, and German philosophy; from the dullness of the English in tastes for poetry that result in a "lamentable mediocrity"; from her "rage" against the distress of the poor of Clovelly, threatening to turn her into a "bitter radical" and "socialist"; to her study of Darwin and attraction to the idea of "endless fertility and power of development in nature" and its "possibility of everlasting progression" — ideas that take shape in *The Gateless Barrier* (Harrison 185 – 195; Lundberg 77 – 78, 87, 95 – 98). Other letters show impatience with unfair criticism. Malet engaged critics directly: a scathing exchange with James Baker in 1892; a 1902 review of William Leonard Courtney's *The Feminine Note in Fiction*; others to the editor of the *Bookman* and to Janet Hogarth Courtney. Friendlier exchanges included those with her only sister, Rose, and Mrs. Moberly Bell. Others are preserved in the Watt Papers at the University of North Carolina and noted in *An Inward Necessity*. The Kingsley Family Archives has a plethora of letters from readers and critics — likely replies from Malet are yet to be discovered in dusty archives.

Even late in life, Malet loved her art. Sitting in Switzerland for her last known interview in 1925, Malet, possibly for the last time in print, showed pleasure in her art, calling authorship "a curious and absorbing thing. Here I sit in Villeneuve and work away every morning from ten o'clock on, and every afternoon often from five until seven. It's the greatest pleasure life can give. They tell me that if I am ever interrupted at my writing, I turn with a face like that of a devil ready to rend any intruder. The story goes on and on, some days well, some days ill. But when the characters take the bit between their teeth and defy me across the writing table, then I know that the story is going well" (Gilman).

Letter 1. Mary St. Leger Kingsley Harrison [Lucas Malet] to Clifford Harrison, 30 September 1884[2]

To do anything very well is admirable, is it not, even if it is to do something wrong? I believe stupidity is the only unpardonable sin, and I am afraid that the majority of people commit it [. . .]. It is one of one's first duties in life to respect the little unreasonableness of people's imaginations [. . .]. I have come to see that half the agonies of life come from a want of delicacy in dealing with the imaginations of others, from the shock that is given sometimes by [. . .] common sense, to imagination; and that we must no more [. . .] insist upon thinking what really is than upon their only suffering from bodily pain, and not from nervous pain.[. . .]. My reading just now consists of a series of sandwiches [. . .] of Darwin's life and Fielding's *Tom Jones*. This sounds abominably robust. But Darwin [. . .] was the most gracious, tender-hearted, modest, humbleminded, unaggressive of men [. . .]. *Tom Jones* is quite in another style. I suppose I ought to be shocked at it. But *realism* is the topmost apple on the topmost bough of modern culture, and if we are to admire it in a contemporary Frenchman, why not in a Georgian Englishman? Then, too, Fielding is the most good-tempered of writers, and a gentleman into the bargain so that even in his undesirable moments he has a certain distinction — and his style is admirable. I have been a little troubled lest my own book[3] should become a trifle hysterical, lest we should sit shrieking at *agony point*. *Tom Jones* is an excellent corrective to any such tendency, keeps one's sense of humour lively, and makes one 'wear one's rue with a difference' — such a difference, that, at times it ceases to look like rue at all, and becomes . . . a very fragrant and pretty little posy. I believe it is immensely important what one reads when one is writing. Each book requires quite a different atmosphere on one's own mind, and that atmosphere must be maintained by the company one keeps [. . .] and by the books one reads. I don't mean books of reference, but of general reading, I believe a contrast is best, and so I have been stoking myself with Walter Scott, Sterne, and now Darwin and Fielding. Walt Whitman remains prince upon poets, *Brooklyn Ferry* and one or two others, notably the one containing the refreshing statement that 'the ugliness of human beings is now acceptable to me' being gone through pretty frequently.

Letter 2. Mary St. Leger Kingsley Harrison [Lucas Malet] to Rose Kingsley,
Vevey, Switzerland, 14 [n.m.] 1891[4]

Darling R.

I want to have written you a long & interesting letter all about nothing at all;
but I actually dawdled about the garden for a good hour after luncheon, and
then when I came in — after two cigarettes — I have not slept at all for two nights
& really needed comfort — I retired stayless to the sofa & there did slumber till
tea time. So all the day has gone, post time is coming & my letter unwritten.

It is very pleasant to be able to walk better — Hay is being made violently on
the great lawns. The two small Russian Grand Dukes [waiting?] in long blue
cloth coats & their hats tied down over their ears as though they were waiting in
mid winter in Siberia. (Clara[5] declares them to be "cross-eyed" & "the curiousest
looking children" she adds that they "always make a noise like cats". Meanwhile
their gigantic male porter gives her cigarettes, brooches, I don't know what all,
and makes love to her in Russian. She has left trails of lovers on the way ever
since we left Tilbury. But there is safety in number. I believe she is really quite
discreet; & lately she has been more than attentive and careful of me. I think
she knows she would not get a mistress who gave her such good times again in
a hurry.

I am beginning to be well enough to long for work to do. The idleness becomes
monotonous. But it is useless, I can't write yet for a long while, I am afraid. It
seems a pity; it is so quiet and peaceful here, that one *might* do beautiful work.

I must stop because of post.

Much dear love & thanks to mother for her letter.
Yr. devoted
MSLH

Letter 3. James Baker to Mary St. Leger Kingsley Harrison [Lucas Malet],
Clifton, England, 19 January 1892[6]

Dear Mrs. Harrison,

Back in the summer I read "The Wages of Sin" & it made me inexpressibly
sad, & the more so when I thought that it was a daughter of Charles Kingsley
who had written it. How much I revere his memory may be gleaned from the
facts, that my first attempt at a poem was written after hearing him preach in
Clifton College chapel, from my walk to his tomb at Eversley which I described

in the Belgravia Magazine [. . .]. & it was my reverence for his memory, which intensified my sadness at your book; for it does no good to one class at whom it probably was aimed. The central point which horrified me is in Paris I think impossible, & how could such a woman after such a life be a model? Faces & limbs would be unpaintable, except as a wreck. Any man of the type of your central character would have fiercely [shrunk from?] the incubus. To me the whole book is impossible; but the horror of it is that it is read & gloated over by young fineminded women & they thus know of a life which it is better they should not know of, though it exists. Do you know why your book was so taken up at the Libraries before it was out? Because a lady from one of the squares, I think Portland, wrote begging Mudie not to touch it; & also to the Grosvenor. Anything "spicy" is always caught at; there is the pity of it: & in spite of clerical approbation, it is the opening up of a vile life that makes your book a success. As you will see, I often review books, but I have never said a word publicly on it, & never intend to. But when I hear of the profit made on the book, I think of its title; though in this I am wrong. I know the [locale?] you have chosen & admire the picture of it you have drawn (I believe when I met you at Clovelly you had some friends at the next farm) but the whole book leaves a bitter sad taste after it & to me an intense regret you should have written it. I have no right perhaps thus to personally address you, but for six months I have debated whether to do so or not & the impulse to write has at last forced me to take up the pen

Letter 4. Mary St. Leger Kingsley Harrison [Lucas Malet] to James Baker, London, 25 January 1892[7]

Sir

I have received yr. letter forwarded by my publishers.

You are good enough to say, at the end of it, that you have "perhaps no right to personally address me". In my opinion, you distinctly have no such right. Had you chosen to express your opinion of my book, "The Wages of Sin" in print, I should not, in the least, have resented your doing so. What is given to the public may be judged publickly without offense.

But a letter, such as you have elected to address to me is, I consider quite unpardonable — contrary to all rules of courtesy. It is extremely painful to the recipient. It should be extremely painful to the writer.

Nor can I imagine what end you propose to gain by this writing to me. That it will affect the circulation of the book in question, you must know, is impossible. That it will alter my opinion as to the worth of that book, or, in any degree, influence my future writing, is, if you will consider the matter without prejudice, equally impossible.

All, and more than all, which you are pleased to say to me was, I must remind you, said to my father about his novel "Yeast". "Yeast" has survived the dislike of its critics. It is conceivable that "The Wages of Sin" may do so likewise.

In conclusion, I would counsel you, in future, to spare yourself the discomfit of writing, and your fellow authors the discomfit of reading, such useless and ill-judged letters.

This reply closes a distressing and wholly superfluous correspondence.

I remain yrs obediently,
Lucas Malet.
To James Baker Esq.[8]

Letter 5. Mary St. Leger Kingsley Harrison [Lucas Malet] to Ernest Hodder Williams, Kensington, England, 11 October 1901[9]

Private[10]

Dear Sir

Thank you for your letter, and I also thank Mr. Robertson Nicoll[11] for his friendly offer to insert any explanation or vindication of my novel which I may desire to make, or have made, in the pages of The Bookman.

It has been my rule never to answer adverse critics, and I do not see any necessity to depart from that rule on the present occasion. Controversy is very amusing to the spectators, but is otherwise, I venture to think, as essentially unprofitable as it is obviously undignified.

With the almost unqualified praise my book has received from critics of such standing as Mr. William Archer, the author of "The Englishman in Paris," my friend Mr. William Barry, and Mr. Lowry of the Morning Post, and the generous and discriminating appreciations of it which have appeared in the Daily Telegraph, Chronicle, Church Times, Literature, Vanity Fair, Churchwoman, Onlooker, Westminster and St. James's Gazettes, Lady's Pictorial, Publisher's Circular, Army and Navy Gazette — to mention only a few of the many reviews which have reached me — I am more than satisfied. Private letters arrive daily which show that a large proportion, at all events, of my readers understand and value the purpose of the book. Under these circumstances I can well afford to be silent.

As to the article in the British Weekly, to which you call my attention, it was based on ever so partial and superficial a view of my novel, was — if you will pardon my saying so — so conjured in thought and inaccurate in terminology, that I could not regard it very seriously. It might deter a few timid persons from reading my book, which, perhaps, is just as well. But that it should seriously affect the judgment of any fairminded and intelligent reader I can hardly suppose.

Again thanking you and Mr. Nicoll for your
   kind thoughts of me in this matter,
I remain, dear sir,
Yrs faithfully,
Mary St. Leger Harrison
Lucas Malet.
To E. Hodder Williams

Letter 6. Mary St. Leger Kingsley Harrison [Lucas Malet] to
Mrs. Moberly Bell, London, 19 October 1901[12]

Dear Mrs. Bell

I wish I could go to the tea on Friday. But I have only been up fr a few days on business, & am now starting fr Eversley. I hope to settle here in November & will let you know, if I may, when I am back.

I am so glad you like the book. As to it's *shocking*, I cannot suppose it likely to shock you or any one else save Dean Swift's "nice man", who you may remember was defined as a "man with nasty ideas". I had hoped, having my moments of optimism even yet, that he was dead long ago. But I have recently discovered that he still lives, and even writes literary notices in one of the leading daily papers, while the rest of his staff are taking holiday! — I have the cynical consolation of knowing he has helped to sell my book. But I am not exactly attached to him all the same — Do you wonder? — I know the book is not meant for babes. That if babes alone are to be considered, not only will no more fine novels be written, but most of the fine ones already written will be put on the Index — not of the Catholic Church, but of[13] great goddess Conventionality, who[14] some persons consider a bit of a hypocrite, after all! I hope the American trip was a success.

Always yrs,
Sincerely
Mary St. Leger Harrison

Letter 7. Mary St. Leger Kingsley Harrison [Lucas Malet],
speech to New Vagabond Club, 23 December 1901[15]

Mr. Chairman, Ladies and Gentlemen

Our Chairman has put before you so justly and so sympathetically the difficulties which beset the path of the woman of letters that I find myself in the
welcome position of having nothing left to say. She has said all that I might have
said, and said it ten times better [. . .]. Let me emphasize one point [. . .] namely
our prayer for impartial and impersonal criticism of our literary work. Whether,
following the example of those great women and great writers George Sand,
George Eliot, Currer Bell, we elect to masquerade before the reading public in
doublet and hose, or whether we freely reveal our name and our identity, this one
favour, ladies and gentlemen, we all ask. Those who sell their wares in the open
market must expect to hear a trifle of rough talk and to be jostled by the crowd.
In proportion they and their wares are honest, that will do them no harm. We
make no sentimental appeals to your chivalry in respect of your verdict on our
work. We only ask for fair play — for a clear stage and no favour. We ask that our
work be judged on its own merits, not in relation to some imaginary portrait
of our unlucky selves supposed to be discoverable in that work. . . . And so we
beg you when you read, still more when you review, not to say — "Should I quite
like my Mother, or my sister, or my aunt to have written this book?" — Restrain
such explosions of vicarious family feeling. . . . We pray you to say simply — "Is
this book, as a whole, sound in itself? Is it good as style, good as craftsmanship?
Is it a sincere comment on manners, a sincere exposition of character? Does it
help — by ever so little — to reveal the springs of human action, of human passion? Does it . . . enlarge my knowledge of the joy and the mystery and tragedy of
life, thereby making clear that wide tolerance, that sane and fearless humanity
to make for which is, after all, the very highest function of the Novelist's art?

Letter 8. Mary St. Leger Kingsley Harrison [Lucas Malet] to
Janet Hogarth Courtney, Paris, 21 March 1902[16]

Dear Madam,

I have read more than once, and with very great care and interest, your article
on my novels in this month's Fortnightly.[17] I cannot but thank you for many
kind and pleasant things you say in it.

I do not, of course, wholly sympathise with your point of view, or endorse your conclusions — as far, that is, as I apprehend them. We look at life, at questions both of religion and art, from different angles. But that, far from lessening my appreciation of the compliment you pay me in writing so serious a study on my work, rather increases it.

Your article raises many questions which are, to me, of considerable importance, and which I should like to discuss with you more at length. But I have not very much time or energy for letters, outside my necessary correspondence — which is rather wearisomely large. I shall be settled in London again (27 Egerton Crescent, Egerton Gardens, SW), at the end of next month; and it would give me much pleasure if you would come and have tea with me one afternoon.

I am not a preacher. Still less have I any desire to *e'pater les bourgeois*.[18] At my age — let alone a question of good manners — one has not the smallest pleasure in shocking anybody. I merely, like the man of science, register the results of my observation and experience. It is a matter almost of mathematics — given such a temperament, such antecedents, such environment, this, and nothing else, will be the necessary result.

As to the question of holiness and the saints — I cannot, of course, agree. Katherine Calmady and Julius March are far nearer the ideal, than are poor Elizabeth Lorimer, or Lydia Casteen[19] — or even (if I may mention great things on the same page as small ones,) sweet Dinah Morris,[20] dreamer of fair dreams, which found their ultimate in a peculiarly attractive husband and the joys of motherhood. Puritanism produces exquisite, if rather unconvincing individuals. But as a system it breaks down — judging both by the history of families and churches — in a few generations. After the Commonwealth, you get a rather alarming reversion to type, in the form of the Restoration. After the New England transcendentalists, you get the existing society, extraordinary in its extravagance and superficiality, of New York.

Forgive the length of my letter. It at least testifies to the interest your article has aroused in me.

I remain,
yrs faithfully,
Mary St. Leger Harrison. Lucas Malet.
To Miss Hogarth

Notes

1. Over the course of the interview with Archer, Malet touched on having read Scott, Dumas, Stevenson, Fielding, Richardson, Hardy, Meredith, Dickens, Balzac, Lamb, Ruskin, Thackeray, Calverley, Samuel Johnson, Hawthorne, Kipling, *Faust, David Copperfield, Pendennis, The Cloister and the Hearth, Henry Esmond, A Tale of Two Cities, Hamlet,* and *Tartuffe.*

2. Reprinted from Clifford Harrison's *Stray Records; or personal and professional notes,* 188 – 195.

3. In 1884, Malet would have been writing her second novel, *Colonel Enderby's Wife* (1885).

4. Kingsley Family Archives, Ely, Cambridgeshire, England; hereafter Kingsley Family Archives. Rose Georgiana Kingsley (1884 – 1925), Malet's only sister and a model for the renouncing women of Malet's early novels.

5. Clara O'Doul, Malet's lady's maid, who accompanied Malet on her journey through Italy and Switzerland in 1891.

6. Kingsley Family Archives. James Baker was an acquaintance and admirer of Charles Kingsley and could not stand the idea that Malet wrote of subjects about which he felt sure her father would disapprove; thus he was worried about Kingsley's legacy. Both a draft and Malet's reply still exist. Among other edits, she substituted "rules of straightforward honest warfare" with "rules of courtesy."

7. University of Bristol, Bristol, England.

8. Seeking the last word, Baker scrawled across the letter, "Wrote sadly that a daughter of Charles Kingsley should have stooped to the type of writing & pointed out the impossibility of the central & horrifying incident in Paris. She afterward wrote a still worse book with very filthy chapters." Baker never forgave Malet for the plot twist that led the seduced woman, Jennie, to turn to prostitution in Paris to feed herself and her child when the artist fell ill.

9. Department of Manuscripts (MS #16 368), Guildhall Library, London.

10. When Malet published her masterpiece, *The History of Sir Richard Calmady* (1901), acclamation for her achievement and daring was almost drowned out by condemnation of it, not in small part because a woman wrote the story of the rake reformed. Malet launched a campaign to challenge her critics. The literary bible, *Bookman,* was among those journals most faithful to reviewing Malet's work, but she was not always satisfied. Incensed by a review in *Bookman,* she fired off this letter marked "Private" to the editor, Ernest Hodder Williams.

11. Sir William Robertson Nicoll (1851 – 1923), the founding editor of the *British Weekly* in 1886 and of the *Bookman* in 1891.

12. Princeton University Library (AM 20826), Princeton, New Jersey.

13. ‹the›

14. ‹is›

15. Sladen Collection (Misc. Letters 25. I. f105 – 07), Richmond Library, London.

16. Berg Collection, NYPL.

17. See J. Courtney, "Lucas Malet's Novels."

18. French phrase which means, literally, to "astound the middle class," i.e., to be pretentious.

19. Julius March is a cleric and Katherine Calmady the perfect mother, both saintly characters in Malet's *The History of Sir Richard Calmady*; Elizabeth Lorimer is the self-ish widow turned selfless heroine in *Mrs. Lorimer*; Lydia Casteen is the self-sacrificing daughter to a tyrant father in *A Counsel of Perfection*.

20. Dinah Morris is not a Malet character; she is one of the main characters in George Eliot's *Adam Bede*.

Works Cited

Archer, William. "Real Conversations . . . Mrs. Mary St. Leger Harrison ('Lucas Malet')." *The Critic* 42:2 (February 1903): 162–169. Rpt. *Real Conversations*. Ed. William Archer. London: William Heinemann, 1904. 216–234.

Baker, James to Lucas Malet, 19 January 1892, KFA; draft of her 25 January response to Baker. Kingsley Family Archives, held privately in Ely, Cambridgeshire, Angela Covey-Crump, Executrix.

Benson, E. F. *Our Family Affairs 1867–1896*. NY: H. Doran, 1921.

Courtney, Janet [E. Hogarth]. "Lucas Malet's Novels." *Fortnightly Review* 71 (March 1902): 532–540.

Courtney, William Leonard. "Lucas Malet." *The Feminine Note in Fiction*. London: Chapman & Hall, 1904. 87–114. Rpt. Norwood, PA: Norwood Editions, 1976.

Dickens, Mary Angela. "A Talk with 'Lucas Malet'." *The Windsor Magazine* 10 (October 1899): 522–524.

Dolman, Frederick. "'Lucas Malet' at Home. A Chat with the Daughter of Charles Kingsley." *The Young Woman: A Monthly Journal and Review* 4:41 (February 1896): 145–149.

Gilman, Dorothy Foster. "An Afternoon in Switzerland with Lucas Malet." *Boston Evening Transcript Book Section* 6 (6 June 1925): 1.

Halsey, Francis Whiting, ed. *Women Authors of Our Day in Their Homes, Personal Descriptions and Interviews*. NY: James Pott & Co., 1903.

Harrison, Clifford. *Stray Records; or personal and professional notes*. London: R. Bentley & Son, 1893.

"Lucas Malet: An American Visitor's Portrait of the Novelist." *NY Daily Tribune* (27 February 1898): 18.

Lundberg, Patricia Lorimer. *"An Inward Necessity": The Writer's Life of Lucas Malet*. NY, Bern, Oxford: Peter Lang, 2003.

Malet, Lucas. *The Survivors*. London: Cassell, Hutchinson, 1923.

Oldham, C. E. Review of *The Wages of Sin*. *The Newberry House Magazine* 7 (1892): 161–169.

"The Progress of Women in Literature." *Universal Review* 2 (October 1888): 295–301.

Schaffer, Talia and Kathy Alexis Psomiades. *Women and British Aestheticism*. Charlottesville and London: U P of Virginia, 1999.

Smith, Laura Alex. "Western Women of Note: Lucas Malet (Mrs. Harrison)." *Western Weekly News* (29 January 1898): 3.

Whitelock, William Wallace. "A Visit to the Home of Charles Kingsley's Daughter and a Talk with Her." *New York Times Saturday Review* (26 October 1901): 784.

[Women Writers Club Dinner, 17 June 1901]. *British Weekly* 20 June 1901: np.

Chapter 9

MOLLY YOUNGKIN

Henrietta Stannard (1856–1911), Marie Corelli (1855–1924), and Annesley Kenealy (1861–1934?)

The Society of Authors, founded in 1884 by Walter Besant, was the first organization to advocate fair practices in the literary marketplace with regard to copyright and pay for the numerous authors writing in a developing industry. Through a variety of social and professional activities and its monthly journal, the *Author*, the Society became a major force in public discussion of authorship issues by the mid-1890s, when it boasted over 1,000 members. As the primary advocate for authors in late-Victorian culture, the Society succeeded in settling numerous disputes between authors and publishers; educating authors about the law so they could make informed decisions about how their work would be published; and laying the groundwork for important copyright law, such as the 1911 Copyright Act, which made the copyright owner the central figure in all transactions concerning literary work.

For the most part, authors who were members of the Society benefited greatly from its presence in the literary marketplace, but the relationship between the Society and women writers was a tenuous one. While women were permitted in the Society early on — Charlotte Yonge was one of the first honorary members — the membership and the Society's policy-making committee were dominated by men. Further, women could not be elected to the Society's Council, which advised the committee, until 1896. As a result, women writers who belonged to the organization often felt excluded from the Society's decision-making process in at least an informal way, and at times, they were excluded in an unequivocally direct manner. The most obvious form of exclusion came in 1890, when Besant

formed the Authors' Club, a smaller social club within the Society established
to improve the sense of camaraderie among members.

As is evident from articles appearing in the *Author*, male members of the
Society feared the admittance of women into spaces they perceived as belonging
to themselves, and they made this fear public when Besant laid out the plan for
the club.[1] In December 1890, in the pages of the *Author*, Besant made it clear that
any club sponsored by the Society should include its female as well as its male
members, in the spirit of acceptance exhibited by the Albemarle Club[2] ("News
and Notes"). But, when members of the Society responded to Besant's call for
feedback on the project, especially whether they should create an Authors' Club
(which would emphasize social gatherings) or an Authors' House (which would
be more of a work space for writers than a social space), the male members of
the Society overwhelmingly voted for a club rather than a house.[3] Further, the
male members objected to the presence of women in the club. As Besant states
in his summary of the voting, "The ladies who voted for a Club did not raise a
word against the admission of men, but many of the men, speaking for a club,
urged strongly upon us the necessity of excluding ladies" ("Notes and News"
[16 February 1891]). Although Besant himself seems to have recognized that it
would be unfair to exclude women from the club, he and a subcommittee of six
other men ultimately decided that the club would be for men only, with women
admitted on Wednesday afternoons and for special events ("Notes and News" [1
August 1891] 83; "Authors' Club" [1 August 1891]; "Authors' Club" [1 April 1893]
401).

While the Authors' Club controversy stands as a representative example of
women writers' exclusion from activities that might have supported and en-
hanced their professional lives, women ultimately did gain more participatory
roles in the Society, such as serving on the Council. Women writers also found
ways to create their own professional support system, despite exclusion from
certain activities by the Society. Shortly after the controversy over the Authors'
Club, Henrietta Stannard and other female members of the Society formed
their own club, called the Writers' Club ("Ladies' Club"). But the road to acceptance within the Society was a gradual one, and individual women continued to
struggle with their respective statuses within the Society well into the twentieth
century. The letters I have selected reflect these differing struggles in order to
illustrate the complex role gender played in the development of professional
authorship.

Henrietta Stannard, who wrote under the pseudonyms "Violet Whyte" and
"John Strange Winter" and was the author of *A Blameless Woman* (1895), joined
the Society of Authors in 1888 and played an influential role in the Society in the

late 1880s and early 1890s, despite the fact that women did not hold official positions in the Society at the time. In fact, Stannard can be credited with helping to convince the Society to elect women to official positions within the organization in 1896, since she spoke out on this issue at one of the Society's annual meetings ("Society of Authors" 224). Further, Stannard was friends with Walter Besant and regularly wrote to him and the Society's secretary, S. Squire Sprigge, about the organization's activities and policies. Included here is a letter to Sprigge from Stannard written in 1889, in which she offers advice about women writers who might be interested in joining the Society. As the letter indicates, Stannard was eager to help the Society improve its interactions with women, but it also is true that Stannard did not hesitate to criticize the organization and Besant himself when she felt it necessary.

Not only was Stannard a key figure in the founding of the Writers' Club after women were excluded from the Authors' Club, but she also took a public stance when Besant, who was known for his ambivalent attitudes toward literary women, wrote an article offensive to women in the profession. In 1892, when Besant published an article in the *Author* titled "On Literary Collaboration," in which he suggested that every literary man find a young woman who was willing to help him develop his characters but not demand payment for her help, Stannard responded strongly in her own periodical *Winter's Weekly*. She wrote, "One would not have expected that Mr. Walter Besant, who is supposed to be as full of chivalry as he is generally full of common sense, would have let his latest advice to young authors appear in the full light of day" (338). In making such criticism public, Stannard tried to exert her influence over the way women were treated by those with power in the literary marketplace.

Like Stannard, Marie Corelli had a relatively amicable relationship with the Society of Authors, but her sense of ease within the organization occurred only once she had been elected to its Council in 1912 and could exert her influence on the Society's activities and policies in a formal manner. Corelli, best known for her novel *The Sorrows of Satan* (1895), became a member in 1892 but was inconsistent in her membership until after she had been elected to the Council. As is seen in the letter dated 30 August 1912, Corelli initially felt herself to be an outsider to the Society, but once a member of the Council, she used the Society's resources to help negotiate her own transactions with publishers and others in the literary marketplace. The letter dated 12 September 1912 highlights Corelli's use of the Society's resources to stop the unauthorized production of a play version of *The Sorrows of Satan*. In addition to the letter included here, the Society archive includes a number of other letters, memos, and documents regarding Corelli's fight to keep her rights as author of the novel on which the play was based.[4] Also included here are letters written by Corelli that highlight her commitment to helping other authors new to the profession, especially women writers, and to implementing policies that would help all authors retain fair pay for their work.

In contrast to Stannard and Corelli, Annesley Kenealy had a significantly more strained relationship with the Society. Kenealy, daughter of the lawyer Edward Kenealy and sister of the doctor and novelist Arabella Kenealy, was active in the suffrage movement and was the author of *Thus Saith Mrs. Grundy* (1911), *The Poodle-Woman* (1913), and *A Water-fly's Wooing* (1914). *The Poodle-Woman* was written to inaugurate the "Votes for Women Novels" series, which was published by Stanley Paul and featured stories about suffragettes. Initially, Kenealy was quite happy with the work of the Society, since she credits it with helping her find Stanley Paul and leave John Long, who had published *Thus Saith Mrs. Grundy*.[5] But, as is evident from the letter dated 21 January 1913, Kenealy became frustrated with the Society when it refused her help in detailing the charges of unfair practices of John Long, which the *Author* had highlighted in its January and February issues in 1913 ("Committee Notes" [1 January 1913] 99–100; "Messrs. John Long").

Kenealy's frustration grew when, in 1916, the Society ran articles about her own case against W. H. Smith & Son—which refused to stock Kenealy's *A Water-fly's Wooing* for fear of a libel suit from the dressmaker Enos Limited—and seemed to give Kenealy less support for her case than she expected. The details of this libel suit are well documented in the January through March 1916 issues of the *Author*, but the letters included here make evident the Society's unwillingness to let Kenealy tell her side of the story directly. When Kenealy writes to W. J. Locke, a member of the Society's Council, about her frustration, his flippant reply shows the eagerness among at least some members of the Society to suppress her voice. Furthermore, the typescript document with Kenealy's comments in the margins indicates Kenealy's resistance to such suppression. Next to the summaries of the case that appeared in the *Author*, the letters and corrected typescript expose one of the more subtle ways the voices of women writers were filtered and sometimes suppressed by the Society.

Letter 1. Henrietta Stannard to S. Squire Sprigge, 31 May 1889[6]

Dear Mr. Sprigge,

Nothing — not even a letter from Mr. Besant — would have induced me to go to the dinner last night. I met Mrs. Lynn Linton[7] just outside the [Al'?] yesterday afternoon & she told me she wasn't going. Neither did Miss Praed.[8]

I would gladly do anything to oblige the Society — but — if you like, I give you my opinion of the chance of them joining[9] —

Miss Braddon[10] — I'll ask her but she is a very[11] woman. *Doubtful.*
Miss R. Broughton[12] — Lives at Oxford. I never met her.
Mrs. Ritchie[13] — Never met her.
Miss B. Edwards[14] — Will ask her when I see her. Always moving about.
Mrs. Annie Edwardes[15] — Lives at Folkestone. Hardly ever in town. Doubtful.
Violet Fane[16] — Quite a dilletante writer.
Ouida[17] — Lives in Florence. *Most* doubtful.
S. Maxwell[18] — Never met her.
G. Fleming[19] — do.
Mrs. Burnett[20] — Will ask her. Very doubtful.
Mrs. Clifford[21] — Never *heard* of her. — Oh! my spouse says I have met her.
Miss O. Schreiner[22] — Wrote one book. Was President of the Lady Dinner.
Mrs. H. Ward[23] — Don't know her.

If you will take a woman's advice don't have any lady novelists *enlisted.* Write & ask them to become members in the name of the Society — nothing fetches a woman so thoroughly as that form of invitation. It implies a recognition of genius which is irresistible.

Ever truly yours
H. E. V. Stannard

Letter 2. Marie Corelli to George Herbert Thring,[24] 23 August 1912[25]

Dear Sir,

I am exceedingly sorry that the letter you wrote to me on July 4th has not been answered till now — owing to my absence from home during which (owing to kindly solicitude for my rest) no letters were furnished.

I am honoured by my election as a member of the Council — and if you will tell me the exact measure of my responsibility, both financially and socially,

I have no doubt I shall be able to accept the position — it is as a 'Shareholder' — that I wish to know exactly my standing and liability.

Sincerely apologising for delay, which was inevitable,
Believe me
Sincerely yours
Marie Corelli

Letter 3. Marie Corelli to George Herbert Thring, 30 August 1912[26]

Private

Dear Sir.

Many thanks for your letter. I am quite willing to accept my election as a Member of the Council — and to do what I can to promote the interest for which the Society exists. Perhaps I may just mention that though I was one of the first subscribers — (I having begun to publish at 14 years of age) some 22 years ago, I have never once been mentioned in the journal "The Author" during that time! Not that it *matters* — but such a number of people *are* mentioned who can sincerely be called 'authors' — that this has always seemed to me curious and amusing.[27]

I cannot undertake any financial outlays beyond my Share — as I am already a sort of bank for needy journalists and writers who are 'down on their luck' —, that is why I must refuse to guarantee any sum for the "collection of fees" — such as your second letter insists though I am sorry to be compelled to do so.

Sincerely yours
Marie Corelli

Letter 4. Marie Corelli to George Herbert Thring, 12 September 1912[28]

Dear Sir.

I have much pleasure in signing the enclosed.

I send for your perusal some 'cuttings' (which you need not return) on the evident paying success of the *unauthorised* play made out of my novel "The Sorrows of Satan."[29] Can nothing be done for *me*, the author of the book? The play has been literally pilfered. Whole sentences taken out of the book for dialogue

— and I never have had a single *penny*! — nor was my permission to dramatise even asked. It seems a little *hard*!

Sincerely yours
Marie Corelli

Letter 5. Marie Corelli to George Herbert Thring, 23 February 1916[30]

Private

Dear Mr. Thring.

I herewith enclose my cheque for Ten Guineas, for the Life Membership in The Authors Society — and at the same time wish to express my earnest sense of obligation and appreciation to the Society for the valuable aid it has afforded me. I hope my *substantial* feelings on this head will not end here! — but that even when I have 'passed on' so useful and admirable an institution may still benefit from my having existed.

Sincerely yours
Marie Corelli

Letter 6. Marie Corelli to George Herbert Thring, 20 January 1917[31]

Private

Dear Sir.

In regard to the subject of your recent letter, I am enclosing to you (confidentially) portions of a letter received from Watt, respecting Methuen's propositions.[32] Both for my own sake and that of my fellow-authors *I have refused to accept reduction.* The 'painful position' of a publisher with a title and a large estate, invoking expensive maintenance, trying to recoup himself out of his already plundered authors' brains, is indeed harrowing!! I see H. & S. are still at 'Charity Books' making 5. per cent![33]

Sincerely
Marie Corelli

Letter 7. Marie Corelli to George Herbert Thring, 9 April 1918[34]

Private

Dear Mr. Thring,

Will you look at enclosed? This poor lady is an invalid, and I fear might be victimised by the man who asks her to pay for the output of her volume. It would be a cruelty — and if you would write to her — or send me a letter to send to her, we might rescue her from a pitfall.[35]

Sincerely yours
Marie Corelli

Letter 8. Marie Corelli to George Herbert Thring, 13 September 1918[36]

Private

Dear Mr. Thring.

Can you help me to understand why Methuen's should wish me to allow them to raise the price of my old novels (of which they have the plates ready anyway) to 7/6d and 8/. (a prohibitive amount assuming all *new* ones at 6/. of which the plates have to be made? And to only grant the same royalty to the authors as when the books are sold at 6/.?

It seems extraordinary! One would have thought might be raised, owing to scarcity of labour, etc — but why those already stereotyped, should suddenly 'soar' is a mystery! Can you help me? I am not at all disposed to agree to it.

Sincerely yours
Marie Corelli

Letter 9. Annesley Kenealy to George Herbert Thring, 21 January 1913[37]

Dear Sir,

I am extremely sorry that my letter *re* John Long is not likely to appear in *The Author.*[38]

The accts & money due to me at Xmas have not been presented or paid to me. And I intend to make a personal application in court & to speak very candidly regarding his dishonest methods. John Long pays a Lout — she is a member of The Writers' Club — to bring him young promising writers. He then cajoles them into nefarious agreements. It is a Literary White Slave Traffic, & I think the Authors' Society, for new & young writers' sakes, shld 'go' for him again & again until he reforms or his business is spoilt.

John Long himself told me *re* a young woman, a personal friend of his whom I also knew, that he had made an agreement with her for years, of such a nature that if she sold a hundred thousand copies[39] of a book she cld never make so much as £5 out of it. He is just bringing out her second book. I hear so many tragic stories of authors who semi-starve through him (as I shld have done only that The Society was able to rescue me) that I am most indignant.

Sincerely yrs
Annesley Kenealy

Letter 10. Annesley Kenealy [to W. J. Locke], [12 February 1916][40]

W. H. Smith & Son are going to cap their five year boycott & slander of my books, by selling up my furniture & sending me out into the street. I intend to protest publicly. If you do not approve of such agitation ask yourself how you wld like to be brought to semi-starvation by such methods as I proved in Court.

Meanwhile, I got no support from The Authors' Soc: (despite their promises) and you see how they are attacking me in the *Author* & *denying me the right to reply* altho. Smith's lawyer writes what he likes.[41] Doubtless those in authority are looking for knighthoods & rewards. Justice to writers is a minor matter.

Letter 11. W. J. Locke to George Herbert Thring, 14 February 1916[42]

My dear Thring

Can't we do something to have this unhappy woman[43] put away into a lunatic asylum? W. H. Smith is selling up her furniture? Why? Surely she is mad &[44] when allowed lone.

Yrs truly
WJ Locke

Letter 12. Society of Authors to Annesley Kenealy and W. H. Smith and Son, [March 1916][45]

---

[46]*Miss Kenealy and W. H. Smith & Son*[47]

We have received a very long letter from Miss Annesley Kenealy criticising the report of this case which appeared in the January number, and offering some observations upon the case itself. It is not possible for us to publish this letter at length, but its general effect may be summarised as follows: —

Miss Kenealy says that by her Statement of Claim her action was founded not upon any statement made by Messrs. W. H. Smith & Son to her Publisher, but upon subsequent communications by the Defendants to other circulating libraries. It would we think be more correct to say that the cause of action included both the statement to Miss Kenealy's Publisher, and statements alleged[48] to have been made to the representatives of other circulating libraries.

Miss Kenealy agrees with Messrs. Bircham & Co. that Mr. Jeans did not in his evidence state that he had received a letter with regard to her book from the Circulating Libraries Association, but states his evidence showed that he had been informed by Mr. Marshall, Librarian to Messrs. W. H. Smith & Son, of the course the latter had taken as regards her book, and it was this act of Mr. Marshall's of which she complained. Miss Kenealy also complained of a communication made by the Defendants to Boots Library substantially to the same effect.[49]

Miss Kenealy points out that these communications from the Defendants were in fact injurious to her, though the Judge has held that they gave her no right to recover damages at law.[50] The suggestion was that the description[51] of a dressmaker called "Sonia" in her book might give rise to legal proceedings as being a libel on the well known firm of "Enos" because the fictitious "Sonia" of the novel was said to occupy premises in Mount Street as does the firm of "Enos" and because if "Sonia" were spelt backwards it would be like "Enos"![52] Messrs. Enos themselves never at any time made any complaint, but this suggestion of possible risk of a libel action has, in Miss Kenealy's view, seriously injured her professional position, as well as put her to expense in amending a substantial number of copies of her book.

So far Miss Kenealy. In their letter to the Editor published in the February number Messrs. Bircham & Co. express surprise at our being of opinion that whatever the legal rights may be, Miss Kenealy had a substantial ground of complaint against Messrs. W. H. Smith & Son. Now every one must form his own opinion as to whether the risk of libel proceedings on account of the references to "Sonia of Mount Street" was in any real sense substantial or not.[53] It seems to us remote, and almost fantastic, and events have proved it to be in fact unfounded, and in our view what Miss Kenealy was entitled to complain of was that this vague fear should have been communicated by representatives of the Defendants (whose suggestions[54] are naturally taken seriously) to other members of the trade, with results certain to be troublesome, and not unlikely to prove seriously injurious to the author.

Notes

1. For more on the connection between the structure of the Society and male-dominated clubs of the period, see Simon Eliot's "Sir Walter, Sex, and the SoA" (2001).

2. According to an April 1899 article entitled "Ladies' Clubs" in the *Nineteenth Century*, the Albemarle Club was founded in 1874 for both women and men. Other sources list 1881 as the founding date, but the club is included in Charles Dickens Jr.'s 1879 *Dickens's Dictionary of London* as a club for "ladies" over eighteen and "gentlemen" over twenty-one. At the end of the century, there were 800 members, 600 of whom were women. The club is perhaps best known for its role in the Oscar Wilde trial. The Marquess of Queensbury left the card "To Oscar Wilde posing as a somdomite [sic]" for Wilde at the Albemarle.

3. Female members were split evenly between the club and the house, but because female members constituted only twenty percent of Society membership, the club was chosen instead of the house by the male members who controlled the overall vote.

4. In insisting upon her authorial rights, Corelli used the Society's resources in a manner similar to that of her male counterparts. For example, the Society's author files for Thomas Hardy and George Moore show that these men also turned to the Society for help with negotiating difficult financial matters. Hardy used the Society's resources to assert copyright claims of foreign translations, and Moore enlisted the Society's help when the publisher Heinemann wanted him to pay the court costs associated with a libel suit brought against both author and publisher over the title of Moore's novel *Lewis Seymour and Some Women*. Ms. 56721, Individual Author File, Thomas Hardy, Society of Authors Archive, British Library, London; Ms. 56757, Individual Author File, George Moore, Society of Authors Archive, British Library, London; hereafter Society Archive, British Lib.

5. Individual Author File, Annesley Kenealy (Ms. 56734), Society Archive, British Lib.

6. Miscellaneous Letters, 1889 (Ms. 56865), Society Archive, British Lib.

7. Eliza Lynn Linton (1822–1898), best known for what would now be called her anti-feminist articles throughout the 1860s in the *Saturday Review*, which were collected as *The Girl of the Period* in 1869. Before these articles, however, Linton's views were not entirely antifeminist; she wrote a number of novels about the trials of everyday women,

such as *The Grasp of the Nettle* (1865), *Lizzie Lorton of Greyrigg* (1866), and *Sowing the Wind* (1867).

8. Mrs. Campbell Praed, neé Rosa Caroline Murray Prior (1851–1935), author of political romances and novels influenced by mysticism. In the 1890s, her novels included *The Soul of Countess Adrian* (1891), *Outlaw and Lawmaker* (1893), and *Christina Chard* (1894).

9. Braddon and many of the other women writers listed in this letter wrote popular but also controversial fiction. By the 1890s, Braddon had written some decidedly realist novels and had earned respect for a more traditional literary technique. Likewise, Clifford, Edwards, Broughton, and Ouida wrote sensational or melodramatic fiction, while Schreiner and, to some degree, Ward wrote New Woman novels. That the Society would consider these popular yet controversial writers for membership indicates a certain level of awareness about the power of women writers in the literary marketplace, even if male members did not wholeheartedly welcome women into the newly professionalized vocation of the realist writer.

10. Some of Braddon's correspondence is included in this volume.

11. ‹indecipherable word›

12. Some of Broughton's correspondence is included in this volume.

13. Anne Thackeray Ritchie (1837–1919), the oldest child of William Thackeray, author of *The Story of Elizabeth* (1863).

14. Possibly Amelia B. Edwards (1831–1892), author of *Barbara's History* (1864); or Matilda Betham-Edwards (1836–1919), author of *The Lord of the Harvest* (1899); or Mrs. Harry Bennett Edwards (1844–1936), author of *Pharisees* (1880).

15. Annie Edwardes (1830–1896), author of *A Girton Girl* (1886).

16. Mary Montgomerie Currie (1843–1905), author of *Denzil Place* (1875).

17. Marie Louise de la Ramée (1839–1908), author of *Under Two Flags* (1867).

18. S. Maxwell has not been identified.

19. Julia Constance Fletcher (1853–1938), who wrote under the pseudonym George Fleming. Well liked by Oscar Wilde, she was the author of *For Plain Women Only* (1885) and *Little Stories about Women* (1897). Fletcher was born in the United States but spent significant time in Europe, especially Rome.

20. Frances Hodgson Burnett (1849–1924), author of *Little Lord Fauntleroy* (1886) and *The Secret Garden* (1911).

21. Sophia Lucy Clifford (1853–1929), author of *Mrs. Keith's Crime* (1885). Clifford joined the Society of Authors and attended some of the annual dinners. Ms. 56867, Miscellaneous Letters, 1891–1921, Society Archive, British Lib.; Ms. 56865, Miscellaneous Letters, 1889, Society Archive, British Lib.

22. Olive Schreiner (1855–1920), author of *The Story of an African Farm* (1883).

23. "Mrs. Humphry Ward" or Mary Ward (1851–1920), author of *Marcella* (1894). Ward joined the Society of Authors. Ms. 56867, Miscellaneous Letters, 1891–1921, Society Archive, British Lib.

24. In 1892, George Herbert Thring succeeded Sprigge as secretary of the Society.

25. Individual Author File, Marie Corelli (Ms. 56683), Society Archive, British Lib.

26. Individual Author File, Marie Corelli (Ms. 56683), Society Archive, British Lib.

27. In fact, Corelli had been mentioned in the *Author* before this time. In November 1895, she was discussed in an article about authors who were no longer sending out their books for review ("On Sending Books" 139); in addition, in the same issue, the release of *The Sorrows of Satan* was cited ("Book Talk" 143). Then, in February 1897, her popularity was highlighted in the "Notes and News" column (223).

28. Individual Author File, Marie Corelli (Ms. 56683), Society Archive, British Lib.

29. In the early twentieth century, there were multiple performances of the "unauthorized" dramatic version of *The Sorrows of Satan*. The newspaper clippings mentioned here are held in Corelli's file in the British Library.

30. Individual Author File, Marie Corelli (Ms. 56683), Society Archive, British Lib.

31. Individual Author File, Marie Corelli (Ms. 56683), Society Archive, British Lib.

32. Methuen's actions are not directly discussed in the *Author*, but Corelli's concerns here appear to be part of a larger discussion about the rising price of books undertaken by the Society in 1917. When the Society heard from a number of its members that publishers were either raising the prices of their books or asking authors to accept smaller royalties, in part because of the rising price of paper during the war but also for their own profit, the Society responded by passing a resolution stating that while it was acceptable for publishers to raise the price of novels during the war, such increases must be limited to the amount needed to cover the increase in the price of paper ("Committee Notes" [1 February 1917] 103). Further, publishers could not ask authors to accept smaller royalties ("Price of Novels" 118). Corelli's file in the Society archive includes a typewritten form letter from Thring, sent 24 March 1918, asking members to sign a statement to this effect. Corelli's signature appears at the bottom of the letter. Individual Author File, Marie Corelli (Ms. 56683), Society Archive, British Lib.

33. Charity books, often sold at the holidays to benefit charitable organizations, became a topic of interest within the Society in the fall of 1916, when the Society's committee decided to set out guidelines for the production and distribution of such books. The Society questioned the "charitable" aspect of these books and suggested that if anyone were being charitable in the production of these books, it was not the publishers or consumers but the writers who provided the content of the books for free. The Society resolved that any charity book must have the Society's approval in order to be published. Further, writers who belonged to the Society should refuse to contribute to any charity book that had not obtained such permission. Corelli signed the resolution put forth by the Society. For more on this issue, see October 1916 through May 1917 issues of the *Author*, especially "Charity Books" and "Annual Meeting."

34. Individual Author File, Marie Corelli (Ms. 56683), Society Archive, British Lib.

35. There is no direct reference to this case in the *Author*, but the topic of amateur women writers victimized by publishers had been discussed within the Society for some years. One of the earliest articles on this subject, "A Hard Case," ran in 1890 and detailed the case of a young woman asked to pay for the publication of a collection of poems. See

also "A Case of Collaboration" and the frequent articles in the 1890s about the S.P.C.K. (Society for Promoting Christian Knowledge), which Besant believed treated women writers especially poorly.

36. Individual Author File, Marie Corelli (Ms. 56683), Society Archive, British Lib.

37. Individual Author File, Annesley Kenealy (Ms. 56734), Society Archive, British Lib.

38. Presumably, Kenealy had read about a letter from John Long to the Society of Authors, in which he stated that authors once amiable to his company became more difficult once they joined the Society. This letter was excerpted in the January 1913 issues of the *Author* as part of the report of the committee's most recent meeting, and the printing of the excerpt drew further response from Long, in which he complained about the Society's decision to print only a portion of his letter. In the February issue, the Society printed the entirety of the letter as well as others it had received from Long regarding the effect of the Society's activities on authors. See "Messrs. John Long, Ltd., and the Society of Authors."

39. ‹she›

40. There is no date written on the postcard in Kenealy's hand, but the front side is postmarked 12 February 1916. Also, there is no greeting on the card, but the front indicates the recipient as W. J. Locke, who was a member of the Society's Council. Individual Author File, Annesley Kenealy (Ms. 56734), Society Archive, British Lib.

41. Two articles concerning Kenealy's case ran in the January 1916 issue of the *Author*, published shortly before Kenealy wrote this letter. In the first, the Society took the position that W. H. Smith was within its rights to refuse to circulate Kenealy's book on the basis that Enos Limited might bring a suit against the library ("Kenealy v. W. H. Smith"). In the second, it was revealed that Kenealy had twice resigned from the Society because of the Society's lack of involvement in her case. Included in this article was the text of Kenealy's second resignation letter, in which she claimed that the Society no longer was committed to protecting its members ("Miss Kenealy and W. H. Smith" [1 January 1916]). The *Author* also ran a letter from Smith's lawyers, Bircham & Co., in the February 1916 issue, in which the lawyer states that the report in the first article about the case was "misleading" ("Correspondence").

42. Individual Author File, Annesley Kenealy (Ms. 56734), Society Archive, British Lib.

43. Since the letter from Locke to Thring is dated only two days after Kenealy's postcard to Locke (letter 10) was postmarked, and since the two documents ended up in Thring's possession, I assume that both documents were sent to Thring by Locke on 14 February 1916 and that the woman referred to in this letter is Kenealy.

44. ‹indecipherable word›

45. Individual Author File, Annesley Kenealy (Ms. 56734), Society Archive, British Lib.

46. Above the title, written in Kenealy's hand, is the following: "This is full of inaccuracies & inexactitudes & twistings & suppressions. It is like one of Wm Asquith's speeches when he wishes to evade facts. Publish it if you will — But I should *protest*."

47. This letter is a typescript document, which the staff of the *Author* evidently planned to print in the journal. The document was sent to Kenealy for her to look over and correct; the "Committee Notes" in the March 1916 issues of the journal state that

the committee had received a letter from Kenealy and would write to her to say that they would publish a portion of her statement in the journal, "subject to her approval" (123). Kenealy responded to the document in the margins and then returned it; I have included Kenealy's handwritten corrections and comments in these footnotes. Perusal of the *Author* indicates that the document was never published, though portions of it, and portions of Kenealy's comments, appear in the third article about the case, which appeared in the March issue. In this final article, the Society claims that while W. H. Smith did nothing wrong in refusing to circulate Kenealy's book, the Society believed that Smith caused unnecessary harm to Kenealy's reputation by telling other libraries of its decision and by encouraging them to follow suit. In this respect, the Society believed that Kenealy "had good ground of complaint whatever the legal rights of the case" ("Miss Kenealy and W. H. Smith" [1 March 1916]).

48. Here Kenealy has underlined this word and written in the left-hand margin: "There is no alleged about it. The statements were sworn to in Court."

49. In Kenealy's hand, she writes: "This is not correct. Boots Head Librarian produced in Court a communication from Mr. Marshall Smiths Head Librarian saying 'We warn you to have nothing to do with Annesley Kenealys book, "A Waterfly's Wooing" We are advised by our lawyers that anybody handling it runs a great risk of a Libel Action.'"

50. In the left-hand margin, Kenealy notes: "The Judge held nothing of the kind. He ‹said› wld not let the case go to the Jury. I showed in Court that no Publisher wld take another book of mine until the case came to Court. I was obliged to amend 1400 copies of the book, a large number of bound volumes costing 11 per vol to amend."

51. ‹s›

52. ‹"›

53. Written in bottom margin, Kenealy says: "That is not the point. The point is (& the Authors' Soc: has allowed this point to become procedure in Law) that no Library has a right to circularise The Circl. Libraries Assoc: stating that a book is libellous when the person alleged to be libelled makes no complaint. This third party complaint of Libel is unprecedented in Law."

54. Kenealy has underlined the word "suggestions" and written at the end of the typescript document: "It was not a suggestion. It was a typed statement issued to several Libraries by Smith & Son & also by Day's Library, stating that anybody circulating my book ran the risk of a libel action from Enos Ltd of 103 Mount St."

Works Cited

Anonymous. "Annual Meeting." *The Author* 1 May 1917: 193–195.

———. "Authors' Club." *The Author* 1 August 1891: 85–86.

———. "Authors' Club." *The Author* 1 April 1893: 400–401.

———. "Book Talk." *The Author* 1 November 1895: 143–146.

———. "A Case of Collaboration." *The Author* 1 March 1893: 311.

———. "Charity Books." *The Author* 1 February 1917: 119–120.

——. "Committee Notes." *The Author* 1 January 1913: 99–101.

——. "Committee Notes." *The Author* 1 February 1917: 102–105.

——. "Committee Notes." *The Author* 1 March 1916: 122–124.

——. "Correspondence." *The Author* 1 February 1916: 119.

——. "A Hard Case." *The Author* 15 May 1890: 8–9.

——. "Kenealy v. W. H. Smith and Son." *The Author* 1 January 1918: 89.

——. "Ladies' Club." *The Author* 1 October 1891: 134.

——. "Ladies' Clubs." *The Nineteenth Century* 45 (April 1899): 598–611.

——. "Miss Kenealy and W. H. Smith and Son." *The Author* 1 January 1916: 98.

——. "Miss Kenealy and W. H. Smith and Son." *The Author* 1 March 1916: 133.

——. "Mssrs. John Long, Ltd., and the Society of Authors." *The Author* 1 February 1913: 150–151.

——. "News and Notes." *The Author* 15 December 1890: 200–201.

——. "Notes and News." *The Author* 16 February 1891: 252.

——. "Notes and News." *The Author* 1 August 1891: 82–83.

——. "Notes and News." *The Author* 1 February 1897: 223.

——. "The Price of Novels.—Declaration by the Committee of Management." *The Author* 1 February 1917: 118–119.

——. "On Sending Books Out for Review." *The Author* 1 November 1895: 139–140.

——. "Society of Authors." *The Author* 1 February 1896: 223–225.

Besant, Walter. "On Literary Collaboration." *The Author* 1 March 1892: 328.

Eliot, Simon. "Sir Walter, Sex, and the SoA." *Reconstructing the Book: Literary Texts in Transmission.* Eds. Maureen Bell, Shirley Chew, Simon Eliot, et al. Aldershot, England: Ashgate, 2001. 100–111.

Stannard, Henrietta. "Editor's Thoughts." *Winter's Weekly* 19 March 1892: 338–339.

Chapter 10

ELIZABETH MacLEOD WALLS

Mary Chavelita Dunne Bright
[George Egerton] (1859–1945)

Mary Chavelita Dunne Bright [George Egerton] seems today to be almost a caricature of the now familiar figure of the short-lived, though profoundly influential, New Woman of the late nineteenth century. Irish, unconventional, and sexually independent, Egerton personified the outsider among English literati —and, indeed, she seemed to cultivate this status. Born Chavelita Dunne to an Irish sailor and his wife in 1859, Egerton lived a nomadic existence throughout her young adulthood. Thanks to the financial intervention of her aunts, Egerton was educated in Germany, and worked sporadically on the Continent, in England, and in the United States. In her youth, Egerton lived with a married, Norwegian intellectual who prompted her interest in Ibsen and Nietzsche. The Norwegian died at the height of their affair. Living on a small inheritance bequeathed her by this lover, Egerton gained some financial independence and moved to London, where she soon met and married George Egerton Clairmonte. Having adopted her husband's name as a pseudonym, Egerton completed *Keynotes*, her best-known work, while living in Cork County, Ireland; she then marketed the book among London publishers with alacrity and success. Egerton published additional volumes of short stories with less success; bore a child and divorced her philandering husband in 1901; married a well-known drama producer, Golding Bright, shortly thereafter; and faded into relative obscurity within only five years of publishing her first volume of stories.

Though this brief biographical sketch may seem befitting of the prototypical New Woman, Egerton in fact was not a caricature of protofeminist womanhood; she was, rather, an innovator upon which numerous British women writers from the 1890s fashioned their ideologies and public images. Egerton provided an identifiable — in today's vernacular, "pop cultural" — persona for the so-called New Woman, who was known simultaneously as a particular authorial and fictional type associated with popular fiction in the 1880s and 1890s. Specifically, New Woman novels offered rhetorical sites in which Victorian women, speaking in the guise of idealistic protagonists, could offer sharp criticisms of marriage, patriarchy, and society often from within the domestic space, thereby developing a pointedly "domestic feminism."

When famed *fin-de-siècle* publisher John Lane presented Egerton's first collection of short stories, *Keynotes*, through his Bodley Head Press, Egerton herself instantly became synonymous with New Womanhood. The book's appearance in 1893 may have presaged the novelist Ouida's pronunciation of the New Woman as "meet[ing] us at every page of literature written in the English tongue" in 1894 (qtd. in Ardis 11), but Egerton's text certainly aided in defining this burgeoning genre of both woman and fiction. For example, the cover of *Keynotes* was replete with fantastic, utopian images of a woman brandishing the key to her own freedom. In this sense, the volume met all of the criteria by which Lane's publications are today identified — or, in Talia Schaffer's words, the text was "published on handmade paper, with an exquisite woodcut for a frontispiece, a stamped gilt design on the cover, special type, in a limited edition, and perhaps with a Beardsley drawing on the cover" (49). Titillated by Aubrey Beardsley's illustration and Egerton's frank discussions of the secret side of domesticity (sexuality, adultery, and pregnancy), readers embraced the text and reified Lane's approach. Thus, Lane began to publish other New Woman writers under the same banner, what became known as his "Keynotes" series, each adorned with the requisite Beardsley woodcut embellished with a highly stylized key.

However important Egerton was to establishing the image of New Womanhood, her own fiction ironically represents a departure from the genre of New Woman fiction, much of which is characterized by the dour plight of the domestic feminist. New Woman protagonists are by and large daring and vociferous at first; they explore their own intellectual and artistic capacity; they pursue independence. Yet they almost invariably marry the wrong man and are then consigned to a life of quiet rebellions. In contrast to these "boomerang books," as Ann Ardis has defined their particular plot, Egerton's collections of short stories — *Keynotes*, *Discords* (1894), *Symphonies* (1897), and *Fantasias* (1898) — are unique insofar as Egerton's stories combine elements of tragedy, comedy, fantasy, and sensationalism to create myriad impressions about women's subjection and subversion. The overarching ethos of Egerton's fiction is playful, and her unusual depictions of women's experiences in Victorian Britain created a new species of comedy mixed with social commentary in the nineteenth-century literary marketplace.

This playful rendering of the New Woman's experience is especially poignant in *Keynotes*, both because of the timeliness of the volume's publication and because, as Kate McCullough has argued, *Keynotes* articulated "the province of women's writing, staking a claim to a territory for women which is wholly different from an already-mapped male territory" (206). Egerton specifically looked to female sexuality as a new landscape of unexplored female power. According to McCullough, "Defining sexuality as the main constituent of female identity, [Egerton] represents female erotic sexuality as innate and 'natural' [...] and potentially socially disruptive as well" (207). Egerton's reclamation of sexuality and maternity as politically and "socially disruptive" was, in 1893, relatively new to the corpus of New Woman fiction. Maternity and sexuality figure prominently throughout *Keynotes*, *Discords*, and Egerton's later collections of stories. Yet these reappearing tropes are not merely the predictable signifiers of women's domain but also indicators of Egerton's true fascination: women's available means of power and persuasion. Over and again in Egerton's short stories, her protagonists celebrate and cultivate self-awareness using private reflection, decision-making, and ultimately action as a way of gaining agency within the home.

Yet, ironically, it is only through public, male intervention that contemporary readers have gained access to Egerton's own interior life — her own socially disruptive private world. As was true of virtually all of the New Woman writers, Egerton's fame diminished rapidly during the waning years of the century; she soon found herself outcast by the English literary world — but this time not because she was radical but because she was Victorian, aesthetic, didactic, and thus passé. Only a few years beyond Queen Victoria's death, Egerton's career had stalled. After grappling with the vagaries of fame, Egerton reemerged within the first two decades of the twentieth century to promote her own plays produced by Golding Bright. However, none met with success (George Bernard Shaw summarizes one as amounting to "really nothing but a happy ending spread over half an hour" [White 60]), and eventually Egerton succumbed and faded into obscurity. Yet, the 1930s saw a resurgence of fascination in writers from the nineties, what Evelyn Waugh classified as "another of those revivalist movements to which European, and particularly English, taste is so fatally liable" (122). In a revivalist gesture reminiscent of anthropologists' fascination with a lost civilization — an analogy Egerton herself would have found appropriately sardonic — young male modernists found, interviewed, and restored the reputations of certain New Woman writers; chief among them was George Egerton.

A Leaf from the Yellow Book, a sampling of Egerton's letters and diary entries compiled by her nephew, Terence de Vere White, in 1958, reveals not only the high value Egerton placed on her "life as a woman," as she described it, but also the wry sarcasm through which she viewed her subject position in the art world. Recognizing an affinity with fellow New Woman writer and aesthete John Oliver Hobbes, for example, Egerton observes humorously in a letter to her son, "[w]omen of our kind are best fitted to be the subject of an *amitié amoureux*.[1] We are unsatisfactory as wives. [. . .] One cannot live with us and idealize us" (71). Egerton also recognized the almost comic frustration endemic to her second-rate status in the new, modernist literary milieu. For example, in her letters and diary entries written just before the outbreak of World War I, Egerton expresses her dismay at modernist indifference to her opinions, suggesting in her diary that she is "[v]exed at being made fun [of] for saying 'Things are serious'. No faintest conception of the situation. The usual dying state of apathy induced by the vegetable existence fed by Boots Library of modern fiction" (84).

A similarly ironic tone runs throughout Egerton's critical estimation of the male modernists' fiction. In November of 1929, Egerton wrote of the "Aldous Huxley, Powys, Lawrence school," noting with her tongue firmly in her cheek: "I can read them with enjoyment, as I can eat gelatine or mousse with truffles" (129). Again to White in July of 1931, Egerton interrogated the literary standards of the day, asking, "[w]hy read [T. S.] Eliot? I've no use for poses in literature or life" (143). And later, in March of 1934, Egerton refers to James Joyce's *Ulysses* as "sheer ballyhoo" (154). Egerton regretted with equal fervor, however, her own lack of influence on the literary scene, declaring finally, "I no longer desire to create plays or write books" now that "George Egerton is merged in 'Mrs. Golding,'" and representing little else to her contemporaries (112).

Thus Egerton, ultimately little more than "Mrs. Golding" to herself and to others, spoke from the draped silence of her marital identity in private letters and within the wordy cloister of her diary. She developed her voice within this hidden medium with a skill similar to that employed by her own protagonist in "A Cross Line." That is, within the privacy afforded by her own lost identity, Egerton endowed herself with the power of telling secrets, of remarking furtively on modernist literature and consequently provoking responses from peers such as George Bernard Shaw and family members — not unlike her protagonists' provocation of readers in the 1890s. Elaine Showalter reads the intense interiority promoted by New Woman writers such as Egerton as the chief cause for the demise of feminist fiction after the nineteenth century. "In retrospect, it looks as if all the feminists [. . .] represent a turning-point in the female tradition," Showalter notes, and thus "[t]he private rooms that symbolize their professionalism and autonomy are fantastic sanctuaries, closely linked to their own defensive womanhood" (215). Yet it seems that the "fantastic sanctuary" of Egerton's life, given to us posthumously through the life-writing she bequeathed to her nephew and to her (somewhat self-serving) admirer, Terrence Ian Fytton Armstrong, has the power today of reinvesting her writing with genuine political and literary importance, of explaining the need for shielding and, at appropriate moments, exposing the revolutionary artist and woman within.

The letters collected here were written by George Egerton to Terrence Ian Fytton Armstrong (1912 – 1970) at the height of nineties revivalism in the 1930s — and, coincidentally, just as Egerton had begun to despair of ever being taken seriously as a writer. Armstrong joined the cadre of other nineties revivalists by capitalizing on the novelty of Egerton's existence; he approached her in order to solicit her stories about life in the 1890s, and to gain her support of one of his new books on the subject. Yet Armstrong's correspondence with Egerton provides readers with a record of Egerton's pride regarding her idiosyncratic contribution to English literature, as well as her reluctance to fulfill Armstrong's desire for personal gain at her expense. Armstrong himself is not often culled from the annals of modernity. Between 1930 and 1940, Armstrong published poems and edited anthologies of modern verse and short stories; more specifically, he hoped to revive contemporary interest in the literature, and literary figures, of the 1890s.

In the 1930s, Armstrong pursued publication of an anthology of retrospectives on the nineties, *Ten Contemporaries: Notes toward Their Definitive Biography*, which required that he solicit prefaces and biographical information from forgotten literary figures. Publishing this anthology seemed like an opportunity to satiate the public's renewed fascination with that "exotic" era. However, Armstrong's reproduction of writing from the nineties smacked of exploitation to at least one prospective contributor. As a subject for the anthology, Egerton grew weary of Armstrong's continued pleas for her contribution. After an amicable exchange between them in 1930, Egerton, though desirous of literary recognition, began to question Armstrong's motives for continuing to contact her. In her letter of 20 July 1931, Egerton hints that Armstrong's revival ignores the current plight of writers from the 1890s, in particular their now laughable popularity. By October of this same year, with plans for Armstrong's anthology well under way, Egerton rejected Armstrong's use of nineteenth-century writers to further his own literary reputation. Egerton further questioned Armstrong's desire to use her and other writers from the nineties to write prefaces to sections of the anthology—to give credibility to his endeavor with their written endorsement. To Egerton, Armstrong's desires were transparently self-serving; moreover, his plan seemed to her typical of the narcissistic generation of writers to which he belonged. Armstrong ultimately eschewed her warning, however, and despite Egerton's misgivings, the anthology of nineties poetry was published in 1931—with her contribution intact.

At first blush, Egerton's letters to Armstrong seem to be prime examples of the Victorian matron schooling the upstart modern boy. Yet, in truth, Egerton's letters are anything but censorious. They are charming, sage, and penetratingly honest. Above all, these letters are Egerton's answer, on behalf of the forgotten "shrieking sisterhood"[2] of which she was a part, to future generations oblivious to her literary and political achievement that shocked middle-class British readers and gave entrée to a new generation of modernist writers.

Letter 1. Mary Chavelita Dunne Bright [George Egerton] to
Terrence Ian Fytton Armstrong, London, 12 June 1930[3]

Dear Mr. Armstrong.

I have been unable to reply to your letter before as I have been very tired—The best way will be for you to come and see me some time—

If you are at your work every day it would have to be, I expect after six, or perhaps over Saturday afternoon.

You must make it this month, or leave it until much later as I may be away. You are I fancy very young, people tell me I still am. I say this because of your enthusiastic belief in the endurance of fame and one's own likes—Alas, both alter—

Yours Sincerely
"George Egerton"

Letter 2. Mary Chavelita Dunne Bright [George Egerton] to
Terrence Ian Fytton Armstrong, London, 20 June 1930

Dear Mr. Armstrong.

I have been very ill for over a week and I am afraid it is impossible to see you
tomorrow. It must be deferred until I am better. Don't regret being young, only
don't say "juvenile." I only trouble to write just because you are young, and one
never knows, youth may be worth while, but not if we [elders?] make "only for
a "yawn his head off" — At your age I found the world a great place to be in.
Questions to be answered — [4]

   1 Keynotes was first book published (or offered)
   2 If you find anything under "Mary Chavelita" I would be much interested
     to hear of it
   3 Look up who's who.

M. C. D. B.

Letter 3. Mary Chavelita Dunne Bright [George Egerton] to
Terrence Ian Fytton Armstrong, London, 22 December 1930

My dear Mr. Fytton Armstrong.

Thank you for your charming card. You do authors [like?] Shaw an injustice
he had no need to be any one's "disciple" — not even of a Keynote.[5] The[6] might
have been better placed, that's all. I wonder had I any merit — perhaps just what
Grant Allen said when he was introduced to me: "So you are the little woman
who dared to do what we have all wanted to do and hadn't the courage."[7] no
more — I've never lacked courage and I've always resented station or publishers
calling *my line* because *they* paid a royalty piper. I had forgotten my promise to
see you but I have been gravely ill since june. Just able to tackle life again since
late October.

I was 70 on the 14th. If I am grateful for anything it is that I still know resentment and I suffer fools no more slowly. I don't find anything very new & youth
seems to offer me the things I have always known as 'marvelous' — Perhaps they
are no younger than I am myself — I find a great many good modern books to
read and I like many of the young ones. I am [still?] conscious of time even.

I wish you my best of a good new year.
Sincerely
"George Egerton"

TELEGRAMS: GOLBRIG, LONDON.
TELEPHONE: 5089 MUSEUM.

59 RIDGMOUNT GARDENS,
CHENIES STREET, W.C.1.

Dec. 22º 1930.

My dear Mr Fytton Armstrong!

Thank you for your charming card. You do Arthur Machen an injustice he had no need to be any one's disciple — not even of a Keynote. The lesser lights have been better placed. That's all. I wonder had I any merit, perhaps just what Grant Allen said when he was introduced to me: "So you are the little woman who dared to do what we have all wanted to do & hadn't the courage." no more — I've never lacked courage and I've always resented editor or publisher calling my time because they paid a royalty piper. I had not forgotten my promise to you but I have been gravely ill since June. Just able to tackle life again since last October I was 70 on the 14th If I am grateful for anything It is that I still know resentment and I suffer fools no more gladly. I don't find anything very new & youth seems to offer me the things I always knew

Letter from Mary Chavelita Dunne Bright (George Egerton) to Terrence Ian Fytton Armstrong, 22 December 1930. Harry Ransom Humanities Research Center, University of Texas at Austin.

as marvellous — Perhaps
they are no younger than I am myself —
I find a great many good modern books to read
and I like many of the young ones. I am not
conscious of time ever.

I wish you the best of good new year.

Sincerely

"George Egerton"

Letter 4. Mary Chavelita Dunne Bright [George Egerton] to
Terrence Ian Fytton Armstrong, London, 20 July 1931

I am so distressed because I know I must have hurt you by not saying one word about "Confessions."[8] To have this creative faculty in any direction means that one has an extra [something?] apart in oneself which is capable of being abominably wounded. Artistic sensitiveness is a rare possession. I would not have willingly done this for anything.[9] The little flame which burns inside oneself is one's very own, no one else can light it or keep it alight & when all is said and done it is the most precious belonging one ever has — It is, by the way, mostly a curse to a woman. Frank Confession is my only avenue. I have not opened it since it came.[10] I put it on my table in my little room to read with another book — I have been ill again & worried, (a family affair)[11] and over tired & glad to rest when possible so your "confession[12]" is thus unheard. When more in time I shall read it and let you know. [Good?] use I hope, because at nineteen you have so much time to make new confessions and get absolution for mistakes & start afresh, at three score & ten and a bit one has none to hurt any one.[13]

"G. E."

Letter 5. Mary Chavelita Dunne Bright [George Egerton] to
Terrence Ian Fytton Armstrong, London, 9 October 1931

Dear Terrence II.[14]

I am better and with a kick in me today as I had a letter from Authors' Society[15] which called for 'one from the left' if an old lady can give such a thing. Got up to [write?] it — I am glad for you things are shaping up with your work. I hope it will be always that way for you. I had to fight for every inch of ground I ever got in any territory — the programme is original and seems worth while — You "dare" ask, but I dare and reply. You will get the socalled criticism of the Publicists, called critics, on the press, you will be able to stand. A. M.[16] has supplied [them?] with the gridiron upon which they will grill you. I can't keep you by criticism, why the devil should you mind what I say or what any one says. If you feel you want to say something, say it and say it in your own way and be damned to them. Unless you think you know better than anyone else, I always did, it is useless — A. M. is right, you don't know why you write it — the best comes that way. No, let me believe that, let me believe there is something worth while in you, and know that you can always come for that grain of good faith where sadly lost elsewhere. I am so weary of listening to the people who cant do anything laying down laws. You can always "stop in" when passing, I'll tell you if I don't want you — Later when you arrive, you'll find all the doors open & need to — it may help just now —

I was largely amused, that puckish humour of mine has made me many enemies. I have so often gone off at a tangent at some facet of an affair presumed done & given dire offense. 19, issuing limited edition, annexing worth while folks to give him stories & seen off, and that is what I found so diverting luring the commercial bookseller into a willing agent to give his bride a send off, making groomsmen of them, as it were, to shower the confetti — You are the Play Boy of the Publishing World![17] Dear Terr forgive me. I laugh so rarely now, it is one to you — I dont say anything about the story of that[18] the word, / not because I dont see what is in it, but because I dont feel it is where I can be of much use to you. Say anything you like. Poor T. I.[19] is having a tragic time. John (his brother) may die & his exams must be struggle.

Letter 6. Mary Chavelita Dunne Bright [George Egerton] to
Terrence Ian Fytton Armstrong, London, 18 October 1931

Dear Fytton,[20]

I think you were disappointed that I refused to write a forward to your second story.[21] May I explain? I can understand how the idea for 'Above the River' came to you — tramping through the wild valley amongst the haunted Welsh hills, echoing the voices of people of the Past.

If at all clairvoyant it was inevitable. Wireless was, I fancy, no revelation to A. M. nor was it to me. Somewhere in an old story of mine I spoke of the utterances of man grown too remote to reach the ears of man or beast, yet vibrating eternally in even greater territory through eons of time. I foretold that someday a genius would arise who would emprison all sounds mechanically to free them at will; perhaps even find a way to chase the voices of the past through the ether and force them to speak in the present — the latter has not yet come.

It was inevitable that other stories would follow Above the River — But — it was not inevitable that you should conceive the idea of getting writers of the forgotten Nineties, a period you seem to wish to make peculiarly your own, to write a preface to each of them. That you would ask A. M. to write a forward to Above the River goes without saying — but, why ask me?

Unless that we are so few, it is a case of the survival of the fittest—It is not —and I am not flattered at being asked to write the forward to your lady of ancient calling. I have not made a special study of Harlots.

It's true, looking back, I wrote "Gone Under" but the accident of a board-ship crashing in a time of storm gave me the key to the woman in that.[22]

I know little of the Romans of that time and nothing of the ways of a harlot who [plied?] her [liads?] on the shores of a Welsh river in the Days of Diocletius.

Besides I never write anything worth while unless spontaneously engendered in that which is me. A spark struck by the other hand from that flint-and-steel in my inner self.

There is an odd duality in you. The pursuit of a poetic ideal, a willingness to sacrifice everything for word-magic harnessed to metre, coupled with a sound commercial desire to label it strikingly for the book shop window. This startles me.

It may be I am very old and you are very young, and it is just the new way: To dash with daring optimism in pursuit of us of the Nineties to further your end. The belief in your power to persuade us is amusing.

It would serve you right if I were to remind you of the culinary lady who lives more by her famous axiom than her recipes—I won't. I will tell you instead of a lesson natural of my girlhood: The Two Headed Nightingale.

Her great claim to notice was that she could whilst whistling a tender wistful spiritual with one head, chew nutrisive oatmeal with the other—

Now don't be hurt, dear lad. Art in any form is the eternal breakfast, the only true aristocracy. Commercialism engenders its own autotoxin—I am really anxious to know will the sound of the crumbling of the oatmeal make listeners too irritated to hear the promise in the melodies—or, and that is where I fear to tread, are you so sure, and only you can know that, that the rhythm or the beat of the fairy drums,[23] the blast of Elfin Trumpets will dominate and make one forget the other—

"G. E."

Letter 7. Mary Chavelita Dunne Bright [George Egerton] to
Terrence Ian Fytton Armstrong, London, 10 January 1933

Dear Fytton,

I am sorry to hear in your letter tonight that you had such a sorry experience I was hoping that you were still happily in Widdecombe—You might be better in the hospital I am afraid[24] is more the cause than "overtired." It is a pity about the sales. I have seen so little of you since this spring, and even if I had, I doubt if you would have listened. I could not see any interest in Beardsley like drawings for any number of people. I have never believed in the Nineties as a selling proposition today — for the few only — and poetry however good needs a sure background before one can live by it — I am so distressed to hear it — No use asking you to come around and see me. I can not talk and I only go out to have teeth extracted and am in pain. A pity as I have wonderful strong teeth; difficult to get out at my age, and distressing to lose — Still if it must be — if I am to get better.

When I can, I will tell you —

I enclose a[25] note. I cant get P. O. dont bother about change use for stamps or something. Shall be glad to hear better news from you. Terence is addressing voters in white army or Nationalist body. May have a career. Will certainly be asked to stand later if De V. goes out — 21 in March.[26] This is a stupid letter, but pain does not inspire me to mental effort.

My best wishes for something soon for you. G. E.

Notes

1. Amorous friendship.

2. As New Woman novelists were famously characterized by Eliza Lynn Linton in "The Wild Women as Social Insurgents," *Nineteenth Century* 30 (1891): 596 – 605.

3. All of the letters in this chapter are at the Harry Ransom Center, U of Texas. They are reproduced with the permission of Mr. Javier Marias, copyright holder of Terrence Ian Fytton Armstrong's correspondence.

4. Egerton is presumably answering Armstrong's questions regarding her literary life posed in their initial correspondence.

5. George Bernard Shaw, with whom Egerton corresponded between 1910 and 1920, when she was an aspiring playwright.

6. ‹indecipherable word›

7. As there is no known written record of this remark, Egerton's comment here appears to be the first time this important meeting has been referenced in print.

8. Armstrong published this volume, as well as *Ten Contemporaries*, under a pseudonym, John Gawsworth. *Confession: Verses* (London: Twyn Barlwn Press, 1931).

9. Egerton seems to be referring to one publishing poems for the world to read and criticize, which is precisely what the very young Armstrong did in 1931.

10. Egerton is attempting a play on words, since she is referencing women's modes of expression alongside reading Armstrong's volume, *Confessions*.

11. It is unclear to what family affair Egerton refers here.

12. ‹S›

13. As with several of Egerton's letters written during illness and, as she says, a state of being "over tired," occasionally her lucidity falters. Here she probably meant to write "any more."

14. In the margin alongside the salutation, Egerton wrote: One of my side worries. "G. E." Pleasant Sunday!

15. The Society of Authors, of which Egerton was a member.

16. Arthur Machen (1863–1947), gothic sensation writer who garnered a great deal of attention in the 1890s. As a flamboyant representative of the nineties, Machen was also the recipient of Armstrong's queries and curiosities. And, like Egerton, Machen developed a friendship with Armstrong — and he did indeed supply the forward to Armstrong's story.

17. Egerton probably is referencing Armstrong's preparations for *Ten Contemporaries*.

18. ‹indecipherable word›

19. It is probable that Egerton is playfully referencing her nephew, Terence de Vere White, as "T I" in order to distinguish him from her recipient, Terrence Ian Fytton Armstrong, whom she addresses in her salutation as "Terrence II."

20. At the top of the letter, in large block print, Egerton wrote: A 'NO' TO NINE-TEEN. She underlined this phrase.

21. "Above the River" eventually appeared in *Full Score*, Armstrong's edited collection of stories written by a variety of relatively unknown writers; "Above the River" is Armstrong's own contribution to the collection, which explains Egerton's concern about injuring the young author's feelings. See John Gawsworth [Terrence Ian Fytton Armstrong], ed. *Full Score* (London: Rich and Cowan, 1933).

22. "Gone Under" appeared in *Discords* (1894).

23. ‹and›

24. ‹indecipherable word›

25. ‹indecipherable word›

26. Terence de Vere White (1912–1994).

Works Cited

Ardis, Ann. *New Women, New Novels: Feminism and Early Modernism*. New Brunswick: Rutgers U P, 1990.

Egerton, George. *Discords*. London: John Lane, 1894.

———. *Fantasias*. London: John Lane, 1898.

———. *Keynotes*. London: John Lane, 1893.

———. *Symphonies*. London: John Lane, 1897.

Gawsworth, John [Terrence Ian Fytton Armstrong]. *Ten Contemporaries: Notes toward Their Definitive Bibliography*. London: Joiner and Steele, Ltd., 1933.

McCullough, Kate. "Mapping the '*Terra Incognita*' of Woman: George Egerton's *Keynotes* (1893) and the New Woman." *The New Nineteenth Century: Feminist Readings of Under-read Victorian Fiction*. Eds. Barbara Harmon, Susan Meyer, and Joan Sutherland. NY: Garland, 1996. 205–223.

Schaffer, Talia. *The Forgotten Female Aesthetes: Literary Culture in Late-Victorian England*. Charlottesville: U P of Virginia, 2000.

Showalter, Elaine. *A Literature of Their Own*. 2nd ed. Princeton: Princeton U P, 1998.

Waugh, Evelyn. "Let Us Return to the 1890s but Not to Oscar Wilde." *The Essays, Articles and Reviews of Evelyn Waugh*. Ed. Donat Gallagher. Boston: Little, Brown and Co., 1984. 122–124.

White, Terence de Vere, ed. *A Leaf from the Yellow Book: The Correspondence of George Egerton*. London: The Richards Press, 1958.

Chapter 11

LINDA K. HUGHES

Rosamund Marriott Watson
[Graham R. Tomson] (1860 – 1911)

Born Rosamond Ball in 1860, the poet and woman of letters known as Graham R. Tomson from 1887 to 1894, then as Rosamund Marriott Watson until her death in 1911, was a significant figure among New Woman poets and female aesthetes in *fin-de-siècle* London.[1] She broke into the influential circle of Andrew Lang in 1887 thanks to talent and a pseudonym borrowed to shield her elopement with the painter Arthur Tomson (1859 – 1905) and her visible pregnancy while she waited for a divorce from her first husband, Australian landholder George Francis Armytage (1853 – 1921). Because *Tares*, the volume of poems she published in 1884 while still married to Armytage, was issued anonymously, she entered literary London with a well nigh blank slate. Under the sponsorship of Andrew Lang she quickly became known as a poet who commanded exquisite technique and could easily shift registers from polished verse forms to urban impressions to eerie ballads. She was, moreover, extremely well read and ambitious, aided in her ambitions by a magnetic personality and a brunette beauty that reminded many of Dante Gabriel Rossetti's paintings (Pennell 157).

Though like most *fin-de-siècle* poets she never enjoyed wide sales of her volumes, she acquired prestige from the reception of *The Bird-Bride: A Volume of Ballads and Sonnets* (1889) and *A Summer Night and Other Poems* (1891), which were preceded by her editions of border ballads (1888) and epigrams from the *Greek Anthology* (1889). A fluent and witty prose writer, she also wrote on fashion as a decorative art in poet W. E. Henley's *Scots Observer*, on "Beauty, from the Historical Point of View" in *Woman's World*, the magazine edited by Oscar

Wilde, and on painting in the short-lived *Scottish Art Review* (1888–1890). She acquired even greater authority as a writer when she became a regular reviewer of poetry for the *Illustrated London News* and for the *Academy*, closely associated with Oxford and the prestige enjoyed by university men. In 1892 she added to these roles the position of staff art critic for a new daily newspaper, the *Morning Leader*, and editor of her own magazine, *Sylvia's Journal*, which she revamped into a monthly magazine committed to progressive roles for women and aestheticism's interrelated arts. She could now extend as well as enjoy patronage. Given in addition her numerous literary friendships — with Thomas Hardy, Oscar Wilde, J. M. Barrie, and Lang, as well as a circle of women writers including poets Amy Levy and Alice Meynell — she seemed set to make a lasting mark as a writer.

She jettisoned all she had achieved as Graham R. Tomson when she fell in love with Australian novelist and journalist H. B. Marriott Watson (1863–1921), which led to a ludicrous second elopement (for by then it looked to be a habit) and radical name change in 1894, when she cancelled a forthcoming volume of poems and suddenly adopted the signature of Rosamund Marriott Watson. She alienated many former friends and thenceforward enjoyed no more favors from prominent writers. The prominent 1890s publisher John Lane, however, was a steadfast advocate, and Marriott Watson became a regular contributor to the *Yellow Book* and entered the list of Bodley Head authors. *Vespertilia* (1895), *After Sunset* (1904), and her posthumous *Poems* (1912) were all published by Lane, who also bought the stock of *A Summer Night* and reissued it as a title by Rosamund Marriott Watson. Although she remained a prolific journalist and critic, most of her reviews were anonymous, and even her books on interior decoration and gardens — *Art of the House* (1897) and *Heart of a Garden* (1906) — though successful, did little to enlarge her reputation. When she died of uterine cancer in 1911 — leaving behind two daughters (Eulalie and Daphne Armytage) from her first marriage, a son (Arthur Graham Tomson) from her second, and a son (Richard Marriott Watson) from her third union, never legalized — she was still deemed a gifted poet by those who knew her, but had become a minor literary figure.

The letters reproduced here suggest the confidence of rising star Graham R. Tomson and the greater modesty of Rosamund Marriott Watson; their contrasting tones suggest the penalties that could be imposed on women who too openly challenged the rules. But the larger significance of these letters has less to do with biography than with illuminating the multiple roles performed by nineteenth-century women writers. The first three were all written from Tomson to publisher T. Fisher Unwin (1848–1935) during 1891, when she was completing work on an anthology, *Concerning Cats* (1892), at once decadent and domestic, since it contained untranslated poems by Baudelaire and Verlaine as well as nursery rhymes.

The first letter indicates a woman writer's strategies for seeking sufficient authority to obtain what she wants from other writers and her attention to the nuts and bolts of publishing; it also provides a momentary glimpse of a writer's domestic arrangements. The second exposes her ambition, as she attempts (unsuccessfully, it turned out) to become a house reader for Unwin; perhaps more significantly, the letter reflects her solidarity with other women poets. Broad attacks on the competence of one woman poet could call into question the abilities of all — hence the vehemence of Tomson's response to a causerie attacking the posthumous reputation of Amy Levy. The third letter demonstrates women writers' capacity for aggression in publishing negotiations, though Tomson's anger over shoddy page proofs may have been easier to express because it was her husband's work that had been insulted.

In the fourth letter Rosamund Marriott Watson writes from the interrelated positions of journalist, aesthete, poet, and mother. Her recipient, Albert Bigelow Paine (1861–1937), is best known today as an early biographer of Mark Twain but was also a notable children's writer. Marriott Watson may have encountered his work in the course of her journalism career, since she contributed numerous book reviews of children's literature to the *Athenaeum* beginning in 1903 (Demoor 123–126). Paine quickly became the favorite author of Marriott Watson's son Richard (called Dick), and her initial letter to Paine was a form of joint fan letter from mother and son. The subsequent letter presented here suggests her growing diffidence about her own poems at this stage of her career, even as it glimpses the source of what may be her best prose work, *Heart of a Garden*: the two acres of ground attached to Heathfield Cottage that had originally been laid out by Joseph Paxton, designer of the Crystal Palace for the Great Exhibition of 1851.

The last two letters are to Mrs. Chesson, a poet better known as Nora Hopper (1871–1906), whose *Ballads in Prose* (1894) W. B. Yeats called "'the most distinguished volume we have had out of Ireland this decade'" (Brownson 95). As editor of *Sylvia's Journal*, Tomson had published the prose ballad "Boholaun and I" (a version of the Diarmuid and Grainne legend) in the March 1894 issue, as well as other poems. In 1905 Chesson wrote to her former editor, eliciting a brief autobiographical account of Marriott Watson's literary career — one example of how a woman writer conceived the shape, course, and satisfaction of her writing career. The final letter sets aside Marriott Watson's own claims to write good poetry and prose (not to mention Alice Meynell's) and seeks to assist Chesson through the agency of her husband rather than as a literary figure in her own right. But both letters also attest to the continuing importance of women's networks in Marriott Watson's life: buoyed by Chesson's interest, she offers solacing praise in turn.

Letter 1. Rosamund Marriott Watson to T. Fisher Unwin,
Sussex, England, 7 October 1891[2]

Dear Fisher Unwin,

Many thanks for your note enclosing proofs. Here, at last, is the MS.; not *quite* complete but nearly so. I only want 1/ for my newsagent to send me *Black and White*[3] for June 13th (containing Gosse's[4] contributions; 2/ for one from Henley,[5] which he is going to try and send me very soon. 3/ for two from Charles[6] and 4/ I wrote to Andrew Lang the other day asking him to translate the poem by Joachim du Bellay.[7] Whether he *will* or not remains to be seen! I have marked the poems of doubtful desirability with a sign like this Δ. Mottoes and dedication I must add later. *The Owl and the Pussycat* I asked for a year ago I think, or thereabouts, but the *publishers* (horrid folk!), I *think*, *Warne's*, or *Ward and Lock*, refused, saying they were going to bring out another edition of Lear's[8] verses themselves. Do you think *you* could ask them? Perhaps they would let us have it now, and they would be more likely to listen to you. So would Locker's publishers who are Kegan Paul and Co. His *Loulou and her Cat*, which I particularly want to[9] be allowed to use, was included in *London Lyrics*.[10] Will you intercede? I think it would be more advantageous. I already had an excellent translation of Heine's cat sonnet,[11] and a copy of Wordsworth's *Kitten and Falling Leaves*.[12] I am charmed with *Some Emotions and a Moral*; it is one of your best Pseudonyms.[13] The style, ideas, and method of expression are admirable — and original.

We have had such a week of it — we got through the papering and furnishing in seven days — to say nothing of whitewashing and "moving in."[14] It is very jolly here — you must come down to us soon — and bring a fishing rod — the pond is just teeming with fish.

We dig up our own potatoes, and pluck our own beans and peas —

I think the cat-book will be very good — When would you like to have the introduction? And to about what length would you wish it limited? And how about terms? I think I have asked you everything now, and it is nearly post-time —

With our best regards to you
Always sincerely yours
G. R. Tomson

Letter 2. Rosamund Marriott Watson to T. Fisher Unwin,
Sussex, England, nd[15]

Dear Fisher Unwin,

Mother Tabbyskins is from *Child World*, by the authors of *Poems Written for a Child* — Menella Smedley and her sister Mrs. Hart, 1869.[16] My conflagration has only made the weather more outrageous — it pours still and fills up the intervals with gales that threaten to sweep one with all one's belongings (and everything else to boot) from the face of the earth.

So don't be surprised if you hear that your friend the Minor Poet[17] (that's me) has shared the same fate as Flying Robert of Struwwelpeter fame.[18]

When you feel inclined send me any M.S. you like, to read — (any, *I mean*, that you care to send, whether you *like* them or not). That criticism of Amy Levy's book is neither criticism nor "*causerie*", save the mark![19] 'Tis just *cant* of the worst description, and impertinent as cant always is — Stead[20] might have written it himself — "Life is real, life is earnest," and all the old barrel-organ damnation grind *ad nauseum* — bah! Imagine the jackanapes prating of "common pity, common charity" and of *Amy Levy's* "*indolence*" and "*poor work*"! If I were her brother he should not "scape whipping"; but, after all, one should not take these things seriously, but just for what they're worth, which is — naught at all. [21]We *might* be in town for a day or so, soon — if so we shall hope to see you. If not, you must come and see us first — but anyway don't forget that we shall be here through November.

Yours sincerely,
G. R. T.

P. S. When you *do* see Mrs. Moulton[22] Please greet her for me.

Letter 3. Rosamund Marriott Watson to T. Fisher Unwin,
Charlston, Sussex, England, 28 September [ny][23]

Dear Fisher Unwin,

The proofs have just arrived, and we are *appalled* by the monstrous cari-
catures of the illustrations. Even if, eventually, they look ninety-nine per cent
better than this they will still be unworthy of publication. After going to the
expense of those *most admirable* blocks it does seem such a terrible pity, to have
money and pains (as it were) wasted, by printing so *utterly* unintelligent as this:
I feel distressed very nearly, if not quite, as much on your account as on my
own — or the artist's. We all want the book to be a success, and these things have
alarmed me fearfully; all the more so as the printing of the text is so good and
(comparatively) correct. I do not know what can be done, but feel sure that you
will be able to arrange something, and that you will feel how important "for all
our own goods" is the proper rendering of the illustrations. The very first proofs
of the blocks were so excellent that I could not have imagined that clumsy printing could have so degraded them.

With best regards
Yours sincerely
G. R. Tomson[24]

Letter 4. Rosamund Marriott Watson to Albert Bigelow Paine,
Charlston, Chiswick, England, 30 April 1902[25]

Dear Mr. Paine,

It seems long since I wrote to you last, but illness, & *not* sloth, has been the
cause. I have never properly thanked you for the great Antarctic Romance,[26]
which I read with the greatest delight — & admiration — : "The ice-fields & the
snow", to say nothing of that old Norse nostalgia for the sea, (or rather, say, the
shadow of it that is our common heritage), have always made special appeal to
me; & the way you have handled your material is, I think, prodigious. I feel so
mean — here have you most generously given us books that are more friends
than volumes, & you have not had so much as a paltry sheaf of rhymes from me!
About the new book I am very doubtful — I had meant it to appear this Spring,
but, unlike my confrère, Mr. Jack Rabbit, I have turned diffident & postponed
it once more.[27] Would you care to have either *Vespertilia* or *A Summer Night*, I
wonder?[28] Someday, I expect, your young admirer Dick will be for sending you
some of his own imperishable impromptus.[29]

The garden is looking very lovely now with its masses of tulips & narcissi, (the daffodils are over), underneath blossoming boughs of pear, apple, cherry, & lilac. Dick has a brand-new cricket-pitch in the orchard, which fills his six-year-old soul with sinful pride, & the birds are singing all together like Morning Stars. I only wish the sun would be a little more prodigal of his presence — that is the great blot on our English climate. We have been reading Mrs. Morse Earle's book about your American gardens,[30] & have found it most interesting. What a conscientious worker she seems to be!

With cordial greetings from all here to you & yours,
Believe me
Sincerely yours
Rosamund Marriott Watson

p. s. Can I get *The Arkansaw Bear*[31] anywhere over here? This *isn't* "hinting," & you are not to give it us, but I want to get it for myself.

Letter 5. Rosamund Marriott Watson to Nora Hopper Chesson, Charlston, Shere,[32] England, 2 March 1905[33]

Dear Mrs. Chesson,

I remember you very well indeed. I need hardly say that I have watched your career with great interest, & felt always so gratified by your artistic success, perhaps none the less in that I prophesied aright all those years ago. I still wish that Mr. Lane had published Mr. Anning Bell's picture for "Boholaun & I"[34] as a frontispiece to your prose Ballads.

Of course I heard also of your marriage[35] & wished you all happiness.

It is so difficult to write things about oneself, & I don't feel as if I had anything interesting to tell. I was born in London, & have read poetry and written verse ever since I can remember. I had naturally rather a lonely childhood as all my brothers & sisters were so far older than myself. From my father, who was a very brilliant personality, an ardent bibliophile, (& a very graceful verse-writer) I owe a fairly wide acquaintance with prose & poetry, more especially poetry, in which he had a fine taste.[36] He had a large & well-chosen library in which I spent my happiest hours.

In spite of all this, however, my dearest ambition was to become a painter; but, as an art education did not come within the range of practical politics, I had to give up the idea.[37] As for the influence of poets upon one's work, it is hard to distinguish when one has read and enjoyed so many — but for sheer intimacy of thought & feeling I think the two Rossettis, Swinburne, W. Morris, & (in earlier years) Jean Ingelow, were nearest & dearest. But I am too catholic to be precise.

As for one's debut—the American periodicals were first and kindest to a quite unknown versifier—and then Mr. Lang[38]—well, I owe him more than I can say in the way of sympathy and encouragement, to say nothing of a most kindly laughing at one's faults and *faiblesses*, which was infinitely helpful. Mr. Henley's friendship & encouragement too, I always like to remember. My literary life has been a *very* happy one. But you will be very tired of all this, it sounds so petty & egoistic.

On Wednesday next we return to our cottage at Chiswick for a time; will you not come to tea with me there? that is, if you are not too busy.[39]

Letter 6. Rosamund Marriott Watson to Nora Hopper Chesson, Charlston, Shere, England, 2 April 1905[40]

Dear Mrs. Chesson,

Your book[41] has been a great joy to me; it is a really beautiful thing & I am glad you have written it. How glad you & your husband must be. I should have thanked you for it before this, but your address was left behind here & so I had to wait until we came down to hunt it up.

I wish I had *The Bell & the Arrow* sent me for review, but I have long left off reviewing fiction, & only verse & two or three special subjects come my way now. I found the welter of novels too much for me when my health gave way, but *your* book I should have welcomed gladly—I could have praised it conscientiously & with enthusiasm. Only a poet could have written it, & how few are the poets who can write beautiful & distinguished prose—Indeed I think I know no other. My husband is much struck by it; it has been also sent to him for the *Athenaeum*.[42]

Dick is well & gay & thoroughly enjoying this heavenly spring weather—I hope your little people are in the same case.

I have found the books[43] (one of which I hope you will accept) & the photo, & will send them on to you directly I can find some brown paper & string.

Again, thank you for the Book, & thank you for seeing things through your own enchanted medium, & writing them—'tis a rare gift yours of making your glamour an outward & visible sign of an inward & spiritual grace—

Yours always sincerely,
Rosamund Marriott Watson

Notes

1. For more on Watson's significance, see multiple works by Hughes; Schaffer 87–102, 113–118; and Vadillo 29–30.

2. Harry Ransom Center, U of Texas.

3. *Black and White*, a weekly illustrated paper (1889–1912) that in 1891 was edited by Oswald Crawfurd, a friend of Tomson.

4. Edmund Gosse (1849–1928), biographer, poet, man of letters; he contributed three translations of French noblewomen's epigrams to *Concerning Cats*.

5. William Ernest Henley (1849–1903), poet, art critic, and editor. Some of the era's finest authors published in his *Scots* (later *National*) *Observer* and *New Review*, including W. B. Yeats, Rudyard Kipling, Thomas Hardy, Alice Meynell, Joseph Conrad, and H. G. Wells. Tomson contributed both poems (including "To My Cat") and a fashion column to the *Observer*. No poem by Henley appeared in the anthology.

6. Possibly Charles Whibley, assistant editor of the *National Observer* in 1891 and Henley's right-hand man.

7. Andrew Lang (1844–1912), poet, novelist, man of letters, and anthropologist. No translation by Lang of French poet Joachim du Bellay (1522–1560) appeared in the anthology.

8. Edward Lear (1812–1888), nonsense poet, children's verse writer, and landscape painter. "The Owl and the Pussycat" did not appear in the anthology.

9. ‹use›

10. Tomson's strategy worked in this case: "Loulou and Her Cat," by Frederick Locker (1821–1895), was included. *London Lyrics* was first published in 1857 and went through multiple editions. The poet was known as Locker-Lampson after 1885.

11. The sonnet by Heinrich Heine (1797–1856) in *Concerning Cats* was translated from the German by Alma Strettel (1854–1939), a friend of poet Alice Meynell. Alice Meynell to Katharine Tynan Hinkson, 10 December 1892, Tynan correspondence (KTL1/716/109), John Rylands University, Manchester University, Manchester, England.

12. The Wordsworth poem was also included in the anthology.

13. *Some Emotions and a Moral*, a novel by John Oliver Hobbes (Pearl Craigie, 1867–1906), was published in 1891 as part of Unwin's Pseudonym Library series.

14. The Tomsons regularly removed to the country during summers so that Arthur could pursue his landscape painting.

15. Harry Ransom Center, U of Texas.

16. "Mother Tabbyskins" was included in the anthology; Tomson's citation is correct, though Hart is sometimes identified as Smedley's aunt; see Logan 278.

17. "Minor Poet" is a play on Levy's volume (see note 19).

18. "Flying Robert," in *Struwwelpeter* (1845), by Heinrich Hoffmann (1809–1894), ignores warnings about going outside during storms and is blown into the sky when the

wind catches his umbrella. A citation in the British Library catalogue indicates that an English version of the tales was in circulation by 1848.

19. In 1891 Unwin reprinted *A Minor Poet*, by poet and novelist Amy Levy (b. 1861), who had committed suicide in 1889; in the last year of Levy's life Tomson became one of her friends (see Beckman 177–178). The offending causerie was by Arthur Quiller Couch (A.T.Q.C., "A Literary Causerie") in the 3 October 1891 *Speaker* (413–414). Tomson herself reviewed the Levy reprint (part of the Cameo Series) in the 21 November 1891 *Illustrated London News* (667), which defended both Levy's artistry and her defiance of feminine convention.

20. W. T. Stead (1845–1912), editor of the *Pall Mall Gazette* (1883–1890), to which he contributed the sensational series on white slavery in London entitled "The Maiden Tribute of Modern Babylon" in 1885 (Brake 94–95).

21. ‹It would›

22. Louise Chandler Moulton (1835–1908), American poet and journalist who, beginning in the late 1870s, resided in London every summer, where she formed friendships with literary notables ranging from George Eliot and the Rossettis to Thomas Hardy and Olive Schreiner. Her 19 May 1889 column in the *Boston Sunday Herald*, to which she contributed a weekly column, was headlined "A Poet Who Will Live. Mrs. Graham R. Tomson's New Volume—True Ballad Touch."

23. Harry Ransom Center, U of Texas.

24. Tomson's 30 September letter (Harry Ransom Center, U of Texas) indicates Unwin's reaction: "Many thanks for your re-assuring letter; 'thou hast comforted me marvelous much'—But you have mistaken what I said about the proofs—I meant that the block-maker's proofs were excellent—not the big sheet of cats—I thought *them* horrid! So *there*, M'sieur le Pecheur!" Her playful allusion to Unwin's middle name—*Pêcheur*, a fisher or fisherman—indicates good humor but also a subtly aggressive pun, since *pécheur* signifies a sinner.

25. Huntington Library, San Marino.

26. *The Great White Way; a Record of an Unusual Voyage of Discovery, and Some Romantic Love Affairs amid Strange Surroundings* (1901).

27. In Paine's "How Mr. Dog Got Even," from *The Hollow Tree* (1898), Mr. Dog shows up just as Mr. Jack Rabbit is triumphantly celebrating the predator's absence by reading aloud a new poem, "When Mr. Dog's Away." The "new book" is *After Sunset*. Watson is avoiding such premature "publication."

28. Her volumes of 1895 and 1891 (rpt. 1895), respectively (see Works Cited).

29. Dick (b. 1895) in fact did publish poems. "Yashmak (An Oriental Fantasy)" appeared in the 11 March 1918 *Daily Chronicle* (2) prior to his death (24 March 1918), and "Kismet" was published posthumously in the 21 April 1918 *Observer* (3). The latter has recently been reprinted (Taylor 91).

30. Alice Morse Earle (1853–1911), *Old Time Gardens: A Book of the Sweet o' the Year* (1901).

31. *The Arkansaw Bear; a Tale of Fanciful Adventure* (1898).

32. Shere is the Surrey village near Guildford dating back to Anglo-Saxon times. The

Watsons began living in Shere part-time after Rosamund suffered a nervous breakdown in 1903, and moved there permanently after the autumn of 1905.

33. The Pierpont Morgan Library, New York.

34. *Sylvia's Journal*, March 1894: 190. Robert Anning Bell (1863 – 1933), a member of the New English Art Club, designed Tomson's masthead for *Sylvia's Journal* and illustrated her most important literary contributions (see Hughes, "Female" 176 – 177). ·

35. On 5 March 1901 to literary critic Wilfred Hugh Chesson.

36. Benjamin Williams Ball (1816 – 1883), was trained as an accountant and rose to the position of secretary to a bank; he was also an amateur poet, leaving a volume of his original poems bound in green calf, now lost, to his daughter Rosamond (as she then spelled her name).

37. Rosamund's older brother, Wilfrid Williams Ball (1853 – 1917), enjoyed a successful career as a painter for a number of years, but his abandoning accounting for art seems to have angered his father. It was through Wilfrid ("Wilf") that Rosamund met publisher John Lane: Lane and Ball were early members of the Sette of Odd Volumes, a literary dining club for men.

38. Lang was English editor of *Harper's Monthly Magazine* when Graham R. Tomson submitted "Ballade of the Bourne"; Lang immediately accepted the poem and then began promoting the new poet in his monthly column, "At the Sign of the Ship," in *Longman's Magazine*. Lang also secured publication of Graham R. Tomson's 1889 volume with Longman's.

39. The signature has been cut from the letter.

40. The Pierpont Morgan Library, New York.

41. Presumably *The Bell and the Arrow* (1905).

42. H. B. Marriott Watson was a principal reviewer of fiction for the *Athenaeum* at this time. No review of *The Bell and the Arrow*, however, was published in the *Athenaeum*.

43. Presumably either *Vespertilia* or *A Summer Night*, the books Watson offered to Paine. The photograph has not survived.

Works Cited

[Armytage, Rosamond.] *Tares*. London: Kegan Paul, 1884.

Beckman, Linda Hunt. *Amy Levy: Her Life and Letters*. Athens: Ohio U P, 2000.

Brake, Laurel. *Subjugated Knowledges: Journalism, Gender, and Literature in the Nineteenth Century*. Washington Square: New York U P, 1994.

Brownson, Siobhan Craft. "Nora Hopper ('Mrs. Nora Chesson')." *Dictionary of Literary Biography 240: Late Nineteenth- and Early Twentieth-Century British Women Poets*. Ed. William B. Thesing. Detroit: Gale, 2001. 94 – 99.

Demoor, Marysa. *Their Fair Share: Women, Power and Criticism in the Athenaeum, from Millicent Garrett Fawcett to Katherine Mansfield, 1870 – 1920*. Aldershot, Hampshire: Ashgate, 2000.

Hughes, Linda K. "'Fair Hymen Holdeth Hid a World of Woes': Myth and Marriage in Poems by Graham R. Tomson." *Victorian Poetry* 32.2 (Summer 1994): 97 – 120.

Rpt. *Victorian Women Poets: A Critical Reader.* Ed. Angela Leighton. Oxford: Basil Blackwell, 1996. 162–183.

———. "A Female Aesthete at the Helm: *Sylvia's Journal* and 'Graham R. Tomson,' 1893–1894." *Victorian Periodicals Review* 29.2 (Summer 1996): 173–192.

———. "Feminizing Decadence: Poems by Graham R. Tomson." *Women and British Aestheticism.* Eds. Talia Schaffer and Kathy Alexis Psomiades. Charlottesville: U P of Virginia, 1999. 119–138.

———. "A *Fin-de-Siècle* Beauty and the Beast: Configuring the Body in Works by Graham R. Tomson (Rosamund Marriott Watson)." *Tulsa Studies in Women's Literature* 14.1 (Spring 1995): 95–121.

———. *Graham R.: Rosamund Marriott Watson, A Woman of Letters.* Athens: Ohio U P, forthcoming.

———. "A Woman on the Wilde Side: Masks, Perversity, and Print Culture's Role in Poems by 'Graham R. Tomson'/Rosamund Marriott Watson." *The Fin-de-Siècle Poem.* Ed. Joseph Bristow. Athens: Ohio U P, forthcoming.

———. "A Woman Poet Angling for Notice: Rosamund Marriott Watson." *Marketing the Author: Authorial Personae, Narrative Identities and Self-Fashioning 1880–1930.* Ed. Marysa Demoor. Houndmills, Basingstoke, Hampshire: Palgrave, forthcoming.

Logan, Deborah A. "Menella Bute Smedley." *Dictionary of Literary Biography 199: Victorian Women Poets.* Ed. William B. Thesing. Detroit: Gale Group, 1999. 278–284.

Pennell, Elizabeth Robins. *Nights: Rome and Venice in the Aesthetic Eighties, London and Paris in the Fighting Nineties.* 2nd ed. Philadelphia and London: J. B. Lippincott, 1916.

Schaffer, Talia. *The Forgotten Female Aesthetes: Literary Culture in Late-Victorian England.* Charlottesville: U P of Virginia, 2000.

Taylor, Martin, ed. *Lads: Love Poetry of the Trenches.* London: Constable, 1989.

Tomson, Graham R. "Beauty, from the Historical Point of View." *Woman's World* 2 (July-August 1889): 454–459, 536–541.

———. *The Bird-Bride: A Volume of Ballads and Sonnets.* London: Longmans & Co., 1889.

———. *A Summer Night, and Other Poems.* London: Methuen & Co., 1891.

———, ed. *Ballads of the North Countrie.* London: Walter Scott: 1888.

———. *Border Ballads.* Canterbury Poets Series. London & Newcastle-on-Tyne: Walter Scott, 1888.

———. *Concerning Cats: A Book of Poems by Many Authors.* Illus. Arthur Tomson. Cameo Series. London: T. Fisher Unwin, 1892.

———. *Selections from the Greek Anthology.* London: Walter Scott; NY & Toronto: W. J. Gage & Co., 1889.

Vadillo, Ana I. Parejo. "New Woman Poets and the Culture of the *salon* at the *fin de siècle*." *Woman: A Cultural Review* 10.1 (1999): 22–34.

Watson, Rosamund Marriott. *After Sunset.* London & NY: John Lane, The Bodley Head, 1904.

———. *The Art of the House.* Connoisseur Series. London: G. Bell & Sons, 1897.

———. *The Heart of a Garden.* London: Alexander Moring, 1906.

———. *The Poems of Rosamund Marriott Watson.* London: John Lane, The Bodley Head, 1912.

———. *Vespertilia, and Other Verses.* London: John Lane, The Bodley Head, 1895.

Chapter 12

KRISTIN A. RISLEY

Palma Pederson (1879 – 1950)

The early life of Palma Pederson[1] — or Palma, her *nom de plume* and preferred designation in her letters — resembles the plot of one of her own novels.[2] Born on 18 November 1879 in the coastal town of Porsgrund, Norway, Palma was the youngest of nine children and the only daughter of Per and Marie Anderson. Palma's father was a tailor who, due to drinking, suffered severe financial losses. Such setbacks resulted in Palma and her brother, Joachim (the only surviving children), being sent away from home: Palma to a home for poor and orphaned children, her brother to work for nearby farmers. After Per Anderson was able to reestablish himself as a tailor in Ulefos,[3] the family reunited.

Palma attended country schools, the primary source of her formal education. One legacy of Palma's time in the children's home was her desire to travel to America, an idea inspired by one of her teachers, Charlotte Riis, who had spent time in the United States. Palma was struck with "America fever" and wrote of her predicament to her grandmother, Anne Korsveien, in Coon Prairie, Wisconsin. Palma describes the reply: "In the next letter from her, there came, to my great surprise, the ticket. Thus I came to America."[4] In 1894, at the young age of fifteen, Palma immigrated to the United States (Øverland 247). During her first winter in America, she lived with her grandmother in Bloomingdale and attended public school, and that spring, Palma moved to LaCrosse to become a hired girl in the household of Kristian Pederson.[5] After the death of Kristian Pederson's first wife, he and Palma were married, and she became the stepmother to his three children.

Palma's domestic duties left little time for further education or intellectual pursuits; in her letters, she bemoans the fact that she must devote time to household chores rather than writing. Yet she enjoyed this hobby, which first began in Norway: "Even before I left home, I tried to interpret my joys, sorrows, and other moods in verse and prose. Though my literary attempts were often lacking, it was a satisfaction for me to be busy with my writings."[6] A few of Palma's early verses were submitted to the *Lutheran Herald* by Mrs. E. O. Vik, wife of a local pastor, and these were published, much to Palma's "joy and surprise."[7] Palma's first collection of poetry, *Syrener* (Lilacs),[8] appeared in 1911, but it was not until after her husband's death in 1920 that Palma devoted herself more fully to writing. In the decade that followed, most of her major works were completed: *Under ansvarets svøbe* (Under the Lash of Responsibility), which received the Norwegian Society's literary prize in 1923[9]; the novel *Ragna* in 1924; and *Genier* (Geniuses), a sequel to her first novel, in 1925. Her longest novel, *Sjælekampe* (Battles of the Soul), was also written during this period but was never published. In addition, Palma contributed poems, short stories, and a serialized novel to Norwegian-American periodicals.[10]

Palma's remarkable story is typical of many immigrant and ethnic writers in the early twentieth century who—despite formidable economic, social, personal, and artistic hardships—wrote American literature in languages other than English. Indeed, throughout the nineteenth and twentieth centuries, the United States was home to a rich assortment of ethnic print cultures that produced books and periodicals for their respective immigrant groups. Palma participated in the active literary scene of *Vesterheimen* (literally, "the western home"), a term used by Norwegian Americans to refer to their distinct ethnic, linguistic, and geographic "home" in the United States.[11] The nucleus of this ethnic enclave was the Upper Midwest, the primary area of settlement for Norwegian immigrants. Palma wrote and published the majority of her literary works in the early decades of the twentieth century, just as Norwegian-American literature was experiencing its golden age.

While Palma's letters reveal challenges faced by many ethnic and regional writers, they provide special insights into her situation as a woman writer in *Vesterheimen*, a position of frequent marginalization and "gender-imposed isolation from the male fellowship of other writers" (Øverland 281).[12] Shaped by publishers, editors, critics, scholars, and clergy, the literary milieu of *Vesterheimen* was overwhelmingly male. Moreover, the Norwegian-American literati formed a relatively small, select group; many of those involved knew each other well, which caused tension when it came to debates about the nature of Norwegian-American literature and reviews of each others' work. Ingrid Urberg notes that "Palma felt her gender not only made it difficult to get things acknowledged and published, but she felt that at times it colored the criticism she received" (140).[13] Thus, while Palma's fears and resentments about editors, publishers, and critics may seem exaggerated, her sense of being an underdog amidst the male literary establishment was well founded.[14]

In addition, Palma's preoccupation with others' reception of her works is no doubt related to her position as "the most prolific Norwegian-American female novelist to publish in Norwegian and the only one to consider herself a full-time author" (Urberg 197). Palma's letters are alternately assertive and self-effacing, proud yet plagued with self-doubt. Palma's humor, however, appears frequently, particularly through her sardonic comments regarding those whom she perceives to be against her. As Urberg points out, in letters "Palma seems to have found her true voice" (187). It is therefore regrettable that, here, the letters cannot appear in their original Norwegian, as some linguistic spark is lost in translation. However, if even a portion of Palma's abundant wit and vivacity is captured here, then the letters testify to her spirit and determination.

The translation of Palma's letters posed several challenges. Palma used an older form of Norwegian that is more characteristic of the nineteenth century than the twentieth. This was typical among Norwegian-American writers because many received their formal language training in Norway prior to emigration. Moreover, the Norwegian language in the United States did not undergo the same changes as in Norway; thus, the spoken and written forms used in America became increasingly static and ultimately archaic. The passing of anti-immigration legislation in the 1920s and the gradual slowing of Norwegian immigration meant that fewer newcomers arrived to rejuvenate *Vesterheimen* with their linguistic and cultural practices. Complications in the translation process may be traced to Palma's lack of language training, which results in anomalies of grammar and vocabulary, and her mixing of Norwegian and English syntax, words, and idiomatic phrases. This mixing, which was so common among immigrant speakers that Norwegian Americans invented a new verb for it — "å mixe" (to mix) — appears in some of the letters below and is noted accordingly.[15] Despite these linguistic difficulties, the primary challenges of this translation were in voice and tone — how to render the feistiness and descriptive language that make Palma's letters as entertaining as they are informative.

To provide a sense of cohesion as well as a snapshot of a vital period in Palma's authorship, all of the selected letters date from 1924 to 1925. With the exception of the last letter, the examples are all addressed to Rasmus B. Anderson. By the time Palma came to know Anderson, he was a fixture in Norwegian America, having been a longstanding advocate for Norwegian culture in the United States. Anderson's contributions were many, and he was particularly active as an author, translator, editor, and scholar.[16] Initially, Palma corresponded with Anderson in his role as editor and owner of the newspaper *Amerika*, to which she contributed. Eventually, Anderson became Palma's chief mentor — she addresses him as "master" in the letters — and surely one of the most important influences in her life.[17] The intensity of this relationship is reflected in both the tone and sheer number of letters to him.[18] Palma relies heavily on Anderson for advice and guidance on both personal and professional matters. With regard to her writing, she asks him to read and respond to her work and to intercede on her behalf with editors and publishers. Palma seeks Anderson's approval constantly and, despite his considerable professional stature, seems to attach undue reverence to his opinion.

Palma's treatment of Anderson contrasts markedly with her attitude toward other leading authors and editors of *Vesterheimen*, as shown in references she makes in several of the letters included here. For instance, while Palma assures Anderson that he need not be afraid to use his pen for corrections on her manuscripts,[19] she cautions O. E. Rølvaag about wielding his powers of criticism.[20] In the last letter of the selection, Palma is defensive and even defiant, reminding Rølvaag of his duties as critic and revealing her struggles with what she perceived to be a literary establishment that treated her unfairly. Despite her comments to the contrary, Palma was sensitive to criticism; in another letter to Rølvaag, she tells him, "your criticism wounded me in my very soul so that it bled."[21] Palma considered Anderson her one true ally; while his support and affirmation surely did her good, her alliance with him may also have hindered her relationships with other editors and critics. Anderson could be cantankerous and had feuds with other writers, notably Waldemar Ager (who appears as a negative figure in Palma's letters). Additionally, Anderson favored modes of literary expression that became increasingly outdated in the twentieth century. Lloyd Hustvedt observes that Palma "attempted to write according to the Andersonian prescription, turning to ancient Norway and its gods for inspiration," an approach which certainly had a negative impact on the critical reception and economic success of her literary works among some of her contemporaries (244).

In addition to her interactions with other writers, Palma's letters reveal challenges she faced as an author. Some of her issues were prevalent among ethnic writers and render the literary landscape of *Vesterheimen*. For example, Palma voices a common concern when she worries about an audience for her works, especially given that she writes in Norwegian.[22] In one letter to Anderson, Palma deplores how difficult it is to get anything published since "there is so little interest among folk of Norwegian descent" who "do not bother to buy their own authors' books."[23] Another problem with using Norwegian as a literary language in the United States was the changing orthography, a difficulty that was only heightened by Palma's lack of higher education and formal training.[24] Reviewers noted Palma's linguistic shortcomings, and the criticism prompted her to consult grammar books in order to improve her accuracy and fluency.

Like many ethnic authors, Palma's relationship to her subculture was, at times, conflicted. In her letters, she proclaims her desire to further Norwegian culture in America and awaken pride in her fellows, yet she also rejects *Vesterheimen* at various points, finding it artistically stifling. Expressing her need to escape: "I cannot, I cannot bear to write about anything Norwegian-American or 'pure' Norwegian now. I must get away from the unpleasantness of the Norwegian barn stench and the predominance of the outhouse, and partake of another climate and see other situations."[25]

Palma struggled to get her works published, an endeavor that cost her a great deal personally and financially. She found it mortifying to peddle her own books, yet she also expressed a passionate commitment to the quality and presentation of her texts, negotiating with publishers and paying attention to binding and other details. Indeed, the letters show Palma's increasing savvy with the publishing process. While Palma lacked formal education, she was intellectually curious; in letters, she frequently tells Anderson about the authors she's reading, including Henry Wadsworth Longfellow, Gustav Flaubert, and Hamlin Garland as well as other Norwegian-American authors.[26] Palma identifies strongly with other artists and emphasizes how precious her art is to her, proclaiming, "I must write!"[27] As she details aspects of her writing process, bouts of writer's block, and moments of artistic inspiration or isolation, her commitment to craft is clear. Several themes recur throughout the letters: first, Palma asserts that her talent is God-given and she therefore has a duty to persevere; second, she expresses the hope that her writing might contribute to the betterment of "her people"; and last, Palma views her writing as a personal quest of the female artist, an idea that reappears in her novels.

Palma's first novel, *Under ansvarets svøbe* (Under the Lash of Responsibility), features Gudrun, a character whose story mirrors Palma's own. After suffering alcoholism in her family life, Gudrun leaves Norway for America. She joins her grandmother in Wisconsin and then finds work in LaCrosse as a maid to a banker named Engh. There she discovers her desire to write, but her artistic endeavors are stalled when she marries her employer's brother, Ole Skjoldhammer. Although Gudrun respects Ole, their marriage is primarily based on their shared sense of duty to the Engh children, who are orphaned and in need of care. Thus, Gudrun's artistic hopes suffer "under the lash of responsibility." Gudrun's story continues in the sequel, *Genier* (Geniuses), as she and Ole struggle in their roles as spouses, parents, and artists — Gudrun as a writer and Ole as an inventor. Ole is eventually killed in a test flight of his solar-powered blimp, but Gudrun overcomes both Ole's death and literary critics to publish her book, *Evnerige Mennesker* (Gifted People) to critical acclaim. Other geniuses appearing in the novel include Gudrun's adopted daughter, Charlotte, who is a musician, and Charlotte's husband, Ideus Olson, a farmer who becomes a New York architect. The novel incorporates real-life figures from the Norwegian-American milieu, including Rasmus B. Anderson, Waldemar Ager, and O. E. Rølvaag (all of whom appear in Palma's letters).

Palma's second novel, *Ragna*, features another female artist: the painter Ragna Blili. Like her creator, Ragna begins as a lowly immigrant girl in Norway. After the local minister learns of the girl's talent for drawing, he helps her to study with Trygve Hjort, a famous painter who becomes her tutor and guide (modeled on Anderson). Ragna and Hjort move to New York to continue her artistic instruction, and she eventually becomes a celebrated painter. The primary conflict of the novel occurs when Ragna moves to the Midwest and meets Sigmund Solskjær; she is torn between love and art. The problem is eventually solved when Ragna's mother convinces her that an artistic career and a happy marriage need not be incompatible. The book concludes with a wedding in Norway.[28]

Palma's preoccupation with the female artist links her to a previous generation of American women writers such as Harriet Beecher Stowe and Elizabeth Stuart Phelps, and in several respects, she has more in common with her predecessors than her contemporaries. This is due to the fact that Norwegian immigrant culture tended to be relatively conservative and artistically belated. Additionally, Palma's penchant for idealistic and sentimental narratives seems stylistically and thematically out of step with much twentieth-century writing. Yet the most compelling link between Palma and her predecessors is the desire, expressed repeatedly in her correspondence and fiction, to attain artistic expression, achievement, and recognition.

As an ethnic woman writer of limited resources — financial, educational, and communal — Palma experienced intense isolation and lacked successful models on which to base her career. Perhaps because of this lack, many of her texts work to create such models, portraying characters of ingenuity and perseverance. Orm Øverland concludes that Palma's novels "are [. . .] memorials to a brave woman, who in a male-dominated culture created female characters of extraordinary moral and spiritual strength" (248). Like her predecessors, Palma imagines vocational possibility and personal fulfillment for women beyond their traditional family roles and domestic responsibilities. For immigrant women,

Palma offers something more than material prosperity and social progress. In both her life and her literary works, Palma attempted to articulate a place for the ethnic woman writer: a success story of artistic accomplishment and enlightenment for the immigrant in America.

Letter 1. Palma Pederson to Rasmus B. Anderson,
LaCrosse, Wisconsin, 3 January 1924[29]

My dear master:

— This Christmas has been very busy. There has been something nearly every day. Yesterday the card club met at my place. We are nine ladies and we play "500." On New Year's Day I was invited to luncheon with M. Laumann.[30] Mr. J. Ovren was their houseguest[31] [. . .]. But Ovren is not a little influenced by W. Ager.[32] And he sees — or acts as though he sees — a lot of things differently than when he was with you; in any case, it struck me that way. He looks better this time. He is happier, I believe, because he has his wife and children with him and has his own home. My master, I have considered whether it would be possible for me to get my book Genier[33] ready for the press by the end of the month of February, so I could get it on the market in time for the centennial jubilee in June.[34] I talked about this a little with him. But it seems as though he, since he came to Ager and Eau Claire, no longer takes the same interest in my work. He let me know that I got the last book Ragna way too cheap.[35] I know well enough that they had to reprint several of the copies the 8 that I proofread. But there was also a good deal of sloppy work from the printer, which was impossible to use. If I could only get, for example, John Anderson or Augsburg Pub. Co. to take my new book Genier on commission, or partly on commission.[36] I almost haven't the strength to bear it all. But I must get it published even if I go to the poorhouse afterward. After you get a chance to read my M.S.[37] when I revise it, you can tell me what you think of it and what you believe and advise I ought to do. You know that there will not be another opportunity again like this centennial jubilee, where thousands come to Minneapolis. J. Ovren said right to my face that he had not read Ragna. He said that W. Ager did not like Ragna as well as *Under Ansvarets Svøbe*; yes, he even said that he did not like my last book.[38] I cannot understand his taste. Or does he think he can change my viewpoint? I am glad that I have written and published Ragna. That I have pursued and put forward the ideal in it does *not* make it less valuable, does it?![39] The only friend I really have in Eau Claire is H. Landmark.[40] And now I hear that he will perhaps quit in *February*. Then there will be just Ovren and Ager left. And truth be told I do not have trust in any of them any longer. When I send them my M.S., they will handle it in such a way that it will become impossible for me to get it printed. Ager will try to stop me if he can. Ovren said, Ager is the best author over here; Rølvaag cannot write![41] Ager praises Simon Johnson; he knows that he is too tiresome and boring and that he does not need to fear him.[42] But Palma? She writes at the very least (if I am to believe the many who have told me so) so that she provokes a lion's appetite. My instinct tells me that if Ager could be rid of and stop authors Palma and Rølvaag, he would then perhaps win a Nobel Prize.[43] In any case, that is my view; but it could be that I am right [. . .].

The fondest greetings to you Respectfully yours,
Palma

Letter 2. Palma Pederson to Rasmus B. Anderson,
LaCrosse, Wisconsin, 6 February 1924

My dear master:

— Have read your excellent and interesting article on artist Ole Bull[44]. Thanks, a thousand thanks for being so good as to send me the newspaper. One never tires of reading about him; one constantly yearns to hear more. How interesting it must have been to have been in his company, to have heard him speak, to have heard him play straight from his innermost artist's soul all the wonderful, grand and delightful things he had of dreams, of poems, of feelings [. . .]! You have really lived! Meanwhile, all things considered, I have never lived other than in dreams and imagination [. . .]. I have, in reality, never had anyone I could talk to about that which most interests me. Often I have felt lonesome and deprived on account of that. But maybe I would not have invested so much in my poems and my stories if I had talked myself out? So perhaps it is best the way it is. I wish that I had more "pep," more desire and courage to write, to live, to interest myself in people around me; then I could write and compose better and more realistically, more naturally and clearly, more movingly and truthfully, more edifyingly. But I sit at home [. . .]. And one cannot write if one does not take an active interest in that which one should achieve. It remains just so-so. Oh, I am an ungrateful thing. I ought to thank God that I have it as well as I do. And I do that too, when I manage to think it over.

The fondest greetings
Yours respectfully
Palma

Letter 3. Palma Pederson to Rasmus B. Anderson,
LaCrosse, Wisconsin, 19 February 1924

My dear master:

— Right now I am "blue." I don't know why. But often in the past I have felt relief in writing to my master. Wonder if the judges have announced their decision with regard to the submitted manuscripts. I do not believe, frankly, that *Ragna* will be one of the prizewinners.[45] There will likely be something that is more captivating than my narrative. I will console myself with the knowledge that you thought it should win [. . .]. One thing I do think is that a Norwegian-American author should win; because it is so difficult for us to get anything published and to awaken interest over here and in Norway for something that is produced here in Norwegian. One also has the issue — and perhaps with good reason — that we here are less literary. And still! I would so like to win so I could get more of my work published[46] [. . .]. I am not reading much now. But the more I familiarize myself with and read your translation of Brandes' Creative Spirits,[47] the more interesting and precious it becomes to me [. . .].

Fondest greetings
Yours respectfully
Palma

Letter 4. Palma Pederson to Rasmus B. Anderson,
LaCrosse, Wisconsin, 16 March 1924

My dear master:

I was very glad to receive a letter from you. Glad to know that you are in the best of health and all is well. Dare I bother you with sending back to me the first chapter of the second section.[48] I feel that I have begun it differently than I ought to have done and that I must arrange the beginning of the second section differently than I have in that chap.[49] When I first get a good start, then it goes relatively smoothly afterward; but the beginning is always the worst for me [. . .]. I have a feeling that you will not completely approve of my little excursion to Finland. But we can change this and that after I, God willing, complete the narrative. You probably would think it better if I had taken Norwegians/Norwegian-Americans as my heroes and heroines instead of those I have now. But the truth is, just now I cannot write about either Norway or Norwegians in America. Hope that I, with new strength and skill, can tackle something like that after a year's time. The whole Norwegian nest here has given me a feeling of bitterness that almost grows into contempt and vengeance, of which I must rid myself before I can handle such subject matter. I am so glad to have a friend like Barton; greet him for me.[50] I have been sick with a rather stubborn cold and have coughed a lot at night; but I believe it is clearing up and feel now a bit stronger and more in the mood to work again. Did you read my piece "Norway and the Norwegian Press in America, ["] in *Norgesposten* last week?[51] I myself thought that article was rather good and feel better for having said it.

Fondest greetings to you Yours respectfully
Palma

Letter 5. Palma Pederson to Rasmus B. Anderson,
LaCrosse, Wisconsin, 31 May 1924

My dear master:

— Today I got the manuscript back. So "Ragna" is now home for the "holiday" [. . .]. Yesterday I wrote to Waldemar Ager and asked him when the most convenient time would be to print another of my stories.[52] I think I'll send "Ragna" in. I have the 50 dollars I got as the prize of "The Norwegian Society"[53] plus 33 dollars that I I have received from several of those who have sold "Under ansvarets svøbe," accordingly 83 dollars. If I could now just find a market for my books in Scandinavia [. . .]. In the event that I get them to print it; will you take one of the proofs and go through it. I shall also read it myself this time so there are not all those defects and printing errors like in "Under andsvarets svøbe" [. . .].

With the friendliest greetings to you and your children
Yours respectfully
Palma

Letter 6. Palma Pederson to Rasmus B. Anderson,
LaCrosse, Wisconsin, 29 July 1924

My dear master:

— Ragna is now finished; I sent the manuscript to Fremad Pub. Co. today.
At the same time I requested that they should send sections for proofreading
directly to you. You can then be so good as to send them to me, at my cost. I will
buy stamps to that end in a couple of days. I don't know how many times I have
written the first chap. It was something of a dilettante attempt at that. I was dissatisfied with it [. . .]. Last night I mean — yesterday evening it was so warm that
I could not sleep. I was agitated and nervous. Water seemed to be undrinkable.
Something must have been wrong with the pipes, I think. I got up at midnight
and warmed up the coffee and drank two cups. The result was that I became
wide awake; and my first chap. was still not revised. I sat myself down to rewrite
it and completed it on the typewriter this morning. I did not sleep a wink last
night. I sat out on the veranda and watched the daybreak. Around three-thirty
I lay down a little while but I lay there sleepless. I slept about 10 minutes in the
afternoon. I hope that God will bless my work and be pleased with that which
I have produced! I am so tired. The worst is to get almost no sleep. But that will
surely get better. I think I will get 50 bound and the others covered in a dust
jacket. If I could just get a bookseller or publishing firm to sell my books. The
most distressing thing I know is to be compelled to offer my own books. Norway
could certainly do this much for me. Skandinaven and Augsburg could do the
same[54] [. . .].

Thanking you in the warmest way for your great goodwill I am as always
Yours very respectfully
Palma

Letter 7. Palma Pederson to Rasmus B. Anderson,
LaCrosse, Wisconsin, 1 August 1924

My dear master:

— Received your friendly letter today and another a couple of days ago. It
gladdens me greatly that you are in good spirits and in somewhat healthy vigor.
Ja, I imagine the roses in your garden are beautiful. But everything in the house
and around me has become neglected; so I should get things in order. Besides,
so much money is going to the new book that I will soon be in a bad way, if

something doesn't come in. But it is just for this that I strive and work to get out some of that which I have produced; so it can go as it will with the rest. If I go to the poorhouse at least I have — I hope — something that will live on when I am no more. I have not yet heard any word as to whether or not Ragna has arrived. I shouldn't wonder if W. A. is extremely annoyed.[55] I feel actually that Ragna is the best literary work that has been published in the Norwegian language in America. I have really exerted myself and I believe that I can say that it is really fine and vivid art. I hope in any case that you think so [. . .]. Should *Ragna* live; you live with her in Trygve Hjort.[56] I am so unwaveringly sure of your good will and good intentions [. . .]. I am rather tired. Enclosed are some stamps. Hoping that you will be healthy and in good spirits,

I am with best greetings yours very respectfully
Palma

Letter 8. Palma Pederson to Rasmus B. Anderson,
LaCrosse, Wisconsin, 12 September 1924

My dear master:

— Received a second set of proofs from you today. I was quite satisfied with the last one. But in the previous one I was very dissatisfied with what I had written and I corrected a good deal [. . .]. While I worked there was overcast weather of the worst sort and so dark that I almost couldn't see.[57] I felt as if I were in *Purgatory* and suffered torments of many kinds [. . .]. And I thought that something that tries to pass itself off as a *publishing house*[58] ought to be able to correct a little of the manuscript before they set it in type; even if the author was not quick-minded enough to do it.[59] During the morning today I was called out for a dress fitting. I came home again; and when I opened the door to the hallway the telephone rang as if it would fall off the wall [. . .]. My instinct was not mistaken — or more correctly — my logic was not mistaken. Ja, it was *Landmark*. He counted up all the corrections and it would be double the work. I said, I was rather grieved with regard to this. — But you see yourself that it ought to be changed, I said. — Ja, he could not deny that. And he was quite friendly and courteous. I asked him what he thought of *Ragna*. Ja, he thought it was a good story and that it looked as though it should be popular. I have decided to[60] get 250 books bound in a *good binding*. He asked if it wouldn't be good enough to do it in paper binding and with paper instead of cloth. I said — *no I want it done properly*! He promised that I should get it done for exactly what it cost them. I[61] received a sample book with binding cloth of every color yesterday. I chose an almost Moroccan brown or *deep* wine red; or if they couldn't get that, a handsome dark green. I think you will come to like the binding color. For the other 250 I chose a light blue for the paper cover. I'm going bankrupt but so be it. Even though I am poor and do not have much to live on, at least I'm getting something of *mine* out. That is what I live and strive for; to make the most of my talents in my Lord's service and for the edification and benefit of my fellow men; so it may go as it will with me [. . .]. My heartfelt thanks, I think, you can see in my narrative, without it being necessary that I say it to you. I am so rich in your friendship! I am reading now an excellent and informative book "Great Men and Famous Woman."[62] There are hardly any of them who have not experienced terrible ordeals. Dikens, for ex.![63] I read your article on Leif Erikson in Skandinaven.

With the best wishes for all good things for *you*,
    I am (please forgive this sloppy letter)
Yours respectfully
Palma

Letter 9. Palma Pederson to Rasmus B. Anderson, LaCrosse, Wisconsin, 28 September 1924

My dear master:

— Sent "Sluppefolket" to "Skandinaven" on the 27th of Sep. via special delivery.[64] Wonder if they accept it? At the same time, I sent the poem to *Decorah Posten* and to *Minneapolis Tidende*.[65] In the event that the poem ignites in my people more pride in their descent and more seriousness and interest with regard to the language and spiritual heritage[66] being preserved, then I haven't written the poem in vain. I composed two more verses about the Norse people's participation in the war between the South and the North and in the World War, which I think you will like. I may send it to Normanden or maybe Norgesposten.[67] Perhaps you have by now received the proofs from Fremad Pub. Co. I had a few words from them that Ragna should be finished around the 15-20th October. Uff, if I only had someone to take over the sale for certain; it is most terribly tedious! I flat out *hate!* to sell my own books! However, I am nevertheless glad that I am getting something of mine launched [. . .]. Yes, dear master, it is so joyful that one should come to see with your eyes the Sluppefolket and Leif Erikson and the other *Americans* of Norse descent; and that you[68] got the joy of seeing and hearing it. It is more — much more gratifying that it comes so long afterward; in that the tree that grows slowest strikes the deepest roots and has the greatest capacity for survival and forms the greatest resistance to the storm.

With friendly greetings
Yours respectfully
Palma

Letter 10. Palma Pederson to Rasmus B. Anderson,
LaCrosse, Wisconsin, 16 October 1924

My dear master:

— Hope you liked your trip to (Rio?) and that the trip did not become too exhausting for you. I wait each day for *Ragna*. But when 100 shall be bound in good binding, perhaps it does not go as quickly by hand as one intended. Moreover, one knows for certain, up there in Eau Claire now, that *Palma* is not so easy to satisfy as one first supposed. My heart's highest wish is that *Ragna* will serve as enjoyment and entertainment and — a little more. I cannot write, before I get to thoroughly examine *Ragna*. That *Skandinaven* did not accept Sluppefolket; did not once let me know why, even though I sent it to editor John Benson with *special delivery*, hurt me.[69] But there is one thing that Skandinaven and others [. . .] will find out: — Not yet are all of the Joms Vikings dead, nor is *Palma finished with them!*[70] It's all the same to me. When you are my friend, the rest do not matter. No one can stop me — or more precisely that gift which is given me by God to bring to "Egypt's Pharaoh." I will serve my God and my people [. . .].

Fondest greetings
Yours respectfully
Palma

Letter 11. Palma Pederson to Rasmus B. Anderson,
LaCrosse, Wisconsin, 31 December 1924

My dear master:

— On Monday I was invited to doctor Adolph Gunderson's for 6-o clock dinner.[71] Mrs. Gunderson telephoned me late Sunday evening, after I had gone to bed [. . .]. I had written her a little Christmas letter and thanked her for extreme kindness to me this year [. . .]. She also asked me [. . .] to the Ibsen Club.[72] This time — that is the third time — the club was to have its 25th anniversary. I dared not do anything other than accept the invitation. But the truth is, I was almost sick with reluctance, because I was so little acquainted with the others [. . .]. There were five tables in a large, handsome dining room. Around the two largest tables there were twelve places set and at the two corner tables there were about 8 at each. I sat at the farthest end of one of the tables [. . .]. Think of my surprise, when after Mrs. Olberg after having read all the funny verses, Mrs. dr. Adolph Gunderson stood up and read [. . .] something like this:

We have among us a poet — about whom I now say
she has given us Ragna and so much more besides
and she won the literary prize.[73]

It was, of course, as you see, a humorous verse like the others. Afterward she said: We have here tonight as a guest one of our own authors, Mrs. Palma Pederson. I propose that, in her honor, we drink a toast and give her a threefold hurrah! And you should have heard the hurrahs. I stood there and wondered if I dreamed or was awake [. . .]. Then postmaster Skaar spoke about Ibsen and his writing [. . .]. Then Mrs. Stavren and Mrs. Skaar shouted: — We want to hear Palma Pederson, let Palma Pederson speak! and clapped. I became speechless and tongue-tied as always, I feared it was a very bad "speech." It is strange, all things considered, how bad I am at public speaking! I almost never find the right words to express what I have in my heart [. . .]. Anyway, I saw that some of what I said pleased the ladies [. . .]. So much fuss was made over me on this occasion that my heart really warmed with friendship for them and the whole world. The strangest of all was that it was as if I had come into an atmosphere where I truly belonged — it was as if I had now finally, truly come home. Heartfelt thanks for the old year and a splendid wish for a bright and happy New Year!

Palma

Letter 12. Palma Pederson to Ole E. Rølvaag,
LaCrosse, Wisconsin, 18 June 1925[74]

Dear Mr. Professor:

— You have perhaps received an examination copy of my last book *Genier*. Believing in your good word, I hope that you will review it soon. Keep this in mind: — You do not need to worry if you have something to say. I am not especially thin-skinned and I can, when it comes to my life's calling, take a good deal of criticism. But remember that there have been critics who have believed themselves to know a great deal and who have picked out shortcomings in truly great writers' works, and exposed these to the view of Joe Public,[75] but who themselves have had the greater shame of their own imagined cleverness [. . .]. Posterity will judge our works.

Both you and Waldemar Ager were basically in agreement that Ragna was a *fiasco* as a narrative. And you said: — There is no art to be found in it. I have received letters from men and women who love and understand imagination and what art really is; and a man like Prof. R. B. Anderson, — who surely as well as anyone understands literature and has read nearly all the classic works that are to be found, calls *Ragna* a little masterpiece and he says *Genier* reaches an even higher *standard*. Whatever *this* or *that* learned critic finds regarding flaws and merits — (I have, God help me, written a good deal that is practically worthless) — I myself have my own opinion about *this* and *that*, regarding my own and others' works. Certainly I do not possess the technical polish or learning of perhaps you or others; but my intellect, I believe, can measure up to anybody.

I got 500 printed of Genier, included in that are 100 in so-called fancy binding. They cost me, just for the printing and binding, $338.75. I have already given away approximately 50. Now I am taking the last few pennies I have to pay for it. But do you think I grieve over that. No, it is a kind of joy for me to give the last little *bit* of what I have in the way of fortune and ability to that which God, with his gift of talent, has given me. Do you think I give up: — never! as long as I manage to *think* and *produce*. When I no longer have any money, I will go out and earn money from some simple work, in order to get my works published. I hope you do not take my forthrightness and unrestrained comments and opinions badly, and hoping to see your review of my book in *Skandinaven* or in one or another more worthwhile organ than the last one you wrote the review of Ragna in,

I am with friendly greetings[76]
Yours respectfully
Palma

Sorry that I did not get to see and speak with you at the Centennial jubilee![77]

Notes

1. Biographical information is primarily based on materials from the Knut Gjerset Papers, Norwegian-American Historical Association, Northfield, Minnesota; hereafter N-A Historical Assn. At least one of the documents was written by Palma herself. See also Øverland 247–250 and Urberg 197–200. I refer to the author as "Palma," echoing her usage of the name in her professional and personal writings. Palma's surname appears alternately as both "Pederson" and "Pedersen"; I use the former spelling since it appears in her own documents.

2. For support of this project, I wish to extend my thanks to the staff of the Wisconsin Historical Society, particularly Harold L. Miller. I am also indebted to my colleagues at the Norwegian-American Historical Association Archives in Northfield, Minnesota—especially Forrest Brown and Kim Holland. Finally, I thank Diane K. Risley for her assistance in Madison.

3. The name is also spelled "Ulefoss," a town in Telemark county in south central Norway.

4. Palma Pederson, "Noget af en biografi," ts., Knut Gjerset Papers, N-A Historical Assn., 2. Unless otherwise noted, all subsequent translations from the Norwegian are mine.

5. In one source, this name is listed as Kristian Pederson Fladlien, Pederson being a patronymic and Fladlien being a place name (perhaps a farm name) in Norway. Kristian Pederson was born in Vardal, Norway. Knut Gjerset Papers, N-A Historical Assn.

6. Palma Pederson, "Noget af en biografi," ts., Knut Gjerset Papers, N-A Historical Assn., 2.

7. Palma Pederson, "Noget af en biografi," ts., Knut Gjerset Papers, N-A Historical Assn., 3.

8. English translations of Norwegian titles appear in parentheses. When italicized, these titles represent actual English language editions of the works. English titles that do not appear in italics signify that the book was not translated into English (few of Palma's works were published in English).

9. The Norwegian Society of America (Det Norske Selskab af Amerika) was founded in Minneapolis in 1903 with the goal of promoting Norwegian-American cultural endeavors.

10. The ethnic press was a catalyst in the development of immigrant and ethnic literature in America; newspapers, journals, and magazines served as key publication sources for aspiring writers. Leading Norwegian-American newspapers also sponsored literary supplements: *Skandinaven* of Chicago (1866–1941) featured *Husbibliothek* (Home Library) and *Decorah-Posten* (1874–1972) sponsored *Ved Arnen* (By the Fireside). Palma's serialized novel *Det rette valg* (The Right Choice) appeared in *Decorah-Posten* from 19 February to 12 March 1935.

11. *Vesterheimen* may also be translated as "the home in the west" or "our western home." The latter suggests the collective identity and shared history *Vesterheimen* came

to represent. The term *Vesterheimen*—derived from the Old Norse word for "the Western world"—was formally proposed as a name for Norwegian America in 1875, when scholar Rasmus B. Anderson used the word in an article for the Chicago-based Norwegian language newspaper, *Skandinaven*. See Rasmus B. Anderson, "En tur ikring i Vesterheimen," *Skandinaven* 23 Feb. 1875: np. Anderson, a major influence on Palma Pederson, was professor of Scandinavian languages at the University of Wisconsin–Madison, 1869–1883.

12. Øverland uses this phrase in reference to another Norwegian-American woman writer, Dorthea Dahl (1881–1958), a contemporary of Palma's. Pederson mentions Dahl in her letters, and her comments suggest that she felt Dahl generally received better treatment by the writers and critics of *Vesterheimen*.

13. Ingrid Urberg's dissertation, "A Sense of Place: America Through the Eyes of Norwegian-American Women Novelists," examines Norwegian immigrant women writers' reactions to and portrayals of the American experience in their correspondence and novels. Urberg pays particular attention to identity and place, as well as to discussions of authorship and the female artist. I am grateful to Dr. Urberg for sharing her insights with me.

14. Norwegian-American author, Helen Egilsrud, expressed similar concerns. See Urberg 139–143.

15. Norwegian-American author, Waldemar Ager, illustrates and satirizes this linguistic mixing among Norwegian Americans, often to great comic effect, in his 1917 novel, *Paa veien til smeltepotten* (On the Way to the Melting Pot).

16. Rasmus Bjørn Anderson (1846–1936) was a leading scholar of Scandinavian Studies, teaching language and literature at Albion Academy and the University of Wisconsin–Madison. Anderson served as minister to Denmark from 1885 to 1889 and as editor of the Norwegian language weekly *Amerika* from 1898 to 1922.

17. Palma employs such appellations with other male writers as well; she addresses letters to Ole Amundsen Buslett (1855–1924) with "dear poet" (21 September 1920) and "dear author and poet" (25 November 1923). O. A. Buslett Papers, N-A Historical Assn. She addresses O. E. Rølvaag as "Dear Author" (5 October 1927) and "Mr. Professor" (18 June 1925). Such gestures convey Palma's genuine respect—even admiration and affection in the case of Buslett—for these figures. Moreover, Palma's emphasis on the men's roles as authors and scholars suggests her desire for intellectual kinship with other writers. On occasion, Palma uses titles of respect sarcastically, especially when she feels that she is being slighted or mistreated by the person concerned. This is the case when she refers to O. E. Rølvaag as "Pope Rølvaag" in a letter to Anderson (20 November 1925). Rasmus B. Anderson Papers, Wisconsin Historical Society, Madison; hereafter Anderson Papers, Wisconsin Historical Society.

18. Palma wrote to Anderson several times per week and even twice in one day.

19. Palma Pederson, letter to Rasmus B. Anderson, 31 October 1923, Anderson Papers, Wisconsin Historical Society. Palma is referring to corrections of her manuscript for *Ragna*.

20. Ole Edvart Rølvaag (1876–1931) was professor of Norwegian at St. Olaf College

and a leading Norwegian-American writer, critic, and author of the 1927 novel, *Giants in the Earth.*

21. Palma Pederson, letter to O. E. Rølvaag, 14 October 1927, O. E. Rølvaag Papers, N-A Historical Assn.

22. Norwegian-American authors might write in Norwegian, English, or both. Palma wrote primarily in Norwegian and few of her works were translated into English.

23. Palma Pederson, letter to Rasmus B. Anderson, 12 February 1924, Anderson Papers, Wisconsin Historical Society.

24. Norwegian-American publications typically used a form of Dano-Norwegian from the nineteenth century, sometimes even printing the periodicals in gothic script. Language debates were common within the Norwegian-American community and were discussed in literary journals, newspapers, and church publications.

25. Palma Pederson, letter to Rasmus B. Anderson, 28 November 1925, Anderson Papers, Wisconsin Historical Society. I have translated the Norwegian word "udhus" as the English word "outhouse." This word means "outbuilding" or "farm building" in Norwegian, but given Palma's choice of metaphors, particularly her reference to "barn stench" ("fjøsstank"), the connotation of the English word is fitting.

26. Palma was also involved in local literary clubs in LaCrosse, including the Ibsen Club and Bjørnson Club (she was a founder of the latter), both of which honored Norway's national poets. Palma hoped that the Bjørnson Club might also foster more reading and appreciation for literature among Norwegian Americans. Palma Pederson, letter to Rasmus B. Anderson, 7 (?) February 1931, Anderson Papers, Wisconsin Historical Society.

27. Palma Pederson, letter to Rasmus B. Anderson, 5 April 1923, Anderson Papers, Wisconsin Historical Society.

28. For more detailed plot summaries of the major novels, see Urberg 210–213. Øverland describes some of Palma's works as well (247–249).

29. All except the last of the letters reproduced here are from the Anderson Papers, Wisconsin Historical Society.

30. Palma mixes Norwegian and English, using the word "luncheon" in her sentence; the original reads, "Paa Nytaarsdag var jeg buden til luncheon hos M. Laumann."

31. Johan Ovren (1883–1944), a printer and the author of a book of poems, *Vinlandske digte* (Vinland Poems), the title of which utilizes the Old Norse name for an area on the eastern coast of North America discovered and temporarily settled by Norse explorers around the year 1000. The book was published in 1914 by Rasmus B. Anderson's Amerika Publishing Company in Madison, Wisconsin.

32. Johan Ovren worked as an editor and printer associated with Fremad Publishing Company in Eau Claire, Wisconsin, along with Waldemar Ager (1869–1941). Ager was one of the leading Norwegian-American authors and critics. Palma's references to Fremad and company are numerous. Her suspicion and concern regarding the staff at Fremad, particularly their treatment of her and her work, is evident here.

33. *Genier* (Geniuses) was published in 1925. It is the sequel to Palma's 1923 novel, *Under ansvarets svøbe* (Under the Lash of Responsibility). The book portrays the struggles of Ole and Gudrun Skjoldhammer as they attempt to raise a family and pursue their

artistic dreams, Gudrun as an author and Ole as an inventor. The character Gudrun has much in common with her creator, submitting her work to Norwegian-American editors and publishers and working on a manuscript entitled "Gifted People."

34. Palma refers to the Norwegian-American centennial celebrations of June 1925; major festivities were held at the fairgrounds in Minneapolis and St. Paul. Norwegian emigration to the United States is typically dated from 1825, when the sloop *Restauration* (Restoration) arrived in New York from Stavanger, Norway. Great attention was paid to Norwegian-American contributions to the United States; thus, Palma's desire to release her new novel in time for the centennial is designed to sell books as well as to underscore her participation in the ethnic group's cultural legacy.

35. Palma's novel, *Ragna,* was published in 1924 by Fremad. Like *Genier, Ragna* features a female artist, Ragna Blili, who becomes a famous painter.

36. John Anderson Publishing Company (Chicago) and Augsburg Publishing House (Minneapolis, extant today as the Lutheran publisher Augsburg Fortress) were two of the most prominent Norwegian-American publishing concerns in the late nineteenth and early twentieth centuries. Palma's wistful comments about being published by Anderson or Augsburg suggest the ability of these larger publishing houses to provide their authors with greater exposure (both in terms of advertising and readership) and financial benefits. She often managed and financed the publication and distribution of her own works, which proved to be a great professional and financial hardship.

37. Palma uses "M.S." or "M.S.S." for "manuscript."

38. In general, critics did not receive *Ragna* as warmly as *Under ansvarets svøbe*, which earned the annual prize of *Det Norske Selskab* (The Norwegian Society) in 1923. It is not surprising that Ager should prefer *Under ansvarets svøbe*; in addition to the novel's other merits, its discussion of alcohol abuse was bound to appeal to Ager, a temperance activist.

39. Palma's reference to the "ideal" may refer specifically to the romantic plot of *Ragna*, in which the title character succeeds as an artist and reconciles her love of art with her love of a man, Sigmund Solkjær. More generally, the "ideal" may also be understood in terms of Palma's preferred literary mode of sentimental fiction and her recurring theme of artistic genius.

40. Haakon Landmark served as manager of the Fremad Publishing Company and was a close associate of editor Waldemar Ager.

41. This is quite an assertion, given that Rølvaag was already among the leading writers of *Vesterheimen* and would go on to achieve international acclaim (the only Norwegian-American writer to do so). In other letters, Palma typically groups Ager and Rølvaag together as representatives of "the establishment" that she is barred from joining fully, as well as authors who had it easier than she in terms of publication, recognition, and critical reception. It is therefore interesting that she allies herself with Rølvaag, which is no small compliment in that he was considered by many the most successful example of Norwegian-American authorship.

42. Norwegian-American writer Simon Johnson (1874–1970) lived in North Dakota.

Johnson is remembered for his novels of immigrant life on the prairie, including *Lonea* (1909) and his trilogy: *I et nyt rige* (In a New Kingdom, 1914; translated as *From Fjord to Prairie*, 1916), *Falitten paa Braastad* (The Banktrupcy at Braastad, 1922), and *Frihetens Hjem* (The Home of Freedom, 1925).

43. This sarcastic comment is typical of the irreverent tone that Palma uses toward Ager.

44. Norwegian violinist, Ole Bull (1810–1880), was an important figure in both Europe and America in the nineteenth century. He attained the status of folk hero in his homeland, being one of the artists associated with the flowering of Norway's national romanticism. Bull also formed the (failed) utopian colony "Oleana" in Pennsylvania (1853) and made several trips to the United States to perform concerts and promote Norwegian and Norwegian-American cultural interests. He was a close friend of and major influence on Rasmus B. Anderson. Palma refers to Bull in several of her letters, celebrating his image as a romantic artist and comparing herself to him: "Ole Bull takes hold of the fiddle, Palma Pederson takes hold of the pen." Palma Pederson, letter to Rasmus B. Anderson, 18 March 1923, Anderson Papers, Wisconsin Historical Society.

45. This is a reference to the 1924 competition for the Norwegian Society's annual prize, which Palma had won the previous year.

46. Palma echoes this sentiment in another letter to Anderson dated 27 February 1924: "My fervent wish is to be able to win, not to win praise, but to win recognition, so I could get my works published." Anderson Papers, Wisconsin Historical Society.

47. *Creative Spirits of the Nineteenth Century* (1923) by George Morris Cohen Brandes (1842–1927), a Danish writer and an important figure in Scandinavian literary history. Rasmus B. Anderson translated Brandes's work and had it published in 1923 under the title *Creative Spirits*. Palma refers to *Creative Spirits* in a number of letters; in addition to reading about these renowned figures for edification, she related to some of them as artistic souls who struggled and strove as she did.

48. Although Palma does not name the text, the timing and her comments suggest that she is referring to her unpublished work, *Sjælekampe* (Battles of the Soul). The book is set in Finland and Russia, which explains her subsequent comments about the lack of Norwegian and/or Norwegian-American subject matter and her concern about Anderson's response.

49. Chap. is an abbreviation for chapter; the original letter reads "kap." for *kapitel* in Norwegian.

50. Journalist, historian, and Progressive Party activist in Wisconsin, Albert O. Barton (1869–1947) read and responded to some of Palma's texts and worked on English translations of *Ragna* and her poem "Mississippi." He also collaborated with Rasmus B. Anderson on the biography *Life Story of Rasmus B. Anderson* (1915).

51. The original article was entitled "Norge og den norske presse i Amerika" and appeared in *Norgesposten* 11 March 1926.

52. Palma writes to Ager in his capacity as editor and publisher at Fremad in Eau Claire.

53. A monetary award accompanied Palma's 1923 literary prize for *Under ansvarets svøbe.*

54. In this sentence, Norway refers broadly to the publishing houses in that country; Skandinaven (Chicago) and Augsburg (Minneapolis) refer to two of the leading Norwegian-American publishers in the United States.

55. W. A. signifies Waldemar Ager. Palma had a complicated relationship with Ager, enlisting his help in printing her works but mistrusting him as an editor, printer, reviewer, and fellow author (whom she perceived to be highly critical of her works and in competition with her).

56. Trygve Hjort is a character in *Ragna* modeled on Anderson. Several other characters in the book were also based on real people in the Norwegian-American community.

57. Palma uses the word "gråvær" (literally, gray weather), meaning overcast or cloudy; however, the word also has a figurative meaning of depression or gloom, reflecting the mood described in the letter.

58. ‹has›

59. Regarding the Fremad Publishing Company in Eau Claire, Palma is expressing her disappointment in the treatment of her manuscripts and the quality of the workmanship, a complaint that resurfaces in many of her letters. Palma's self-deprecating remark about the author (herself) is most likely expressed as an ironic paraphrasing of opinions she would attribute to Ager and the others at Fremad rather than the suggestion of her own shortcomings.

60. ‹to›

61. ‹have›

62. *Great Men and Famous Women* (1894) by Charles F. Horne, a multi-volume series of biographical studies. Palma most likely refers to "Part IV: Artists and Authors." She mentions this book again in a letter dated 28 September 1924.

63. English author Charles Dickens.

64. "Sluppefolket" (The Slooper Folk) is the title of a poem by Pederson that commemorates a group of Norwegian emigrants. The Sloopers emigrated from Stavanger, on the southwestern coast of Norway, on 4 July 1825 and arrived on 9 October in New York. The voyage is remembered as the first organized migration of Norwegians to the United States, although Norwegians had emigrated prior to 1825.

65. Palma submits her poem to three Norwegian-American newspapers: *Skandinaven* (Chicago), *Decorah-Posten* (Decorah, Iowa), and *Minneapolis Tidende* (Minneapolis). Given that the poem is designed as a commemorative homage, Palma appears to expect that it may be printed simultaneously in several publications for the betterment of "her people."

66. Palma refers to an artistic and intellectual inheritance among Norwegian Americans, going on to emphasize Anderson's central role in fostering Norwegian culture in the United States.

67. *Normanden* (Fargo, North Dakota) and *Norgesposten* (Brooklyn, New York) were Norwegian-American newspapers.

68. ‹should›

69. John Benson (1862–1939), chief editor of the newspaper *Skandinaven*, based in Chicago. Pederson refers disparagingly to Benson in other letters; apparently, she did not think that he appreciated her or her work to the degree that he should. In a letter to Anderson (31 July 1928), Palma mentions that she does not think Benson is a "friend to the ladies," suggesting her perception that she was treated differently based (in part) on gender.

70. The words "finished with them" are underlined three times each in the original letter. Historically, a "jomsviking" was a member of a Danish band of Vikings based in Jomsborg at the mouth of the Oder in Denmark. Pederson uses the term to convey her fierceness and determination in the face of a literary establishment that she perceives to be largely against her.

71. The first sentence of this letter provides an example of Palma's mixing of Norwegian and English; the original Norwegian sentence includes the English phrase "6-o clock dinner."

72. This was a local Norwegian-American cultural group. The club appears to have included both men and women. The group hosted meetings and special events; such gatherings typically featured a program (in this case, a talk on Henrik Ibsen) and some refreshments or even a banquet. Palma's letter also mentions the singing of "lovely Norwegian songs," including national songs and hymns.

73. The translation is very close to the original, which also rhymes the second and third lines in Norwegian with "mere" (more) and "literære" (literary).

74. Ole Edvart Rølvaag Papers, N-A Historical Assn.

75. The original letter reads "Ola Publikum" [Ole Public] in Norwegian, Ola or Ole being a very common Norwegian name.

76. Rølvaag's review of *Ragna* appeared in *Duluth Skandinav* (Duluth, Minnesota) on 27 February 1925, so Palma's disparaging remark appears to be directed toward that publication.

77. Palma refers to the 1925 Norwegian-American Centennial celebrations in Minneapolis.

Works Cited

Hansen, Carl G. O. "Glimt fra Livet i det norske Amerika: Skrivende Norsk-Amerikanderinder." *Minneapolis Tidende* 22 November 1925: n.p. Clipping from the Carl G. O. Hanson Papers. Norwegian-American Historical Assn., Northfield, MN.

Haugen, Einar. *Immigrant Idealist: A Literary Biography of Waldemar Ager, Norwegian American*. Northfield: Norwegian-American Historical Assn., 1989.

Hustvedt, Lloyd. *Rasmus Bjørn Anderson: Pioneer Scholar*. Northfield: Norwegian-American Historical Assn., 1966.

Lovoll, Odd S. *The Promise of America: A History of the Norwegian-American People*. Minneapolis: U of Minnesota P, 1984.

Naess, Harald S., ed. *History of Norwegian Literature. A History of Scandinavian Literatures 2.* Lincoln: U of Nebraska P, 1993.

Norlie, Olaf Morgan. *History of the Norwegian People in America.* Minneapolis: Augsburg Publishing House, 1925.

Øverland, Orm. *The Western Home: A Literary History of Norwegian-America.* Northfield: Norwegian-American Historical Assn., 1996.

Pederson, Palma. *Genier.* Eau Claire: Fremad, 1925.

———. *Ragna.* Eau Claire: Fremad, 1923.

———. *Syrener.* LaCrosse: n.p., 1911.

———. *Under ansvarets svøbe.* Eau Claire: Fremad, 1924.

Skårdal, Dorothy Burton. *The Divided Heart: Scandinavian Immigrant Experience through Literary Sources.* Oslo: Universitetsforlaget; Lincoln: U of Nebraska P, 1974.

Thorson, Gerald Howard. "America is not Norway: The Story of the Norwegian-American Novel." Diss. Columbia U, 1957.

Urberg, Ingrid. "A Sense of Place: America Through the Eyes of Norwegian-American Women Novelists." Diss. U of Wisconsin – Madison, 1996.

KIMBERLY J. BANKS

Jessie Redmon Fauset (1882 – 1961)

Jessie Redmon Fauset (1882 – 1961) was an essayist, short-story writer, novelist, and literary editor for the *Crisis*. She is remembered for her second novel *Plum Bun* (1928), which highlights the complex relationship between race and sex for an African-American woman artist. Such a focus is significant given Fauset's own position during the Harlem Renaissance, also known as the New Negro Renaissance, a movement remarkable for the number and range of writing done by black writers, the interest among mainstream journals and publishing houses in supporting this work, and the creation of significant journals such as the *Crisis* and *Opportunity* associated with the national organizations of the National Association for the Advancement of Colored People (NAACP) and the Urban League.

The nomenclature of "Harlem Renaissance" is convenient, although there is extended debate about whether the movement was in fact a renaissance and whether the geographical location of Harlem should be privileged. New York is significant as the publishing center of the United States and Harlem as a point of access to such publishing circles. Access to such power has been the source of considerable controversy, because white facilitators of contact between white publishers/editors and black writers such as Carl Van Vechten provided their own constructions of blackness that black writers and intellectuals had to negotiate. While interracial negotiations are generally emphasized in critical discussions of the Harlem Renaissance, Jessie Fauset forces critics to be more attentive to intraracial negotiations. Her position as literary editor of the *Crisis* gave her power to identify and develop emerging artists. At the same time, Fauset could not leverage her position as literary editor to promote her own work.

Early scholarship on Fauset cast her in the role of a midwife to the Harlem Renaissance. Her literary salon in New York and her facilitating role at the *Crisis* are privileged in such a description. In his autobiography, *The Big Sea* (1940), Langston Hughes explains:

> in those pre-crash days there were parties and parties. At the novelist, Jessie Fauset's, parties there was always quite a different atmosphere from that at most other Harlem good-time gatherings. At Miss Fauset's, a good time was shared by talking literature and reading poetry aloud and perhaps enjoying some conversation in French. White people were seldom present there unless they were very distinguished white people, because Jessie Fauset did not feel like opening her home to mere sightseers, or faddists momentarily in love with Negro life. (247)

Here Hughes notes Fauset's resistance to the kind of interracial spectatorship that plagued the Harlem Renaissance as well as her efforts to focus on highbrow intellectual exchange. He also gives her credit for supporting his first publication in the *Crisis* in 1919 with the poem "The Negro Speaks of Rivers." The letters selected for this chapter highlight the important role that Fauset played as a literary editor in her support of the writer Langston Hughes. They also suggest that he provided support to Fauset by listening to and reading her personal and professional frustrations.

In her pioneering critical article reassessing Fauset's work, Abby Arthur Johnson explains, "she helped establish a literary climate favorable to black writers of varying persuasions, even to those who would never have come to her for assistance" (315). Gloria T. Hull offers a more general reassessment of women writers of the Harlem Renaissance when she suggests, "from a feminist perspective, it is ironic that one of the notable ways women contributed to the period was through hostelrying-hostessing-salon keeping, refinements of their traditional domestic roles extended into the artistic and cultural arena" (6).

Almost the opposite of her relationship with Hughes is Fauset's relationship with Alain Locke, the editor of the influential, ground-breaking anthology *The New Negro* (1925). Unlike the mutually supportive relationship between editor and writer Faucet enjoyed with Hughes, when dealing with Locke, Fauset faced his indifference. The 1925 and 1933 selections below provide evidence of a continually strained relationship between the two. He marginalized her at the *Opportunity* dinner which historian David Levering Lewis describes as the "dress rehearsal" for the Harlem Renaissance (90). This dinner provided the contacts and interest necessary for Locke's editorship of a special issue of the *Survey Graphic*, which was eventually expanded into the book *The New Negro*. The dinner was originally organized as a celebration of Fauset's novel *There Is*

Confusion (1924). The fact that her work and her individual importance as a power broker were eclipsed at this dinner is significant in appreciating the racial and gender politics of the Harlem Renaissance. Locke prompted Fauset to write an article for inclusion in his landmark anthology. This article, which becomes "The Gift of Laughter," was adapted from an earlier article, "The Symbolism of Bert Williams" (1922). Included here is one letter from within a series of letters that Fauset writes to Locke asking for further guidance in recasting this article, which he insists be adapted to fit his preferred new title. In "The Symbolism of Bert Williams," Fauset emphasizes the importance of suffering to Bert Williams's life. She says, "His resignation to suffering took the sting out of the malevolence of fate" (259). His life becomes the exemplary text for the motivation that "at length shall we all be free" (259). The thematic of laughter as a racial gift is not well suited to such a favorite thematic of sacrifice. Fauset has to shift the emphasis in her original article in order to make it fit Locke's thematic. In "The Gift of Laughter," she explains that Williams "was sad with the sadness of hopeless frustration. The gift of laughter in his case had its source in a wounded heart and in bleeding sensibilities" (165). This conclusion is a compromise to the new context in which Fauset discussed Williams.

Fauset's attitude toward hardship and sacrifice was not the attitude explained by Hughes in his novel *Not without Laughter*: to "poverty-stricken old Negroes [. . .] no matter how hard life might be, it was not without laughter" (249). For Fauset, hardship and sacrifice proved to be chastening. In *Plum Bun*, after the protagonist, Angela Murray, realizes the implications of her love affair, "she began to see the conventions, the rules that govern life, in a new light; she realized suddenly that for all their granite-like coldness and precision they also represented fundamental facts; a sort of concentrated compendium of the art of living and therefore as much to be observed and respected as warm, vital impulses" (228). In *The Chinaberry Tree*, Fauset offers a gloss on the significance of suffering that echoes a passage from *Plum Bun*. After the protagonist, Joanna Marshall's, disappointment in achieving her ambition,

> her romance would hereafter lie behind her. From this day on she would dedicate herself to one interest, which should be the fixed purpose of her life; now that she thought of it she would give up the idea of dancing, too. Her former lover and her former ambition alike were unattainable; they had merely been means of enriching her experience. Now she would get down to the business of living; no more sighs, no more backward glances. (222)

In her letters to Hughes, Fauset emphasized repeatedly the importance of suffering. They both focused on suffering, but used suffering in very different ways as suggested by their relationship to laughter. Hughes explained in his autobiography that he was most productive as a writer when he was unhappy. Such contrasting approaches were also evident in Fauset's first letter below in which she asserts that the answer to disappointment and disgust is to seek oblivion and the sublimation of pain through art. Mutual support is reinforced in the second and third letters, where she reflects, "Here I was writing you brave advice from Paris only to be unable to follow it myself," and "I hope your jinx has disappeared; I don't know whether or not I'm being pursued by one or whether such and such are in just life." In the final letter between Fauset and Hughes, his poem "Childhood" prompts Fauset to reflect on the need for children to know that "ugliness and pain are so much a part of living as beauty and sweetness." The contrast between Fauset's encouragement of and artistic sustenance from Hughes and her difficult and ultimately antagonistic relationship with Locke provides a complex and dynamic picture of intraracial, heterosocial negotiations within the Harlem Renaissance.

In her correspondence with Hughes, Fauset provides news of her progress or lack thereof on her novel and notes news about other writers and personalities, her reactions to his work, and celebration at the publication of his first book of poems. In her correspondence with Locke, Fauset reveals frustration at his inattentiveness and outrage at his review of her fourth novel, *Comedy American Style* (1933). In the letter dated 9 January [1934], before Fauset states her objections to the review itself, she revisits the dynamics of the pivotal 1924 *Opportunity* dinner and her own marginalization at an event held in her honor. She proceeds to question Locke's talent as a critic and essayist. Finally, she ends with specific attention to the language of the review and what she deems Locke's support of the motto "whatever is white is right." Such a disagreement forces critics to reconsider a schematization of the Harlem Renaissance that pits Old vs. New Negroes, Rear vs. Van-Guard, and Conservative vs. Bohemian writers and intellectuals. Within such a schema, Fauset and Locke would be on the same side. However, given the difference that gender makes during the Harlem Renaissance and Locke's infamous misogyny, the schema suggested above appears to be an exclusively masculinist construction. In Fauset's letter to Locke, the intra-generational conflict proves just as remarkable as what we see in other letters, the cross-generational support between Fauset and Hughes.

Letter 1. Jessie Redmon Fauset to Langston Hughes,[1]
Paris, France, 6 January 1925[2]

Dear Langston:

To-day brought me your letter. It was nice of you to write me on Christmas Day, — a beautiful Christmas thought. And oh when I had given up all thoughts of hearing from you how splendid it was to see your writing again.

You must not let what has happened to you dishearten you too much.[3] If it has made you disgusted, it will be hard for you to forget it I admit, but oblivion is possible and you with your beautiful poet's mind and your glorious memories of Italy must deliberately let yourself dwell on gracious thoughts and fancies until the unpleasant happening is overlaid and buried deep, deep below consciousness. I am proud and grateful that you realized without my telling you the unquestioning quality of my friendship. Long ago, almost ten years now, I learned with bitterness and tears that there is only one way of friendship and that is to be a friend. I am *your* friend and nothing that I hear from any lips but yours (and only from yours as a request) can make me swerve from that stand.

I am so sorry that you couldn't or wouldn't stay in Paris.[4] Yet if you have my last letter sent care of Harold Jackman,[5] you must know that I think it a wise thing for you to choose now the métier which will be the prop of your mature life. Of course you will always write. You can't help it, but you will have to live too and I'm beginning rather tardily to recognize that the possession of a small income or of the ability to make a small regular income means all the difference between freedom and bondage.

You know by now that I am about to leave for Nice and Italy — you have my itinerary and my dates.[6] Indeed I had expected to be in Carcassonne this very minute and would have been but for a series of unexpectedly exasperating happenings. But now I'm glad I had to stay for the delay brought me your letter which otherwise would not have been in my hands until I reached Nice next week.

I have had a charming three months. I've loafed and dreamed and studied and written and destroyed — the stuff I've thrown away! The beginnings of my book which I've discarded! Yet within me I feel a strong impulse. I think I shall do to better piece of work. Sharper, more clearly cut, more psychical. I'm taking my work book with me. (My kindest regards to your mother. I'm so glad she's with you[)]

Thank you for your suggestion. I'm already seen some of the cafés at Montmartre and when I come back I shall see some of the others. I have a friend here who will take me and protect me. I don't believe I'd choose McKay to accompany me to such places. He is a better artist than a man I imagine.[7]

For a brief space I was bewildered when I came over this time.[8] Six months of freedom — more freedom than I'd ever had at one time in my life, enough money to manage on and no restraints. Grown-up though I am and have been now for some time I had never known such independence. I think I have spent it well. I've had some courses, rather stupid ones, at the Alliance Française and at the Sorbonne. And some really profitable work with a young French teacher — this I shall resume when I return to Paris in February. But except for that I'll double all my time to my novel.[9] I wish I could tell you about it. It stands out very clear and firm in my mind — the difficulty is getting it down.

Now I am over that first bewilderment and my life has been — to me — charming. It is lovely just being oneself and not bothering about color or prejudice. I think strangely enough that's why my book progresses so slowly because I'm away from the pressure. Like you I find Americans, black or white, nicer when they are nice than any other people in the world. I used to love the French but this time they leave me cold. The war has spoiled them poor things. I've been lucky enough to run into a group of writers whom I knew slightly in New York. Now I know them much better and they have been glorious. Through them I have seen the Paris cafés up here in the student quarters, have been invited to literary teas and heard literary gossip and am to meet Sinclair Lewis.[10] I shall never forget New Year's Eve day — I went walking with one of them in the forest at St. Germain-sm-Laye. Curiously enough I spoke of you and your beautiful work — you know Langston I think you have the freeest poetic instinct of us all — black & white in the U.S. This man is the one whom I want to see your things.[11] Be sure to send them on. I am sure you must have Jackman's letter by now, so you know my schedule. If not drop a line to my sister Mrs. Helen Lanning 203 West 122nd St., or send a letter to her addressed me; she'll forward it.

Don't go off to sea before I get home, please. As I said I'll be home the day before Easter, certainly Easter Sunday morning. Save up your money and run up to N.Y. for that week-end. If, as I think, you are at Howard,[12] you'll have a holiday anyway and you'll have to live somewhere, so live for those few days in N.Y.

But Langston remember everything passes. It really does — I have suffered and I know. Of course this does not make the pain less severe while it lasts. But the "new sun has brought the New Year". I think it will have peace and healing oblivious in its wake for you.

Sincerely, Jessie Fauset

Letter 2. Jessie Redmon Fauset to Langston Hughes, 23 April 1925[13]

Dear Langston:

I wrote you last week thanking you for the Easter flowers and still more for the exquisite Easter poem or more than Easter poem — a poem of all time.[14] I am so grateful for a manifestation of real spontaneous friendship — it is so rare. Many many thanks again. I write thus for I realize from your note which came this morning that you did not get my letter. Now that I think of it I[15] believe I addressed it to 1719 instead of 1749. Well it will come back to me and then I'll send it to you again.

Today I am in purgatory — through a combination of circumstances, thro' wrongly interpreting certain events of my life I have got myself into a maze — oh today, today I am so unhappy! You see how futile words are! Here I was writing you brave advice from Paris only to be unable to follow it myself![16] Only and how I thank God for this — I know[17] one can get over anything. I know too that "patient endurance attaineth — " not to *all* things but to very many. Already in the little struggle in which I am engaged I have seen one little victory come to me by the simple expedient of sitting still and waiting. But I am not naturally patient or passive. I want what I want horribly always, and I like to be up and getting it, instead of waiting for things to drift my way.

Why should I burden you? Only because friends are rare and you are so truly one. There is nothing you can do except to wish me the best that can come to me and to wish that it may come *soon, soon*. Today it seems to me I can no longer stand pain — and the worst of it is in order to save still greater pain and confusion I myself today must inflict pain on one who has been faithful and true. Oh Langston you think life is hard and complicated! It is, it is! But when one adds to that being a woman! Oh God doesn't like us — doesn't like women I mean! In some way we've interfered with his scheme and he's been paying us back ever since.

Otherwise everything is going well — oh I've lots to be thankful for. My few friends are true, my acquaintances kind. I think my book is good, the future smiles: you'll come to see me in June. Lots of things are lovely.

Don't keep this gloomy letter and don't worry about me. Sunday is my birthday and I'm really going to start a New Year — rising above self and bitterness. Oh I'll be strong yet!

Good-bye dear Langston — write me when you can. I like your letters

Your friend,
Jessie Fauset

Letter 3. Jessie Redmon Fauset to Langston Hughes,
before November 1925[18]

Dear Langston:

What a tresure you are! (Look at that word "treasure"! Now you see how much correcting I'd be able[19] to do of your copy!)

The book review was very nice;[20] as simply and feelingly written, I thought as the book[21] it self. (I'm crazy today! Look at those errors.)

I'm glad you're not reviewing the sam[22]e book for "Opportunity"[23] that you are for us; though of course I think you should do as much prose writing as possible in order to become better known and also to give you practice. Not that one gains much to my way of thinking from doing book reviews; that is a poet does not; book reviewing is just the type of writing to suit a man like Dr. Locke[24] or even such a person as Mr. Charles Johnson,[25] but too much of it could be deadly for you, — and all this in the teeth of the fact that I mean very soon to ask you to do some more reviewing for me.

Thanks greatly for the information; such questions are asked not, as you know, out of a spirit of mean curiosity but because the knowledge of such things often help to shape policies, — small ones.

I hope your jinx has disappeared; I don't know whether or not I'm being pursued by one or whether such and such are in just life. I know in one place in my novel I speak of the "meaningless ferocity" of life. I think that's a very good phrase, don't you? I suspect that to nature, we're not much more than beasts in the jungle undergoing the same laws of chance that jungle folk do. Only we're a little more organized. I've been reading with more pleasure than I've ever read anything else of his, Van Vechten's book on cats.[26] He speaks of the possibility of of [sic] there being some secret free masonry[27] among them. I shouldn't be surprised if there were. I also[28] should not be surprised if our organization meant no more and no less to Life or Nature or whatever the big Pooh-Bah is than theirs. From which bit of cynicism you may deduce my[29] mood.

The mood in turn is a result of the persistent delay about my book.[30] (All this of course is entre nous). It is at Macmillans who asked us by the by for fiction but their literary editor, Littell,[31] is off in Bar Harbor and likely to be there, it appears for centuries. Imagine a publisher's Literary editor in Bar Harbor! Anyway he won't be back until th the [sic] end of October which puts a definite quietus on my book's making its bow before spring.

How is your nice little mother: and your brother[32] with the adorable name and the obvious adoration for you, how fares he?

I could forgive Nugent's[33] rather too deliberate eccentricities but I am not prepared to pardon his untidy[34]ness. Can't you straighten him out on this?

The cold cream came and my beauty is returning. Thank you for that and for the review.[35]

Yes read the "Green Hat".[36] The style I think is tosh, but Doctor DuBois,[37] always more farseeing than I, feels it serves a special purpose of which more anon. Perhaps he's right. Anyway I think the story it self is immensely important, sociologically and psychologically. If you're not in any hurry to read it and I judge you're not (drawing that conclusion from the point where you are in your reading) I'll send it to you but first it must go to some one else.

Write me and come to see me.
As always,
Jessie Fauset

Letter 4. Jessie Redmon Fauset to Alain Locke, 18 August 1925[38]

Dear Alain:

I was very much disappointed in your note because I had hoped that it would contain suggestions as to treatment, length and general trend of the article which you suggested. Your former note led me to expect some specific directions. Will you let me know about this at once please,[39] also,

As to the passage from "There Is Confusion" choose what you want and I will o.k. it.

I have been overwhelmingly busy this week—if you'll special me directions to my house (203 West 122nd St.) I'll work on The Gift of Laughter Saturday and Sunday and will have it in your hands by Tuesday. Be sure to let me know what characters you want stressed besides Williams. With so little time and so little material I had thought I might just mention Hogan, Walker, Cole, Johnson & concentrate on Williams as the fine flower.

Now let me hear from at once
Sincerely,
Jessie

Letter 5. Jessie Redmon Fauset to Langston Hughes, before March 1926[40]

Dear Langston:

I'm so glad and happy and proud for you! I'd congratulate you but I think the public Knopf[41] and Van Vechten[42] are the ones really to be congratulated. So even though the spring is all around you with its urge and the call of the sea stirs your blood. You see that your sojourn "in these United States" has done something for you. I'm so glad you went to the Casino that night and saw Van Vechten again.

I'm keeping "Lullaby"[43] for the Crisis and I'm keeping "Childhood"[44] for myself. I don't want to put this latter in the Crisis but though it hurts me I like to read it occasionally. I see so clearly the horrid little drab town, prejudice, vice, death and all the other evils that so transform life which should be so beautiful. Or should it be beautiful? I think if ever I have a child I shall make plain to her that ugliness and pain are so much a part of living as beauty and sweetness. I wonder if part of our suffering in later years isn't caused by the fact that we are taught that only the nice things are normal.

I was interested in your diagnosis of V. V.[45] I don't know what his motives may be for attending and making possible these mixed parties. But I do know that the motives of some of the other pale-faces will not bear inspection. I've been home five weeks and (as you said to me these things are only for your eyes) already I've seen such remarkable manifestations of a changing social order that I am ready to retire bewildered. However if I'm going to be a writer I have certainly got to face life, get into it, mix with it. Ideals are not a good forcing-bed for ideas.

I was amused at your outburst in rereading your — how many? — 50,000 names again.[46] However of course not even this occupation, interminable as it seems, can last forever. Undoubtedly the brightest kind of a failure is stretching before you.

I wish you'd do me a favor — write me rather frequently for two or three weeks, about anything and that too whether I answer or not. I happen to have a little rough sailing in through here. Don't be as cynical about friendships. There are some rare, unselfish ones — witness ours.

Your friend, Jessie Fauset

Letter 6. Jessie Redmon Fauset to Alain Locke, 9 January [1934][47]

Dear Alain:

I have always disliked your attitude toward my work dating from the time years ago when you went out of your way to tell my brother that the dinner given at the civic club for "There Is Confusion" wasn't for me.[48] Incidentally I may tell you now that that idea originated with Regina Anderson and Gwendolyn Bennett, both members of a little library club with which I was then associated.[49] How you and one or two others sought to distort the idea and veil its original graciousness I in common with one or two others have known for years. And I still remember the consummate cleverness with which you that night as toastmaster strove to keep speech and comment away from the person for whom the occasion was meant.

It has always both amused and annoyed me to read your writings. Amused because as in the case of your multiple articles in the New Negro[50] they are stuffed with a pedantry which fails to conceal their poverty of thought. Annoyed because your criticisms such as the one I've just read in Opportunity point most effectively to the adage that a critic is a self-acknowledged failure as a writer. It has always seemed to me that you who cannot write have had the utmost arrogance to presume to criticize those who are at all possessed of the creative art or even of the art of marshalling facts and recording them. Nor am I alone, Alain, in this thought.

But today's article[51] is positively the worst because in it you have shown yourself so clearly as a subscriber to that purely Negroid school whose motto is "whatever is white is right."

For instance, very slightly, very haltingly you have pointed to certain faults in Mrs. Peterkin[52] and Mr. Bradford.[53] But all this you have quickly glossed over with hearty praise and approbation on other lives.

Also since Mr. Johnson[54] has been approved by the grand white folks you have graciously approved of him too without one word as to his style — what is it mid-Victorian, or purest Locksien[55] or modernistic — with those page paragraphs and parentheses? You've said not a word about the grouping of his facts — all of his acts are equally important aren't they?

But in the case of Mr. McKay[56] and myself[57] — our virtues are barely outlined, our faults greatly stressed and in my own case I am left without a leg to stand on, characterization, style, sentiment, treatment are all wrong. My art is "slowly maturing"; my "championship of upper and middle class Negro life" is not even "singlehanded"; it is "*almost* singlehanded." And what does such an expression as this mean: "Her characterization is too close to type?" — Just nothing! I was telling the story of a real family — how could it be a story of types?

One last point — the one that made me most furious — I wasn't telling the story of "one dark child in a family" etc. If I had been even poor mid-Victorian, sentimental, persevering Miss Fauset would have told the story from a different angle. I was telling the story of a woman who was obsessed with the desire for whiteness.

I am hoping that you will never review another book of mine. I am going to ask Mr. Carter to send you no more of my work. (Later: I've changed my mind about this; now that I've let you know how I feel I don't care how many books you review.)

No dear Alain, your malice, your lack of true discrimination and above all your tendency to play safe with the grand white folks renders you anything but a reliable critic. Better stick to your own field and let us writers alone. At least I can tell a story convincingly.

Very sincerely,
Jessie F. Harris[58]

Your total failure to understand my work goads me to more words. For instance what on earth are you talking about when you speak of my having missed "the deep potential tragedy of the situation and its biting satire"? Who but *you* could succeed in missing both & then just because you wanted to?

Notes

1. Langston Hughes (1902–1967) was a prolific poet, novelist, journalist, and political activist. His career started during the Harlem Renaissance with the publication of "The Negro Speaks of Rivers" (1919) and his collection of poetry, *The Weary Blues* (1926).

2. Langston Hughes Papers (JWJ MSS 26 Hughes, Box 57), Beinecke Lib., Yale U.

3. The incident Fauset refers to here has not been determined.

4. Hughes had been working as a sailor for a number of years, but on his last voyage he felt lucky to still be alive. Not only did Hughes's ship encounter gale-force winds, but also the chief engineer died, one of the mess boys scalded his foot and ankle in an errant pot of boiling cabbage, and the wireless operator had a mental breakdown. In *The Big Sea*, he says, "When we got to Rotterdam, however, I thought maybe there might be a jinx on our ship, so I got off. I had twenty-five dollars coming. I drew it, packed my bags, and caught the night train for Paris" (143). Hughes was in Paris from February to August 1924.

5. Harold Jackman (1901–1961) was a well-known social personality of the Harlem Re-

naissance and friend to poet Countee Cullen (1903–1946), but was not himself a writer or artist.

6. Fauset was in Europe from September 1924 to May 1925. She had studied in Paris from September to December 1924; 5 January 1925 she planned to travel through the Midi, Italy, and Austria; 12–26 January she planned to be in Nice, France; 28 January to 3 February she planned to be in Rome, Italy; 9–23 February she planned to be in Vienna, Austria; between 23 February and 2 April she planned to be back in Paris. Jessie Redmon Fauset to Langston Hughes, 21 December 1924, Langston Hughes Papers (JWJ MSS 26 Hughes, Box 57), Beinecke Lib., Yale U.

7. Claude McKay (1889–1948) was a poet, novelist, short-story writer, and essayist. Fauset would have edited the two-part article "Soviet Russia and the Negro" published in the *Crisis* December 1923 and January 1924 and the article "A Moscow Lady" published in September 1924 (Cooper 196). In addition, McKay's first American collection of poems, *Harlem Shadows* (1922), received excellent reviews. McKay was in Paris from August 1923 to January 1924 and then moved to Toulon.

8. Fauset went to Paris for the first time in 1914 and the second time in 1921 for the Second Pan-African Congress (Sylvander 67).

9. Fauset was working on her second novel, *Plum Bun* (1928).

10. Sinclair Lewis (1885–1951), an American writer, known for his novel *Babbitt* (1922). Lewis was in Paris with his wife, Gracie, in November and December 1924. It is unclear how Fauset met Lewis, but, like Fauset, Gracie took courses at the Sorbonne (Cooper 216; Lingeman 252–254).

11. Fauset never identifies this man's name in her correspondence. Hughes sent twenty poems to Fauset while in Vienna, and she passed them on to her friend. The last mention of her friend's interest occurs in a 16 March letter: "My friend hasn't reported on them yet but when he does I'll let you know or probably I'll tell you for I'll be home soon now." While Hughes had numerous poems appear in *Messenger, Workers Monthly, Bucaneer, Opportunity*, and the *Crisis*, not one of these publications seems directly related to Fauset's intervention (Rampersad *The Life* 103–104). Jessie Redmon Fauset to Langston Hughes, 16 March 1925, Langston Hughes Papers (JWJ MSS 26 Hughes, Box 57), Beinecke Lib., Yale U.

12. Hughes attended Lincoln University in Pennsylvania from February 1926 to May 1930. He had discussed attending Howard University with Alain Locke, who taught there, but Locke was fired in June 1925 after supporting "a bitter student strike and other wide-ranging disputes with the administration" (Rampersad *The Life* 101).

13. Langston Hughes Papers (JWJ MSS 26 Hughes, Box 57), Beinecke Lib., Yale U.

14. The poem was published in the May 1925 issue of the *Crisis*. It did not have a title, but was dedicated "To F. S." It reads "I loved my friend. / He went away from me. / There's nothing more to say. / The poem ends as it began, — / I loved my friend."

15. ‹think›

16. In a letter to Hughes dated 21 December 1924, Fauset wrote, "In one sense I do not want you to go back to school because I think you are one young man whose empiri-

cal knowledge will mean much more to him than his technical. On the other hand life is notoriously unkind to artists and as far as I can see the only way in which one can thwart that unkindness is to have something besides one's natural gift of art or poesy on which to fall back. So I'm going to take the liberty dear Langston to advise you to fix your eye on some professional goal and to reach it. You are a person who will never be spoiled by material possession, yet paradoxically you might be ruined without it. Please forgive for proffering you advice." Langston Hughes Papers (JWJ MSS 26 Hughes, Box 57), Beinecke Lib., Yale U.

17. ‹you›

18. Langston Hughes Papers (JWJ MSS 26 Hughes, Box 57), Beinecke Lib., Yale U.

19. ‹of›

20. Hughes reviewed *The Sailor's Return* by David Garnett (1892–1981) in the November 1925 issue of the *Crisis*.

21. ‹himself›

22. ‹r›

23. *Opportunity* was a journal sponsored by the Urban League that regularly featured the work of Harlem Renaissance artists and awarded literary prizes for the best work. Hughes published a poem "Soledad (A Cuban Portrait)" in the December 1925 issue, but a book review did not appear within the following year under his name.

24. Alain Locke (1885–1954) earned a Ph.D. from Harvard University, was the first African-American Rhodes scholar to attend Oxford University, and was a philosophy professor at Howard University. He played a pivotal role during the Harlem Renaissance not only by editing the *New Negro* but also through his influence over the philanthropist Charlotte Mason (dates unavailable), who provided many young artists with significant financial support.

25. Charles S. Johnson (1893–1956) was the Urban League's national director of research and investigations and editor of *Opportunity* magazine (Lewis 47).

26. It is unclear to which book Fauset is referring. Five years later, Carl Van Vechten (1880–1964) published a quarto on his cat, Feathers, called *Feathers*, and in 1932 republished it as an essay with *Sacred and Profane Memories*. Van Vechten is best known in Harlem Renaissance circles for his controversial novel *Nigger Heaven* (1926), and there was widespread concern about the extent of his influence on younger writers such as Hughes and their willingness to represent less respectable aspects of black life.

27. ‹between›

28. ‹sh›

29. ‹boo›

30. Fauset is still referring to *Plum Bun* (1928).

31. I was unable to identify to whom Fauset refers here.

32. Here Fauset refers to Hughes's mother, Carolina "Carrie" Mercer Langston (1873–1938), and his stepbrother, Gwyn Shannon Clark (1913–?), better known as "Kit."

33. As a writer, Richard Bruce Nugent (1906–1987) was best known for his short story "Smoke, Lilies and Jade" (1926) and for his willingness to explore homosexuality in that

story. He was notorious for his iconoclasm, wearing dress shoes without socks and dress shirts open at the neck.

34. ‹n›

35. In an earlier letter dated 23 September 1925, Fauset asks Hughes to pick up cold cream left at Georgia Douglas Johnson's (1877–1966) house. She writes, "Will you do me a favor? Will you drop in Mrs. Johnson's some time and get a partly filled jar of face cream—Harriet Hubbard Ayers make—which I left there? This may seem a strange thing to ask but the cream is expensive and even the small quantity which I left there is valuable to me and to no one else." Langston Hughes Papers (JWJ MSS 26 Hughes, Box 57), Beinecke Lib., Yale U. Johnson was the famous host of the Saturday night salons in Washington, DC, and a writer in her own right.

36. This book was not reviewed in the *Crisis* within the next year. In an earlier letter Fauset tells Hughes, "Tonight I'm going to see 'The Green Hat'. Have you read it yet? When you do let me k know of your reaction; I'll be very curious to get it. How much I'd like to write a best seller." Jessie Redmon Fauset to Langston Hughes, 23 September 1925, Langston Hughes Papers (JWJ MSS 26 Hughes, Box 57), Beinecke Lib., Yale U.

37. William Edward Burghardt DuBois (1868–1963) was a well-known black intellectual of the twentieth century. In this context, it is important to know that he was general editor of the *Crisis* from 1910 to 1934.

38. Alain Locke Collection, Moorland-Spingarn Research Center, Howard U.

39. Egbert "Bert" Austin Williams (1874–1922) was one of the most successful black artists on the minstrel stage. He was part of the famous duo of Williams and Walker. In an earlier undated letter, Fauset asks, "Can you tell me what you have decided to do with my essay on Bert Williams? Do you mean to use it as it stands or do you still insist on it's being changed—and have you time for this." In the same letter, she offers "that after August 8, I'll be free enough to recast that Williams essay and make it fit into the title 'The Gift of Laughter.' But you'll have to let me know about this shortly." In another undated letter, Fauset sends a draft and explains, "I hope this is nearer what you want. You see after all you've been very indefinite about this. The work was to be mine but the idea is & always has been yours. However I glimpsed dimly from your last letter what you wanted me to drive at. I hope this is o.k." When Fauset finally sends the final article, she explains, "Here is the belated article. I'm sorry about it's belatedness but not very guilty since I never got very clearly from you just what you wanted. However all—s well that ends well." Citation for both letters is Jessie Redmon Fauset, letter to Alain Locke, n.d., Alain Locke Collection, Moorland-Spingarn Research Center, Howard U.

40. Langston Hughes Papers (JWJ MSS 26 Hughes, Box 57), Beinecke Lib., Yale U.

41. Publisher Alfred A. Knopf (1892–1984) was responsible for one of the major opportunities for black writers to publish their work with his company Alfred A. Knopf, Inc.

42. Knopf was Van Vechten's publisher and convinced him to read Hughes's work. Van Vechten provided publishing contacts for a number of Harlem Renaissance writers.

43. "Lullaby" was published in the March 1926 issue of the *Crisis*.

44. This poem was never published.

45. V. V. is Van Vechten.

46. Hughes was working as an assistant to Carter G. Woodson (1875–1950) in 1925 on *Free Negro Heads of Families in the United States in 1830* (1925). There were approximately 30,000 names included in this volume.

47. This letter bears the date 9 January 1933 but it must have been written in 1934 given that Alain Locke's review is a retrospective of 1933. Alain Locke Collection, Moorland-Spingarn Research Center, Howard U.

48. Fauset's brother was folklorist Arthur Huff Fauset (1899–1983). The Civic Club dinner on 21 March 1924 illustrates the dilemma of marginalization of black women writers during the Harlem Renaissance. In *When Harlem Was in Vogue*, Lewis describes the change: "the original idea had been an informal gathering to honor the publication of *There Is Confusion*, a novel by the literary editor of the *Crisis*, Jessie Fauset; [Charles S.] Johnson had turned it into a well-advertised literary symposium" (89). Lewis describes the suspension of Fauset's voice: "While Jessie Fauset, whose novel was the ostensible reason for the gathering, waited her turn, Locke presented Carl Van Doren, editor of *Century* magazine" (93). After a number of speakers, Fauset "thanked the audience for honoring the publication of her novel" and once again surrendered the microphone to other speakers and topics (94).

49. Fauset refers here to the group around the Harlem branch of the New York Public Library. Regina Anderson [Andrews], pseudonym Ursula Trelling, (1901–1993) was an assistant at the library, and Gwendolyn Bennett, like Fauset, was a volunteer. Anderson married William T. Andrews in 1926. In addition to writing poetry, Gwendolyn Bennett (1902–1981) had a regular column in *Opportunity* magazine called "The Ebony Flute" from 1926 to 1928.

50. Locke included four of his own articles in the anthology. The articles were "The New Negro," "Negro Youth Speaks," "The Negro Spirituals," and "The Legacy of the Ancestral Arts."

51. The article, "The Saving Grace of Realism: Retrospective Review of the Negro Literature of 1933," was published in the January 1934 issue of *Opportunity* magazine and republished in *The Critics and the Harlem Renaissance*.

52. Locke reviewed Julia Peterkin's (1880–1961) book *Roll, Jordan, Roll* (1933). He says, "It is illuminating to see the actual types from which she has been making up her characters all these years. That they are real Negroes, the happy but unfortunate illusion that they are the generic Negro, — and that they scarcely are. For one thing, they are too bucolic, too tinted with Miss Peterkin's own Theocritan fancy; and for the other, they are a bit too local and sectional to be generic" ("The Saving Grace of Realism" 273).

53. Locke reviewed Roark Bradford's (1896–1948) book *Kingdom Coming* (1933). He describes Bradford's literary growth as moving from "the superficial, caricaturish interest of the early Roark Bradford into the penetrating, carefully studied realism of his latest novel" (8) where "the Negro characterization is true and deeply sympathetic. But for a forced and melodramatic ending the novel would have been a masterpiece" ("The Saving Grace of Realism" 273).

54. Locke reviewed James Weldon Johnson's (1871–1938) autobiography *Along This*

Way (1933). He explains that the work "represents a new and effective step in Negro biography" and its originality "can be attributed to the sober, realistic restraint that dominates it in striking contrast to the flamboyant egotism and sentimentality of much of our previous biographical writing" ("The Saving Grace of Realism" 272).

55. "Locksian style" is a phrase coined by Fauset and like the other terms in the list, "mid-Victorian" and "modernistic," she uses it to describe "page paragraphs and parentheses."

56. Locke reviewed Claude McKay's novel *Banana Bottom* (1933). He describes the novel as a "complete success so far as local color and setting are concerned" and a moderate success in terms of "the story of Bita whose life dramatizes a provincial duel between peasant paganism and middle class Puritanism" ("The Saving Grace of Realism" 273).

57. Locke reviewed Fauset's novel, *Comedy American Style* (1933). He offers the balm that "it makes a distinct contribution in its theme" and then undercuts its value because "it fails to capitalize it fully by forceful style and handling [. . .]. Yet Negro fiction would be infinitely poorer without the persevering and slowly maturing art of Miss Fauset, and her almost single-handed championship of upper and middle class Negro life as an important subject for fiction" ("The Saving Grace of Realism" 273).

58. In 1929, Fauset married insurance broker Herbert E. Harris (? – 1958).

Works Cited

Allen, Carol. *Black Women Intellectuals: Strategies of Nation, Family, and Neighborhood in the Works of Pauline Hopkins, Jessie Fauset, and Marita Bonner.* NY: Garland, 1998.

Cooper, Wayne F. *Claude McKay: Rebel Sojourner in the Harlem Renaissance: A Biography.* Baton Rouge: Louisiana State U P, 1987.

Fauset, Jessie. *The Chinaberry Tree & Selected Writings.* 1931. Boston: Northeastern U P, 1995.

———. *Comedy American Style.* 1933. NY: Negro U P, 1969.

———. *Plum Bun: A Novel without a Moral.* 1928. Boston: Beacon Press, 1990.

———. "The Symbolism of Bert Williams." *Crisis* May 1922. Rpt. *The Crisis Reader.* Ed. Sondra Kathryn Wilson. NY: Modern Library, 1999. 255 – 259.

———. *There Is Confusion.* 1924. Boston: Northeastern U P, 1989.

Hughes, Langston. *The Big Sea.* 1940. NY: Hill and Wang, 1993.

———. *Not without Laughter.* NY: Knopf, 1930.

Hull, Gloria T. *Color, Sex, and Poetry: Three Women Writers of the Harlem Renaissance.* Bloomington & Indianapolis: Indiana U P, 1987.

Johnson, Abby Arthur. "Literary Midwife: Jessie Redmon Fauset and the Harlem Renaissance." *Phylon* 39 (1978): 143 – 153. Rpt. *Remembering the Harlem Renaissance.* Ed. Cary D. Wintz. NY: Garland Publishing, Inc., 1996. 313 – 323.

Kellner, Bruce. *Carl Van Vechten and the Irreverent Decades.* Norman: U of Oklahoma P, 1968.

Lewis, David Levering. *When Harlem Was in Vogue.* NY: Penguin Books, 1997.

Lingeman, Richard. *Sinclair Lewis: Rebel from Main Street*. NY: Random House, Inc., 2002.

Locke, Alain. *The New Negro: Voices of the Harlem Renaissance*. 1925. NY: Atheneum, 1992.

———. "The Saving Grace of Realism: Retrospective Review of the Negro Literature of 1933." *Opportunity* (January 1934): 8 – 11, 30. Rpt. *The Critics and the Harlem Renaissance*. Ed. Cary D. Wintz. NY: Garland Publishing, Inc., 1996. 272 – 276.

Rampersad, Arnold, ed. *The Collected Poems of Langston Hughes*. NY: Random House, Inc., 1994.

———. *The Life of Langston Hughes*. Vol. 1. NY: Oxford U P, 1986.

Sylvander, Carolyn Wedin. *Jessie Redmon Fauset, Black American Writer*. Troy, NY: The Whitson Publishing Company, 1981.

Wilson, Sondra Kathryn, ed. *The Crisis Reader: Stories, Poetry, and Essays from the N.A.A.C.P.'s Crisis Magazine*. NY: Modern Library, 1999.

CONTRIBUTORS

Kimberly J. Banks is an assistant professor of English at the University of Missouri–Kansas City teaching courses in African American literature and twentieth-century American literature. Among her recent scholarship, she has completed a book, *Framing Diasporic Memory: Walrond, Hurston, McKay, and Dunham Negotiating Nostalgia*, and published an article on representations of lynching in African American literature in *African American Review*.

Jennifer Cognard-Black is an assistant professor of English at St. Mary's College of Maryland, where she teaches Anglo-American literature and fiction writing. Her critical work has appeared in *American Literary Realism*, the *National Women's Studies Association Journal*, and *Popular Culture Review*. She is the author of *Narrative in the Professional Age: Transatlantic Readings of Harriet Beecher Stowe, George Eliot, and Elizabeth Stuart Phelps* and a writing textbook, *Advancing Rhetoric*. She is a Pushcart Prize nominee whose short stories have appeared in numerous journals and magazines.

Frances Smith Foster, Charles Howard Candler Professor of English and women's studies at Emory University, has edited two volumes of Frances E. W. Harper's works: *A Brighter Coming Day: A Frances E. W. Harper Reader* and *Minnie's Sacrifice, Sowing and Reaping, Trial and Triumph: Three Rediscovered Novels by Frances E. W. Harper*. She has published extensively on Harper and nineteenth-century African American women writers.

George V. Griffith's published work on Eliot and America has included studies of Eliot's reception in the American press, adaptations of her works on the American stage, and film adaptations of Eliot's novels. His transcription of the Phelps correspondence originally appeared in *Legacy*. He is professor of English at Chadron State College in Nebraska.

Sharon M. Harris, Lorraine Sherley Professor of Literature at Texas Christian University, is the author of *Executing Race: Eighteenth-Century American Women's Narratives of Race, Society, and the Law* and *Rebecca Harding Davis and American Realism* and is the editor of such texts as *Blue Pencils, Hidden Hands: Women Editing Periodicals, 1820–1900* and *Women's Early American Historical Narratives*. Former editor of *Legacy*, Harris was founding president of the Society for the Study of American Women Writers.

Linda K. Hughes, Addie Levy Professor of Literature at Texas Christian University, works on Victorian periodicals in the context of gender and publishing history. Her recent work includes *Graham R.: Rosamund Marriott Watson, Woman of Letters, Elizabeth Gaskell's Shorter Tales, 1859–1865*, and articles on *fin-de-siècle* figures in *SEL: Studies in English Literature* and *Victorian Literature and Culture*. She recently guest-edited a double issue of *Victorian Poetry* entitled "Whither Victorian Poetry?" Hughes is also the author of *The Manyfacèd Glass: Tennyson's Dramatic Monologues* and coauthor of *The Victorian Serial* and *Victorian Publishing and Mrs. Gaskell's Work*.

Patricia Lorimer Lundberg is the founding executive director of the Center for Cultural Discovery and Learning at Indiana University Northwest. She is also a member of the Indiana University Graduate Faculty and has served in administrative posts such as interim associate vice chancellor for academic affairs. Among her recent publications is a biography of Lucas Malet: *An Inward Necessity: The Writer's Life of Lucas Malet*. She is the recipient of several grants and awards, has postdoctoral training in leadership and diversity, and is a member of the President's Council of St. Scholastica Academy.

Linda Peterson, Niel Gray, Jr. Professor of English at Yale University, is the author of *Victorian Autobiography* and *Traditions of Victorian Women's Autobiography: The Poetics and Politics of Life Writing* as well as the editor of Emily Brontë's *Wuthering Heights* and Harriet Martineau's *Autobiography*. She is currently working on a study of nineteenth-century women's entry into the profession of letters.

Jennifer Phegley is an assistant professor of nineteenth-century literature at the University of Missouri–Kansas City. She is the author of *Educating the Proper Woman Reader: Victorian Family Literary Magazines and the Cultural Health of the Nation* and coeditor of *Reading Women: Literary Figures and Cultural Icons from the Victorian Age to the Present*.

Kristin A. Risley is assistant professor of English at the University of Wisconsin–Stout, where she teaches literature and writing. A scholar and translator of Norwegian-American literature, her research has been supported by awards from the American-Scandinavian Foundation and the Norwegian-American Historical Association. She first became interested in Palma Pederson while completing her doctoral thesis, "Vikings of the Midwest: Place, Culture, and Ethnicity in Norwegian-American Literature, 1870–1940," and she continues to study ethnic authors and print cultures. Her most recent publication is an article in *American Periodicals* entitled "Christmas in Our Western Home: The Cultural Work of a Norwegian-American Christmas Annual."

Elizabeth MacLeod Walls has authored articles on gender and modernism in such venues as *Papers on Language and Literature, Rhetoric Review*, and *The Dictionary of National Biography*. She is the recipient of several national research grants, including the Midwest Victorian Studies Association's Arnstein Prize, and is coeditor of a forthcoming book, *The BBC Talks of E. M. Forster, 1929–1960*. MacLeod Walls is executive director of a Lilly Endowment grant supporting continuing education in Nebraska as well as a faculty member at Nebraska Wesleyan University.

Susan S. Williams is an associate professor of English at the Ohio State University. She is the author of *Confounding Images: Photography and Portraiture in Antebellum American Fiction*, and her book on American female authorship in the second half of the nineteenth century is forthcoming. In addition, she is coeditor of *Reciprocal Influences: Literary Production, Reception and Consumption in America* and of the journal *American Periodicals*. She is also a contributor to volume 3 of *History of the Book in America*. Williams is currently working on a project on the abolitionist, editor, and promoter James Redpath.

Molly Youngkin is an assistant professor of English at California State University – Dominguez Hills, where she teaches courses in nineteenth-century British literature and gender studies. Her research focuses on feminist reception of the New Woman novel of the 1890s, with special emphasis on narrative strategies used to depict women's agency. She has published articles on this topic in *Studies in the Novel* and *English Literature in Transition* and is completing a book entitled *Feminist Realism at the Fin de Siècle: The Influence of the Late-Victorian Woman's Press on the Development of the Novel*.